Hookers, Crooks, and Kooks

Part 2
Crooks and Kooks

By

Jana Sloan Broglin, CG

HERITAGE BOOKS
2007

HERITAGE BOOKS

AN IMPRINT OF HERITAGE BOOKS, INC.

Books, CDs, and more—Worldwide

For our listing of thousands of titles see our website
at
www.HeritageBooks.com

Published 2007 by
HERITAGE BOOKS, INC.
Publishing Division
65 East Main Street
Westminster, Maryland 21157-5026

Other books by the author:

Lucas County, Ohio Index to Deaths, 1867-1908
Hookers, Crooks and Kooks, Part I: Hookers

International Standard Book Number: 978-0-7884-4550-7

Dedication

To Grandma Lou

Louie M. (Kennedy) Beard
1910-1988

Who gave me such a love of our family's history.

Preface

While working on *Hookers, Crooks, and Kooks, Volume 1, Hookers*, I noticed other unusual occupations. Along the way, opium dealers, vagrants, gamblers, and even oracles, and those who laid out the dead, were located in the census.

In this volume of *Hookers, Crooks, and Kooks, Volume 2, Crooks and Kooks,* occupations from the old Cher song, "Gypsies, Tramps, and Thieves," were located, as well as quack doctors, phrenologists, stealing chickens, circus performers, ballet dancers (as well as the more notorious "Hurdy Dancer"), clairvoyants, bummers, and drunks were all there to find.

Baseball players are included, although they don't really fit the criteria of a "crook or kook" as the sport was so new, these occupations were rarities. Searches were made for other sports, but only cricket was found with three being listed as a "cricket player."

Actors and actresses were to be included in this volume, but space wouldn't allow their huge number.

People who had died by the census date may also be listed in the census with "dead" as the occupation. When finding a person with this occupation, be sure to check for the corresponding state's mortality schedules. For more information regarding the availability of mortality schedules see Kathleen W. Hinckley's *Your Guide to the Federal Census.*[1]

One of the more unusual entries was for Wm. Cameron in Rio Grande, Colorado. The full "occupation" was "Thief would dignify him. To low for anything." For space, the entry within was shortened to "Thief would dignify him."

As always, it is important to look at the image of the census record. Please note if a name is in question, it has been checked to the image. Not all names are listed as they appear on Ancestry.com. However, the page numbers, counties, and states, are as they appear. Problems with either image or name errors have been reported to Ancestry. If information is not given in the census, such as year or place of birth, three dashes (---) appear within the corresponding column.

---

[1] Hinckley, Kathleen W., *Your Guide to the Federal Census for Genealogists, Researchers, and Family Historians* (Cincinnati, Ohio: Better Books, 2002), 88-95; 185-186.

Introduction

As with the first volume in this series, "Hookers, Crooks, and Kooks" the information was located in the 1880 Federal Census at Ancestry.com <http://www.ancestry.com> using the advanced search options for occupation. Different "jobs" were entered into the field.

Gambling was the most prominent occupation with 1,313 men and women listed. Those of Chinese descent presented problems within the search. Last names were sometimes omitted in the index, so a check of the actual census page may list a person's name differently than found in the online indexes for the 1880 census.

While viewing the listings for "Astronomers" it is wise to remember some may actually be an astronomer as those listed in Ann Arbor, Washtenaw, Michigan, and Cambridge, Suffolk, Massachusetts, both university towns. Others may be astrologers who were looked down upon, so they chose to use the term "astronomer" to hide their true profession.

The term "Tramp" may be referring to those people not working, or, possibly, women who may be prostitutes. These women are located in this volume and not in volume one of this series, "Hookers, Crooks, and Kooks."

Hucksters/hucsters/huksters, are not listed in this volume due to the sheer number of those listed in the census. With 23,571 individuals listed, it could be a volume in itself.

As with the first in this series, all attempts to locate individuals have been done. However, due to the amount of occupations, spelling changes, there may be people who have been missed.

Jana Sloan Broglin, CG
October 2007

(?) Chong; Opium Den; Sacramento; CA; 1858; China; 2D
---, Elizabeth S.; Dead; Milwaukee; WI; 1790; Prussia; 233A
Abbott, H.; Circus; Ohio; WV; 1859; PA; 449B
Abbott, L.T.; Gambler; Jackson; MO; 1837; KY; 226B
Abel, Margaret; Layes out dead; Philadelphia; PA; 1838; PA; 54C
Abele, Joseph; Dead; Adams; IL; 1879; IL; 481B
Abertheny, George; Miserable loafer; Genesee; MI; 1852; MI;
    145C
Abeytia, Carmen; Gambler; Santa Fe; NM; 1850; NM Terr.; 68A
Abner, Lewis; Gambler; Montgomery; TX; 1835; AL; 87A
Abom, John; Tramp; Pinal; AZ; 1866; CA; 373C
Acker, Avery; Dead; Albany; NY; 1879; NY; 369B
Acosta, Tomas; Gambler; San Miguel; NM; 1851; Mexico; 412D
Acre, Frances; Tramp; King George; VA; 1822; VA; 564C
Adalgo, Francisco; Gambler; Marin; CA; 1866; Mexico; 88B
Adam, Effee; Dead; Clark; KY; 1880; KY; 421D
Adams, C.B.; Dead; Middlesex; MA; 1833; MA; 149B
Adams, C.H.; Thief; Philadelphia; PA; 1839; England; 295C
Adams, Fred E.; Gambler; Richardson; NE; 1855; OH; 435C
Adams, Geo.; Thief; Philadelphia; PA; 1836; PA; 293C
Adams, Horace; Gambler; Deer Lodge; MT; 1835; NY; 116A
Adams, John; Gambler; Cook; IL; 1831; NY; 64C
Adams, John Q.; Quack Doctor; Chester; PA; 1826; MA; 115A
Adkins, William; Wandering; Kent; DE; 1864; DE; 77B
Adler, Henry; Gambler; Storey; NV; 1840; Prussia; 122B
Adolphe, J.; Professional Gambler; Orleans; LA; 1860; New
    Orleans, LA; 72C
Agen, John; Tramp on public street; St. Clair; IL; 1854; England;
    483C
Aggie, John; Gambler; Franklin; OH; 1841; OH; 490C
Agnew, Luke; Healer; Cook; IL; 1863; IL; 314B
Ah, App; Gambler; Yuba; CA; 1850; Canton; 426D
Ah, Bat; Gambler; Elko; NV; 1851; China; 56C
Ah, Bing; Gambler; Shasta; CA; 1836; Quong Tong; 95D
Ah, Bo; Opium Shop; Santa Clara; CA; 1840; China; 125D
Ah, Boe; Gambler; Nevada; CA; 1829; Canton; 220A
Ah, Boh; Keeps Opium Den; Shasta; CA; 1845; China; 2D
Ah, Bung; Gambler; Amador; CA; 1852; Canton; 38D

2   Name; Occupation; County; State; Birth; Birth place; Page

Ah, Cam; Opium Smoker; Eureka; NV; 1854; China; 212C
Ah, Cap; Gambler; Union; OR; 1839; China; 177C
Ah, Cha Koon; Gambling House; Amador; CA; 1827; China;
     112A
Ah, Chap; Opium Shop; Santa Clara; CA; 1837; China; 125C
Ah, Charly; Gambler; Nevada; CA; 1852; China; 175B
Ah, Chay; Opium Shop; Santa Clara; CA; 1847; China; 127C
Ah, Chee; Gambler; Madison; MT; 1842; China; 386B
Ah, Chee; Gambling House Keeper; Stanislaus; CA; 1832; China;
     373C
Ah, Chi; Gambler; Fresno; CA; 1845; China; 288D
Ah, Chim; Gambler; Deer Lodge; MT; 1850; China; 111C
Ah, Chin; Gambler; Eureka; NV; 1848; China; 191A
Ah, Chin; Gambler; Butte; CA; 1849; China; 262C
Ah, Ching; Gambler; Sacramento; CA; 1843; China; 333D
Ah, Ching; Keeps Gambling House; Amador; CA; 1821; China;
     112A
Ah, Ching; Gambling House Keeper; Stanislaus; CA; 1822;
     China; 373C
Ah, Chong; Gambler; Amador; CA; 1854; Canton; 38D
Ah, Chong; Gambler; Kern; CA; 1848; China; 586C
Ah, Chong; Gambler; Tuolumne; CA; 1820; Canton; 164B
Ah, Choo; Keeper Opium Den; Sacramento; CA; 1830; China; 2C
Ah, Choo; Gambler; Eureka; NV; 1845; China; 191B
Ah, Chou; In Jail for Selling Opium; Eureka; NV; 1850; China;
     180A
Ah, Chow; Gambling House; Nevada; CA; 1825; China; 83D
Ah, Choy; Gambler; Eureka; NV; 1859; China; 206D
Ah, Chu; Gambling House; Amador; CA; 1837; China; 111D
Ah, Chuan; Gambler; Butte; CA; 1840; China; 148A
Ah, Chuck; Gambler; Butte; CA; 1832; China; 262C
Ah, Chuck; Gambler; Nevada; CA; 1829; Canton; 220B
Ah, Chuig; Opium Dealer; Butte; CA; 1840; China; 264D
Ah, Chum; Gambler; Amador; CA; 1830; Canton; 38C
Ah, Chung; Opium Den; Mono; CA; 1856; China; 126D
Ah, Chung; Keeping Opium Den; San Joaquin; CA; 1826; Mikoo;
     12A
Ah, Chung; Keeps Opium Den; Shasta; CA; 1863; China; 2D

Ah, Chung; Gambler; Boise; ID; 1838; China; 118B
Ah, Chung; Gambler; Idaho; ID; 1845; Canton; 166C
Ah, Chung; Gambler; Ormsby; NV; 1842; China; 74C
Ah, Chung; Gambler; Butte; CA; 1840; China; 262C
Ah, Chung; Gambler; Butte; CA; 1849; China; 262C
Ah, Chung; Gambler; El Dorado; CA; 1838; China; 65B
Ah, Chung; Gambler; Tuolumne; CA; 1832; Canton; 165C
Ah, Chung; Gambler; Yuba; CA; 1850; China; 454D
Ah, Chung; Gambling House; Owyhee; ID; 1827; China; 353C
Ah, Chung; China Gambling House; Storey; NV; 1853; China;
    236B
Ah, Chung; Gambling House; Storey; NV; 1823; China; 237D
Ah, Cong; Gambler; Alameda; CA; 1860; China; 126A
Ah, Coon; Gambler; Butte; CA; 1850; China; 261B
Ah, Cow; Gambler; Tuolumne; CA; 1820; Canton; 165C
Ah, Coy; Gambler; Alameda; CA; 1848; China; 126A
Ah, Coy; Keeps Gambling House; Shoshone; ID; 1830; China;
    361A
Ah, Cum; Gambler; Ormsby; NV; 1840; China; 41A
Ah, Daugh; Gambler; Boise; ID; 1830; China; 118A
Ah, Din; Gambler; Trinity; CA; 1851; China; 570D
Ah, Ding; Gambler; Eureka; NV; 1845; China; 191A
Ah, Ding; Gambler; Washoe; NV; 1853; China; 277A
Ah, Duck; Gambler; Boise; ID; 1836; China; 118B
Ah, Fah; Gambler; Placer; CA; 1827; Canton; 316D
Ah, Fat; Gambler; Idaho; ID; 1846; Canton; 166C
Ah, Fat; Keeps Gambling House; Boise; ID; 1850; China; 132A
Ah, Fauk; Stealing Chickens; Trinity; CA; 1820; China; 580A
Ah, Fee; Gambler; Eureka; NV; 1848; China; 191B
Ah, Fen; Gambler; Nevada; CA; 1839; China; 188A
Ah, Fong; Opium Dealer; Sacramento; CA; 1854; China; 1B
Ah, Fong; Gambler; Yuba; CA; 1855; Canton; 428C
Ah, Foo; Gambler; Washoe; NV; 1852; China; 277A
Ah, Foo; Gambler; Butte; CA; 1840; China; 262C
Ah, Foo; Gambler; Yuba; CA; 1845; China; 454D
Ah, Fooey; Gambler; Eureka; NV; 1848; China; 212D
Ah, Fook; Gambler; Baker; OR; 1850; China; 8D
Ah, Fook; Gambling House; Storey; NV; 1840; China; 237D

4   Name; Occupation; County; State; Birth; Birth place; Page

Ah, Foon; Gambler; Idaho; ID; 1840; Canton; 166C
Ah, Foot; Gambler; Nevada; CA; 1841; China; 188A
Ah, Foy; Gambler; Kern; CA; 1858; China; 586C
Ah, Foy; Gambler; Nevada; CA; 1839; China; 188A
Ah, Fung; Gambler; Butte; CA; 1849; China; 148A
Ah, Fut; Opium Shop; Alameda; CA; 1844; Canton; 664C
Ah, Gee; Gambler; Nevada; CA; 1855; China; 175B
Ah, Gee; Gambling House; Owyhee; ID; 1830; China; 353C
Ah, Gee; Vag. ; Nevada; CA; 1826; ---; 83D
Ah, Geu; Opium Dealer; Sacramento; CA; 1840; China; 1B
Ah, Gin; Gambler; Baker; OR; 1838; China; 8D
Ah, Ging; Gambler; Washoe; NV; 1848; China; 276C
Ah, Git; Gambler; Butte; CA; 1850; China; 262C
Ah, Goo; Peddling Opium; Sierra; CA; 1846; China; 167A
Ah, Goom; Gambler; Marion; OR; 1845; China; 47C
Ah, Goon; Gambler; Butte; CA; 1833; China; 262C
Ah, Goon; Gambler; Yuba; CA; 1834; Canton; 429A
Ah, Gop; Gambler; Union; OR; 1841; China; 177C
Ah, Gow; Gambler; Butte; CA; 1849; China; 262C
Ah, Gow; Gambler; Trinity; CA; 1850; China; 570C
Ah, Guey; Gambler; Alameda; CA; 1805; China; 126A
Ah, Gun; Dealer in Opium; Sierra; CA; 1833; Canton; 177D
Ah, Gun; Gambler; Eureka; NV; 1857; China; 191A
Ah, Gun; Gambling House Keeper; Stanislaus; CA; 1830; China;
     373C
Ah, Hee; Gambler; Calaveras; CA; 1850; China; 346C
Ah, Hen; Gambler; Nevada; CA; 1838; Canton; 220A
Ah, Heng; Gambler; Amador; CA; 1847; China; 112A
Ah, Him; Gambler; Deer Lodge; MT; 1848; China; 110A
Ah, Hin; Opium Shop; Santa Clara; CA; 1849; China; 126B
Ah, Hin; Gambler; Sacramento; CA; 1830; China; 333D
Ah, Hing; Gambler; Eureka; NV; 1842; China; 191A
Ah, Hing; Gambler; Butte; CA; 1843; China; 261B
Ah, Hing; Gambler; Butte; CA; 1860; China; 262C
Ah, Ho; Keeps Opium Shop; Santa Clara; CA; 1844; China; 127C
Ah, Hoe; Gambler; Deer Lodge; MT; 1830; China; 111C
Ah, Hoey; Gambler; Fresno; CA; 1844; China; 289A

Ah, Hone; Keeps Opium Den; Shasta; CA; 1848; China; 2D
Ah, Hong; Gambler; Madison; MT; 1834; China; 386B
Ah, Hong; Gambler; Butte; CA; 1854; China; 262C
Ah, Hoon; Gambler; Storey; NV; 1848; China; 236B
Ah, Hop; Gambler; Eureka; NV; 1845; China; 212C
Ah, How; Keeper of Gambling House; Alameda; CA; 1840;
    Canton; 500A
Ah, Hoy; Gambler; Tuolumne; CA; 1850; Canton; 165C
Ah, Hoy; Gambler; Eureka; NV; 1845; China; 203B
Ah, Hoye; Gambler; Boise; ID; 1840; China; 118B
Ah, Hoyer; Gambler; Amador; CA; 1838; Canton; 46D
Ah, Hu; Gambler; Ada; ID; 1835; China; 19A
Ah, Hum; Gambler; Calaveras; CA; 1830; China; 346C
Ah, Hun; Gambling House; Nevada; CA; 1842; China; 83D
Ah, Hung; Gambler; Tuolumne; CA; 1845; Canton; 165C
Ah, Hut; Gambler; Amador; CA; 1860; Canton; 38D
Ah, Ileu; Gambler; Josephine; OR; 1822; China; 160C
Ah, Ing; Gambler; Deer Lodge; MT; 1853; China; 110B
Ah, Jake; Gambler; Placer; CA; 1846; China; 301B
Ah, Jake; Gambling House; Nevada; CA; 1840; China; 84A
Ah, Jim; Gambler; Nevada; CA; 1849; China; 175A
Ah, Jim; Gambler; Nevada; CA; 1836; China; 175B
Ah, Jim; Gambler; Nevada; CA; 1845; China; 175B
Ah, Jim; Gambler; Trinity; CA; 1849; China; 570C
Ah, Jim; Thief; Trinity; CA; 1840; China; 580A
Ah, Jo; Gambler; Storey; NV; 1858; China; 236B
Ah, John; Gambler; Nevada; CA; 1844; China; 175A
Ah, Jon; Gambler; Nevada; CA; 1855; China; 175B
Ah, Kah Un; Gambler; Deer Lodge; MT; 1850; China; 111C
Ah, Kat; Gambler; Yuba; CA; 1829; China; 454C
Ah, Kee; Opium Dealer; San Joaquin; CA; 1836; Mikoo; 12A
Ah, Kee; Opium Seller; Santa Cruz; CA; 1850; China; 521C
Ah, Kee; Gambling House; Yuba; CA; 1840; Canton; 444C
Ah, Ken; Gambler; Butte; CA; 1819; China; 149C
Ah, Kin; Gambler; Deer Lodge; MT; 1842; China; 111C
Ah, King; Gambler; Ada; ID; 1842; China; 19B
Ah, King; Gambler; Boise; ID; 1835; China; 118B
Ah, King; Gambler; Boise; ID; 1845; China; 136A

Ah, Ko Chung; Gambler; Amador; CA; 1840; China; 112B
Ah, Kum; Gambler; Amador; CA; 1847; China; 112B
Ah, Kum; Gambling House; Nevada; CA; 1850; China; 83D
Ah, Kwong; Gambler; Butte; CA; 1840; China; 261B
Ah, Lan; Opium Healer; Amador; CA; 1842; Canton; 46D
Ah, Lang; Opium Merchant; Baker; OR; 1844; China; 47A
Ah, Laugh; Gambler; Boise; ID; 1839; China; 147D
Ah, Lay; Gambler; Trinity; CA; 1854; China; 570C
Ah, Layo; Gambler; Washoe; NV; 1834; China; 276D
Ah, Lee; Opium Shop; Santa Clara; CA; 1840; China; 126B
Ah, Lee; Gambler; Deer Lodge; MT; 1841; China; 111C
Ah, Lee; Gambler; Butte; CA; 1845; China; 134A
Ah, Lee; Gambling; Yuba; CA; 1844; Canton; 427A
Ah, Leong Pu; Gambler; Amador; CA; 1816; China; 112A
Ah, Leu; Gambler; Lewis and Clark; MT; 1847; China; 277D
Ah, Lib; Gambler; Santa Clara; CA; 1845; China; 124B
Ah, Lim; Gambler; Elko; NV; 1840; China; 55A
Ah, Lin; Opium Den; Mono; CA; 1846; China; 126D
Ah, Lin; Dealer in Opium; Sierra; CA; 1842; Canton; 177D
Ah, Lin; Gambler; Storey; NV; 1851; China; 237D
Ah, Ling; Gambler; Yuba; CA; 1854; Canton; 428C
Ah, Linn; Gambler; Yuba; CA; 1861; China; 454C
Ah, Lock; Gambler; Sacramento; CA; 1839; China; 332A
Ah, Long; Opium Dealer; Placer; CA; 1840; Canton; 379B
Ah, Long; Gambler; Santa Clara; CA; 1831; China; 126A
Ah, Look; Gambler; Butte; CA; 1852; China; 261B
Ah, Look; Gambler; Placer; CA; 1847; China; 338C
Ah, Loong; Gambler; Butte; CA; 1830; China; 262C
Ah, Loop; Gambler; Elko; NV; 1840; China; 59D
Ah, Lou; Gambler; Eureka; NV; 1837; China; 213B
Ah, Lou; Gambler; Nevada; CA; 1852; Canton; 220B
Ah, Loug; Gambler; Nevada; CA; 1842; Canton; 152C
Ah, Lough; Gambling House; Calaveras; CA; 1825; China; 343A
Ah, Louis; Opium Den; Plumas; CA; 1842; China; 421C
Ah, Loy; Gambler; Butte; CA; 1850; China; 264D
Ah, Loy; Gambler; Tuolumne; CA; 1820; Canton; 165C
Ah, Luck; Gambler; Santa Clara; CA; 1830; China; 126A
Ah, Lum; Opium Den; Storey; NV; 1825; China; 236B

Ah, Lum; China Gambling House; Storey; NV; 1845; China; 236B
Ah, Lum; Tramp; Napa; CA; 1835; China; 379B
Ah, Lun; Gambler; Alameda; CA; 1840; China; 126A
Ah, Lun; Gambler; Butte; CA; 1838; China; 262D
Ah, Lung; Gambler; Ada; ID; 1850; China; 19A
Ah, Man; Gambler; Trinity; CA; 1851; China; 570C
Ah, Mang; Gambler; Washoe; NV; 1850; China; 277A
Ah, Meo; Gambler; Amador; CA; 1836; China; 112A
Ah, Mew; Gambler; Sacramento; CA; 1840; China; 332A
Ah, Ming; Gambler; Eureka; NV; 1854; China; 191B
Ah, Mong; Sells Opium; Siskiyou; CA; 1841; China; 252A
Ah, Mong; Keeps Gambling House; Boise; ID; 1814; China; 132A
Ah, Moon; Gambler; Lewis and Clark; MT; 1838; China; 278A
Ah, Moon; Gambler; Amador; CA; 1839; Canton; 47A
Ah, Mow; Gambler; Boise; ID; 1840; China; 118B
Ah, Mow; Gambler; Butte; CA; 1845; China; 261B
Ah, Muck; Dealer in Opium; Sierra; CA; 1836; Canton; 177D
Ah, Mun; Gambler; Amador; CA; 1844; China; 112A
Ah, Mung; Gambling House; Storey; NV; 1842; China; 237C
Ah, My; Opium Smoker; Inyo; CA; 1830; China; 489B
Ah, Nam; Gambler; Trinity; CA; 1848; China; 570D
Ah, Nang; Gambler; Mariposa; CA; 1840; China; 166D
Ah, Ne; Gambler; Baker; OR; 1834; China; 8D
Ah, Nook; Gambler; Nevada; CA; 1839; China; 175B
Ah, Now; Gambler; Sacramento; CA; 1858; China; 332A
Ah, On; Gambler; Idaho; ID; 1851; Canton; 166C
Ah, Ong; Gambler; Boise; ID; 1845; China; 118B
Ah, Oolong; Gambler; Madison; MT; 1828; China; 386B
Ah, Ougun; Gambler; Amador; CA; 1855; China; 112B
Ah, Ouie; Fancy-free; Amador; CA; 1836; Canton; 38C
Ah, Own; Keeps Gambling House; Calaveras; CA; 1835; China;
    345B
Ah, Pan; Stealing Chickens; Trinity; CA; 1840; China; 580A
Ah, Ping; Gambler; Butte; CA; 1832; China; 262C
Ah, Pon; Gambler; Yuba; CA; 1850; Canton; 428C
Ah, Pow; Gambler; Trinity; CA; 1852; China; 570D
Ah, Puhat; Gambler; Washoe; NV; 1841; China; 277A
Ah, Quan; Stealing Chickens; Trinity; CA; 1850; China; 580A

8   Name; Occupation; County; State; Birth; Birth place; Page

Ah, Quay; Gambler; Trinity; CA; 1820; China; 570C
Ah, Quay; Gambling House; Storey; NV; 1851; China; 237D
Ah, Quee; Gambler; Butte; CA; 1839; China; 148B
Ah, Quee; Gambler; Butte; CA; 1848; China; 262C
Ah, Qui; Gambler; Fresno; CA; 1840; China; 289A
Ah, Qui; Gambler; Fresno; CA; 1840; China; 291A
Ah, Quon; Gambler; San Francisco; CA; 1854; Sam Yap; 635C
Ah, Quong; Gambler; Butte; CA; 1841; China; 148B
Ah, Quong; Gambler; Butte; CA; 1839; China; 262D
Ah, Quony; Gambler; Trinity; CA; 1846; China; 570C
Ah, Quy; Gambler; Butte; CA; 1839; China; 262C
Ah, Ring; Gambler; Butte; CA; 1839; China; 262D
Ah, Sam; Gambler; Eureka; NV; 1847; China; 192C
Ah, Sam; Gambler; Butte; CA; 1836; China; 133D
Ah, Sam; Gambler; Butte; CA; 1832; China; 148A
Ah, Sam; Gambler; Nevada; CA; 1849; China; 175A
Ah, Sam; Gambler; Nevada; CA; 1839; China; 188A
Ah, Sam; Keeps Gambling House; Ada; ID; 1842; China; 19B
Ah, Sam Yung; Gambler; Amador; CA; 1821; China; 112B
Ah, See; Sell Opium; San Joaquin; CA; 1824; Mikoo; 11B
Ah, See; Gambler; Ada; ID; 1830; China; 19A
Ah, See; Gambler; Nevada; CA; 1830; Canton; 220B
Ah, See; Keeps Gambling House; Shoshone; ID; 1825; China;
     360D
Ah, Shung; Keeps Gambling House; Amador; CA; 1843; China;
     112B
Ah, Sin; Gambler; Deer Lodge; MT; 1838; China; 111C
Ah, Sin; Gambling House; Amador; CA; 1817; China; 111D
Ah, Sin; Gambler; Deer Lodge; MT; 1841; China; 111C
Ah, Sin; Gambler; Storey; NV; 1848; China; 237D
Ah, Sin; Gambling House; Amador; CA; 1817; China; 111D
Ah, Sing; Opium Den Keeper; Sacramento; CA; 1838; China; 1B
Ah, Sing; Gambler; Idaho; ID; 1846; China; 171C
Ah, Sing; Gambler; Butte; CA; 1828; China; 147D
Ah, Sing; Gambler; Butte; CA; 1844; China; 262C
Ah, Sing; Gambler; Trinity; CA; 1860; China; 570C
Ah, Sing; Gambler; Yuba; CA; 1848; Canton; 426D
Ah, Sing; Gambler; Yuba; CA; 1825; China; 481C

Ah, Sing; Gambling House; Storey; NV; 1858; China; 237D
Ah, Som; Gambler; Yuba; CA; 1850; Canton; 428D
Ah, Song; Gambler; Trinity; CA; 1854; China; 570D
Ah, Song; Gambler; Tuolumne; CA; 1843; Canton; 165C
Ah, Soo; Opium Den; San Joaquin; CA; 1855; Canton; 11B
Ah, Sow; Gambling House; Owyhee; ID; 1838; China; 353C
Ah, Sue; Keeps Gambling House; Calaveras; CA; 1850; China; 345B
Ah, Suey; Gambler; Trinity; CA; 1844; China; 570D
Ah, Suey; Gambling House; Trinity; CA; 1845; China; 570D
Ah, Sun; Keeps Opium Den; Eureka; NV; 1830; China; 212C
Ah, Sun; Gambler; Butte; CA; 1849; China; 148B
Ah, Taunge; Gambler; El Dorado; CA; 1828; China; 65B
Ah, Tay; Opium Shop; Santa Clara; CA; 1840; China; 127D
Ah, Tay; Gambler; Ormsby; NV; 1842; China; 70D
Ah, Tay; Gambler; Butte; CA; 1845; China; 149C
Ah, Thug; Gambler; Yuba; CA; 1830; Canton; 428C
Ah, Tie; Gambler; Tuolumne; CA; 1809; Canton; 165C
Ah, Tim; Gambling House; Sacramento; CA; 1843; China; 332A
Ah, Tin; Gambler; Butte; CA; 1847; China; 148B
Ah, Tom; Gambler; Madison; MT; 1845; China; 386B
Ah, Tom; Gambler; Nevada; CA; 1840; China; 188A
Ah, Tone; Gambler; Tuolumne; CA; 1840; Canton; 164A
Ah, Tong; Gambler; Elko; NV; 1845; China; 69A
Ah, Tong; Gambler; Nevada; CA; 1854; China; 175B
Ah, Tony; Opium House; Trinity; CA; 1837; China; 570D
Ah, Toon; Gambler; Idaho; ID; 1850; Canton; 166C
Ah, Tow; Gambler; Tuolumne; CA; 1840; Canton; 165C
Ah, Toy; Gambler; Boise; ID; 1843; China; 118B
Ah, Tsing; Gambler; Deer Lodge; MT; 1844; China; 111C
Ah, Tu; Gambler; Idaho; ID; 1840; Canton; 166C
Ah, Tuck; Gambler; Eureka; NV; 1843; China; 213B
Ah, Tuey; Gambler; Nevada; CA; 1841; China; 188A
Ah, Tun; Opium Smoker; Alameda; CA; 1848; Canton; 664C
Ah, Tung; Gambler; Storey; NV; 1838; China; 147D
Ah, Ty; Gambler; Nevada; CA; 1854; China; 175B
Ah, Wah; Gambler; Washoe; NV; 1854; China; 277A
Ah, Wah; Gambler; Butte; CA; 1845; China; 149C

Ah, Wan; Gambler; Lewis and Clark; MT; 1829; China; 276B
Ah, Wan; Gambler; Tuolumne; CA; 1840; Canton; 165C
Ah, Way; Gambler; Boise; ID; 1841; China; 136A
Ah, Why; Keeps Gambling House; Calaveras; CA; 1829; China;
    345B
Ah, Wing; Gambler; Eureka; NV; 1845; China; 191A
Ah, Won; Opium Den; Nevada; CA; 1850; Canton; 149B
Ah, Wong; Opium Store; Storey; NV; 1843; China; 147D
Ah, Wong; Gambling House Keeper; Boise; ID; 1844; China;
    118B
Ah, Wong; Gambler; Storey; NV; 1859; China; 147D
Ah, Wong; Gambling House Keeper; Boise; ID; 1844; China;
    118B
Ah, Wough; Gambler; Boise; ID; 1847; China; 118B
Ah, Wun; Gambler; Amador; CA; 1834; Canton; 35A
Ah, Wy; Gambler; Amador; CA; 1834; Canton; 38C
Ah, Yah; Gambler; Deer Lodge; MT; 1830; China; 110A
Ah, Yang; Gambler; Boise; ID; 1840; China; 118B
Ah, Yawk; Gambler; Amador; CA; 1823; China; 111D
Ah, Yeck; Gambler; Placer; CA; 1842; China; 301B
Ah, Yen; Gambler; Shoshone; ID; 1840; China; 360D
Ah, Yick; Keeps Opium Den; Shasta; CA; 1856; China; 2D
Ah, Ying; Gambler; Sacramento; CA; 1844; China; 332A
Ah, Yip; Gambler; Yuba; CA; 1850; Canton; 428D
Ah, Yon; Gambler; Nevada; CA; 1840; China; 175A
Ah, Yon; Keeps Gambling House; Ada; ID; 1853; China; 19B
Ah, Yook; Gambler; Butte; CA; 1850; China; 262C
Ah, Yot; Opium Den; San Joaquin; CA; 1845; Canton; 12C
Ah, You; Gambler; Eureka; NV; 1840; China; 192C
Ah, You; Gambler; Butte; CA; 1844; China; 262C
Ah, Young; Gambler; Yuba; CA; 1855; Canton; 428D
Ah, Yun; Gambling House; Owyhee; ID; 1852; China; 353C
Ah, Yun; Gambler; Sacramento; CA; 1836; China; 333D
Ah, Yun; Gambler; Tuolumne; CA; 1840; Canton; 165C
Ah, Yun; Gambler; Tuolumne; CA; 1831; Canton; 165C
Ah, Yung; Gambler; Washoe; NV; 1856; China; 277A
Ahan, Matiws; Tramp on public street; St. Clair; IL; 1846; IL;
    483D

Ahern, William; Ball player; Rensselaer; NY; 1858; NY; 108B
Ahl, Gottlieb; Tramp; Onondaga; NY; 1834; Wurtenburg; 225C
Akers, Anna; Dead; Taylor; IA; ---; IA; 60B
Akers, Wm. H.; Gambler; Clark; IN; 1844; IN; 137C
Alaxender, Spencer; With Circus; Rock; WI; 1851; NY; 225D
Albert, Peter; Dead; Sandusky; OH; 1825; OH; 160B
Albrice, Thomas; Gambler; Presidio; TX; 1848; MS; 86C
Alby, Alb; Tramp; Grant; OR; 1849; ME; 45B
Aldrich, Harison; Dead; St. Louis; MO; 1842; MO; 315C
Alen, John; Tramp; Hennepin; MN; 1859; ---; 272A
Alexander, Elijah W.; Phrenologist; Erie; OH; 1834; PA; 50B
Alexander, John; Gambler; Franklin; OH; 1838; OH; 398A
Allen; Dead; Calhoun; AR; ---; AR; 107B
Allen, Abe; Vagabond; Morgan; GA; 1828; GA; 278A
Allen, Charles; Gambler; Saratoga; NY; 1855; OH; 456B
Allen, David; Gambler; Deer Lodge; MT; 1851; NY; 126B
Allen, Frank; Circus Rider; Franklin; OH; 1856; NY; 476B
Allen, James; Pimp; Wayne; IN; 1849; TN; 323C
Allen, John; Tramp on public street; St. Clair; IL; 1862; NJ; 482B
Allen, Mary; Dead; Travis; TX; 1879; TX; 33D
Allen, Ruben H.; Dead; Cook; IL; 1875; NY; 151C
Allen, Thomas; Tramp; Buchanan; MO; 1832; NY; 41A
Allen, William; Dancer; New York; NY; 1852; NY; 245B
Allnetty, Clark; Tramp; Dallas; AR; 1858; KY; 184C
Alloway, Henry; Gambler; Warren; MS; 1848; KY; 346A
Alma, Roda; Dead; Ingham; MI; 1806; ---; 475C
Alt, Eddie C.; Dead; Grant; WV; 1878; WV; 242A
Altekruse, Charlotta; Dead; St. Louis; MO; 1851; Germany; 287B
Alvan, Wilhelmina; Astronomer; San Francisco; CA; 1839; NY;
    95D
Amakeen, Frank; Dead; Henrico; VA; 1862; VA; 242A
Ambrosia, Theresia; Medium; Philadelphia; PA; 1851; PA; 332B
Amerson, Mattie; Dead; Crawford; GA; 1879; GA; 665B
Amler, Harry; Travels with Circus; Cook; IL; 1840; Ireland; 96B
Amos, R.B.; Circus; Ohio; WV; 1848; IN; 448D
An, Fong; Fortune Teller; San Francisco; CA; 1849; Wampoa;
    428C
An, Hop; Gambler; Idaho; ID; 1850; Canton; 166C

Anaguistick; Thief; Piute; UT; 1864; UT Terr.; 545B
Andersen, Anna C.; Dead; Montcalm; MI; 1816; Denmark; 270A
Anderson, Ellen; Fortune Teller; Hamilton; OH; 1841; Baden;
        56B
Anderson, Gabel; Worked on farm (dead); Iberia; LA; 1854; LA;
        329B
Anderson, James; Tramp; Erie; NY; 1867; NY; 236B
Anderson, John; Tramp; Dutchess; NY; 1831; NY; 106C
Anderson, John; Tramp on public street; St. Clair; IL; 1858;
        Sweden; 481D
Anderson, Lana A.; Dead; Graves; KY; 1879; KY; 303D
Andrews, Frank; Tramp on public street; St. Clair; IL; 1838; NY;
        483D
Andrews, Julia E.; Clar. Healer; Will; IL; 1829; Canada; 199B
Andrews, Louis; Circus Actor; St. Louis; MO; 1851; MO; 386D
Andrews, Michael; Dead; Cuyahoga; OH; 1863; NY; 331B
Andrews, W.K.; Gambler; Storey; NV; 1838; MA; 143D
Ang, Gee; Gambler; Eureka; NV; 1850; China; 191A
Ang, Yu; Gambling House; Storey; NV; 1860; China; 237D
Angell, Arthur; Dead; Fillmore; NE; 1880; NE; 469B
Ankeny, Thomas J.; Gambling; Beaverhead; MT; 1858; PA; 20C
Anndedown, Mrietta; Clairvoyant Physician; Worcester; MA;
        1841; MA; 434C
Ansley; Dead; Indiana; PA; 1880; PA; 416D
Anson, Adrian C.; Baseball player; Cook; IL; 1852; IL; 292B
Anthony, Charles; Magnetic Bath House; Fulton; IN; 1818;
        France; 72B
Anthony, Sarah A.; Clairvoyant; Philadelphia; PA; 1815; NJ;
        311B
Anton, Herr; Magician; St. Louis; MO; 1845; Italy; 364B
Antony, C.; Circus; Ohio; WV; 1852; Switzerland; 449A
Aratuas, Pablo; Circus Performer; Maricopa; AZ; 1851; Zacateras;
        81C
Arble, Sophia; Dead; Blair; PA; 1858; PA; 87A
Arentz; Dead; Adams; IL; ---; IL; 472D
Ariola, Cresencia; Circus Actor; Atascosa; TX; 1846; Mexico;
        322A

Arlinghouse, C.H.; Gambler; Deer Lodge; MT; 1834; Germany; 126B

Armijo, Jose M.; Gambler; Conejos; CO; 1850; NM Terr.; 179B

Armistead, Harry; Dead; Carroll; MS; 1879; MS; 135B

Armstrong; Dead; Washington; IL; 1880; IL; 364C

Armstrong, Joseph; Gambler; Deer Lodge; MT; 1854; PA; 137C

Arney; Dead; Allegheny; PA; 1880; PA; 253B

Arthur, William; Arthur the Magician; Philadelphia; PA; 1840; MD; 437B

Ashford, George; Pimp; Eau Claire; WI; 1853; WI; 515A

Ashley, I.W.; Circus; Ohio; WV; 1852; NY; 448D

Ashton, C.; Gambler; Pima; AZ; 1849; TN; 331B

Ashton, Thomas; Gambler; Santa Fe; NM; 1849; OH; 74B

Asken, James; Tramp on public street; St. Clair; IL; 1846; MO; 482B

Aspinwall, Franklin E.; Phrenologist; Albany; NY; 1854; NY; 422C

Aspinwall, William H.; Gambler; Washington; D.C.; 1845; NY; 219C

Atkins, Elizabeth; Tramp; Surry; NC; 1824; NC; 69A

Atkinson; Tramp; St. Louis; MO; 1834; MO; 511D

Atkinson, William H.; Vagrant; Muskingum; OH; 1863; OH; 282A

Austin, Edw'd P.; Astronomer; Suffolk; MA; 1838; MI; 277D

Aut, Sallie; Ballet dancer; Philadelphia; PA; 1856; PA; 383B

Avery, Mathew; Dead; Wilcox; AL; 1868; ---; 191C

Ayer, Alber W.; Gambler; Rockingham; NH; 1814; NH; 22D

Aymar, Bella; Circus Performer; New York; NY; 1864; Brazil; 74A

Aymar, Lottie; Circus Performer; New York; NY; 1859; NY; 74A

Aymar, Maggie B.; Circus Performer; New York; NY; 1840; PA; 74A

Aymar, Walter; Circus Performer; New York; NY; 1839; NJ; 74A

Aymar, William; Circus Performer; New York; NY; 1863; Brazil; 74A

Babb, Jasper; Tramp; Adams; OH; 1825; OH; 54B

Babcock, Ella M.; Dead; St. Croix; WI; 1875; WI; 225C

Baca, Maria; Dancer; Santa Fe; NM; 1859; NM Terr.; 85A

Bachmann, John; Tramp on public street; St. Clair; IL; 1832;
      Wurtemburg; 484A

Back, William; Gambler; San Bernardino; CA; 1855; CA; 508B

Bacon, Fannie; Tramp; Hawkins; TN; 1840; TN; 196A

Bader, Rudolph; Dead; Allegheny; PA; 1879; PA; 241A

Badonuex, Marie; Clairvoyant; Providence; RI; 1846;
      Switzerland; 194A

Bagby, G.W.; Gambler; Tulare; CA; 1848; IL; 101B

Bagley, Andrew; Circus Man; Winona; MN; 1855; ---; 257C

Bagley, Sarah O.; Doctoress (Mental Cure); Essex; MA; 1825;
      MA; 381D

Bagley, William; Circus; St. Louis; MO; 1859; TX; 57A

Bailey, F.H.; Circus Man; Hamilton; OH; 1818; NY; 124A

Bailey, George; Base ball player; San Francisco; CA; 1859; IA;
      136D

Bailey, George G.; Prof. ball player; Marshall; IA; 1858; IA; 109B

Bailey, James; Dead; Clay; KY; 1810; KY; 552D

Bailey, Jane; Dead; Clay; KY; 1856; KY; 552D

Bailey, John B.; Boxing master; Suffolk; MA; 1818; MD; 251B

Baine, James; Tramp; Lapeer; MI; 1821; Scotland; 315B

Bairzley, Annie; Layer out of the dead; Philadelphia; PA; 1830;
      PA; 46D

Baker, Estell; Dead; Susquehanna; PA; 1864; PA; 359B

Baker, Frederic; Tramp; Peoria; IL; 1862; Germany; 10D

Baker, Iram; Magnetic Healer; Arapahoe; CO; 1818; NY; 354D

Baker, Major; Gambler; Sedgwick; KS; 1845; KS; 250A

Baker, Marcellus; Boxing master; Suffolk; MA; 1846; ME; 116D

Baker, Philip; Baseball player; Washington; D.C.; 1855; PA; 378B

Baker, S.C.; Pico Gambler; Carroll; AR; 1852; MO; 152B

Baker, Schell; Tramp; Vigo; IN; 1860; IN; 147B

Baldwin, Taylor; Gambler; Jefferson; KY; 1849; IN; 149C

Ball, Albert; Fortune Teller; Franklin; OH; 1825; VA; 350C

Ballard, John; Tramp; Buchanan; MO; 1839; MO; 41A

Balli, Ricardo; Vagrant; Hidalgo; TX; 1837; Mexico; 231A

Ballio, Guiseppe; Tramp; Genesee; NY; 1847; Italy; 506B

Balten, Robert; Dead; Madison; KY; 1878; KY; 348B

Bandiz, Charles; Tramp on public street; St. Clair; IL; 1856;
      Baden; 482B

Bane, Jas. C.; Quack Doctor; Putnam; WV; 1814; WV; 4C
Bank, Geo.; Gambler; Robertson; TX; 1864; TX; 371A
Banks, H.; Tramp; Douglas; NE; 1855; PA; 291B
Baptiste, Joseph Jean; Drunkard; St. James; LA; 1835; LA; 615C
Barber, Susan; Fortune Teller; Monmouth; NJ; 1823; NJ; 471A
Barden, Hamal; Magnetic Healer; Oneida; NY; 1831; NY; 82A
Bardmer, Henry; Tramp on public street; St. Clair; IL; 1858; NY;
    481D
Barela, Juan; Vagabond; Huerfano; CO; 1845; NM Terr.; 231D
Barger, Emma V.; Layer out of the dead; Philadelphia; PA; 1845;
    PA; 575A
Barker, David; Circus; Ohio; WV; 1840; NY; 448D
Barlow, Lucinda A.E.; Dead; Grundy; MO; 1878; MO; 369A
Barlow, Pinkey; Dead; Grundy; MO; 1879; MO; 369A
Barlow, Thomas; Ball player; New York; NY; 1852; NY; 113A
Barnes, Aaron; Phrenologist; Suffolk; MA; 1815; MA; 112C
Barnes, Agnes H.; Clairvoyant; Suffolk; MA; 1848; Scotland;
    318B
Barnes, William; Gambler; San Francisco; CA; 1832; IN; 127C
Barnhart, Sarah; Hurdy dancer; Deer Lodge; MT; 1858; Germany;
    136B
Barnmul, N.C.; Gambler; Deer Lodge; MT; 1854; NY; 135C
Barnum, Jack; Prisoner for arson; Randolph; GA; 1858; GA; 118C
Barr, Daniel; Circus; Ohio; WV; 1852; KY; 448D
Barr, Sarah; Dead; Allegheny; PA; 1857; England; 221B
Barrera, Gabino; Proffessional Thief; Zapata; TX; 1835; Mexico;
    453A
Barrett, Russell; Phrenologist; Fulton; OH; 1835; NY; 169C
Barrett, William; Gambler; Natchitoches; LA; 1845; NY; 609B
Barris, Carman; Circus Rider; Maricopa; AZ; 1862; Mexico; 81C
Barron, Morris; Gambler; New York; NY; 1834; NY; 143B
Barry, John; Tramp; New York; NY; 1845; Ireland; 581D
Barry, William; Tramp; Franklin; NY; 1862; NY; 645D
Barsch, Albert; Tramp on public street; St. Clair; IL; 1850;
    Prussia; 482A
Bartel, S.B.; Quack Doctor; Kent; MD; 1815; France; 103A
Bartholomew, George; Circus Horse Trainer; Alameda; CA; 1834;
    MI; 340C

Bartlet, Frank; Thief; Franklin; OH; 1847; MI; 481C

Bartlet, John; Tramp; Union; NJ; 1852; CT; 171C

Bartley, William; Tramp; Butler; PA; 1840; PA; 51B

Barttell, R.T.; Circus; Ohio; WV; 1848; KY; 448D

Baskerville, Albert E.; Dead; Henderson; IL; 1861; IL; 35C

Bass, Samuel; Circus Driver; Bergen; NJ; 1844; PA; 434B

Bassett, Louisa; Clairvoyant; Providence; RI; 1830; NJ; 308C

Bastian, Harry; Spiritual Medium; Cattaraugus; NY; 1843; NY;
        175C

Bat, Ting; Pimp; San Francisco; CA; 1850; Kwontung; 375D

Batchellor, George H.; Manager of Circus; Providence; RI; 1830;
        RI; 1B

Battle; Foot racing; Shawnee; KS; 1861; MO; 264B

Bauer, Charles; Tramp on public street; St. Clair; IL; 1826;
        Bavaria; 482A

Baumann, Nik; Tramp on public street; St. Clair; IL; 1853; Hesse
        D.; 482A

Baunon, John; Thief; Westchester; NY; 1857; NY; 107D

Baury, Thos.; Circus; Ohio; WV; 1840; England; 449A

Baxter, Fred; Gambler; Arapahoe; CO; 1854; NJ; 98D

Baylor, Millard; Dead; Northumberland; PA; 1880; PA; 523A

Beadinkopf, H.; Magician; Baltimore; MD; 1848; MD; 88A

Beak, Martin; Gambler; Jefferson; KY; 1851; KY; 378D

Beal, Reah; Fortune Teller; Wayne; MI; 1845; OH; 114B

Beal, William; Plays baseball; Sumner; KS; 1861; NJ; 275C

Beals, Dolly; Dead (Drowned); St. Joseph; IN; 1874; IN; 431C

Beals, Owen; Dead (Drowned); St. Joseph; IN; 1876; IN; 431C

Beatty, Geo.; Thief; Westchester; NY; 1857; MI; 109C

Beaty, Mary; Dead; Fairfield; SC; 1860; SC; 95C

Beaver, Jacob; Thief; Dutchess; NY; 1845; NY; 194B

Beck, Frank; Gambler; Montgomery; OH; 1852; OH; 81A

Beck, James; Astrologer; Salt Lake; UT; 1854; England; 169A

Beck, John; Circus; Ohio; WV; 1852; NY; 448D

Beck, Louguria; Dead; Autauga; AL; 1871; AL; 66C

Becker, Christ; Tramp on public street; St. Clair; IL; 1845;
        Nassau; 482A

Beckwith, Emma; Clairvoyant; New York; NY; 1838; MA; 406C

Beckwith, Emma; Clairvoyant; Providence; RI; 1842; RI; 336A

Beddford, J.; Tramp; Pima; AZ; 1850; Montreal, Canada; 312A

Beeby, Robert C.; Gambler; Lake; CO; 1850; LA; 352A

Beecher, George C.; Magnetice Healer; Ontario; NY; 1832; NY;
    100D

Beechler, George; Quack at Medicine; Upshur; WV; 1829;
    Germany; 155C

Beer, Mary C.; Dead; Carbon; PA; 1877; PA; 488D

Begneut, Henry; Tramp; Orleans; LA; 1862; LA; 29B

Beighle, Nellie; Spirit Medium; San Francisco; CA; 1850;
    Canada; 275C

Belcheir, D.; Billiard player; Oakland; MI; 1858; Canada; 330C

Bell, Amelia A.; Dead; Sullivan; IN; 1872; IN; 531A

Bell, Charles; Clown; Shelby; IN; 1851; England; 285A

Bell, Maria; Dead; Sullivan; IN; 1859; OH; 531B

Bell, Thomas; Tramp; New York; NY; 1823; England; 581D

Bell, Thomas; Thief; Franklin; OH; 1855; OH; 483C

Bell, Thomas A.; Dead; Owen; KY; 1863; KY; 172B

Bell, Wm.; Tramp; Douglas; NE; 1861; TN; 260D

Bellinger, Bej.; Tramp; Colleton; SC; 1855; SC; 410C

Bellville, J.M.; Circus; Ohio; WV; 1836; Scotland; 449A

Belville, C.; Circus; Ohio; WV; 1853; VT; 449A

Benbrook, C.L.; Gambler; Pinal; AZ; 1855; AR; 400D

Benedict, Phelps; Deadbeat; Schoharie; NY; 1838; NY; 74D

Benedie, Viola; Fortune Teller; Cuyahoga; OH; 1833; Prussia; 8D

Beneditto, Ben; Gambler; Orleans; LA; 1850; Cuba; 453A

Bengert, Frederick; Dead; Adams; IL; 1876; IL; 470D

Benke, James; Tramp; Hennepin; MN; 1861; MA; 272A

Bennett, Chas.; B. ball player; Worcester; MA; 1850; MD; 182D

Bennett, George C.; Gambler; Mobile; AL; 1849; AL; 302A

Benson, Christian; Tramp; Iowa; WI; 1818; Norway; 81D

Benson, Peter; Laborer Vagrant; Winnebago; WI; 1849; Sweden;
    163A

Benton, David; Tramp; Hanson; Dak. Terr.; 1844; MO; 56C

Benton, Winny; Farming dead; Fairfield; SC; 1845; SC; 190B

Benz, Franceska; Dead; Adams; IL; 1870; IL; 472C

Berg, William; Tramp on public street; St. Clair; IL; 1860;
    Prussia; 483C

Berger, Christian L.; Astronomer; Suffolk; MA; 1844; Germany; 252D

Bergholz, Henry; Dead; St. Louis; MO; 1879; MO; 358A

Bergim, M.; Dead; St. Louis; MO; 1831; Ireland; 184A

Berguin, Mingo; Dead head; St. Landry; LA; 1800; LA; 335D

Berhuer, Theodore; Tramp; Pinal; AZ; 1846; Lorraine; 373C

Berk, John; Gypsy; Bradford; PA; 1854; Wales; 61B

Berkhalter, Edwr.; Thief; Franklin; OH; 1861; OH; 482B

Berley, James H.; Tramp; Marion; IN; 1850; IN; 435C

Bernett, Isaac; Gambler; Franklin; OH; 1800; NY; 98A

Berry, Richard; Gambler; Storey; NV; 1830; Ireland; 138B

Best, John; Gambler; Mono; CA; 1848; MO; 132B

Bezant, John; Thief; Westchester; NY; 1845; Scotland; 97D

Bibb, Margaret; Dead; Perry; AL; 1879; AL; 441D

Biddox, Willis; Gambler; Davidson; TN; 1862; TN; 110B

Big John; Gambler; San Bernardino; CA; 1850; CA; 537A

Bigger, William D.; Dead; Panola; TX; 1879; TX; 203B

Biggert, Albert; Tramp; Allegheny; PA; 1852; PA; 336C

Biggs, Francis L.; Dead; Panola; TX; 1867; TX; 199A

Biggs, Mary; Dead; Panola; TX; 1870; TX; 199A

Bilderback, Wm.; Tramp; Buffalo; WI; 1861; IL; 228D

Bill; Gambler; Ormsby; NV; 1840; NV; 77A

Birdsell, Varnham; Dead; St. Joseph; IN; 1880; IN; 416B

Bishop, Amanda; Dead - kept house; Ballard; KY; 1836; KY; 401A

Bishop, George A.; Mag. Healer; Cook; IL; 1829; OH; 563D

Bishopp, R.C.; Circus; Ohio; WV; 1851; IN; 448D

Bissell, Samuel D.; Travels with Circus; Otsego; NY; 1842; NY; 125B

Bissitt, Sarah; Dead; Nash; NC; 1853; NC; 547B

Bissitt, William; Dead; Nash; NC; 1880; NC; 547B

Biven, Elizabeth; Dead; Colleton; SC; 1855; SC; 245B

Black, Dan; Gambler; Warren; MS; 1848; MO; 347C

Black, Daniel; Tramp on public street; St. Clair; IL; 1850; OH; 482B

Black, Elizabeth; Tramp; Randolph; NC; 1840; NC; 86D

Black, Rob't; Circus; Ohio; WV; 1838; IN; 449A

Black, Slick; Gambler; Calcasieu; LA; 1846; TX; 504D

Black, Wm.; Circus; Ohio; WV; 1859; CT; 448D
Blackburn, J.B.; Gambler; Cooke; TX; 1839; MO; 199B
Blackford, James; Circus Actor; Buchanan; MO; 1853; CT; 122B
Blackford, John; Circus Actor; Buchanan; MO; 1856; CT; 122B
Blacks, Dave; Gambler; Tarrant; TX; 1857; MS; 52C
Blair, John; Gambler; Lake; CO; 1840; MN; 353C
Blair, Roland W.; Gambler; Mendocino; CA; 1850; KY; 222A
Blake; Dead; Dubuque; IA; ---; IA; 352B
Blake, George; Gypsy; Bennington; VT; 1840; VT; 519C
Blake, Harry; Gambler; Lake; CO; 1836; IL; 358A
Blake, Mariah; Just dead heart; Accomack; VA; 1801; VA; 184A
Blake, Mary Ann; Dead; Pointe Coupee; LA; 1879; LA; 312B
Blake, Mrs.; Gypsy; Bennington; VT; 1845; VT; 519C
Blakeslee, N.A.; Magnetic Doctoress; New York; NY; 1840; OH;
    224B
Blakesley, Narcissa A.; Clairvoyant Medium; Ocean; NJ; 1835;
    IL; 65A
Blames, William; Gambler; New York; NY; 1827; NY; 548B
Blanc, Jean; Tramp; Orleans; LA; 1820; France; 151A
Blanchard, Ed.; Sec. House Bum; Chemung; NY; 1846; NY; 287D
Blanche, August; Tramp on public street; St. Clair; IL; 1860;
    Switzerland; 483C
Blanchfield, Andy; Ball player; San Joaquin; CA; 1860; MA; 86D
Blank, (Infant); Dead; Indiana; PA; 1880; PA; 416C
Blank, Charles; Tramp; Essex; NJ; 1830; Baden; 470A
Blanton, Ajacks; Gambler; Henderson; NC; 1869; NC; 239D
Bletze, Wm.; Circus; Ohio; WV; 1857; NY; 448D
Blinn, Solomon; Magnetic Physician; Marshall; IA; 1834; OH;
    212C
Blish, H.O.; Circus; Ohio; WV; 1862; OH; 449B
Bliss, Adam; Dead; St. Louis; MO; 1877; MO; 497D
Bliss, Christina; Spiritual Medium; Philadelphia; PA; 1857; Cuba;
    341A
Bliss, Jas. A.; Spiritual Medium; Philadelphia; PA; 1847; MA;
    341A
Blitz, Eugene; Magician; New York; NY; 1851; NJ; 280A
Blue; Tramp; Weakley; TN; 1860; ---; 148B
Bluher, Rudolph; Gambler; Caldwell; TX; 1851; Oldenburg; 243B

Blunt, Charly; Gambler; Oglethorpe; GA; 1859; GA; 246C
Boatman, Forest; Dead at home; Ross; OH; 1870; OH; 165A
Bodemann, Helene; Dead; Milwaukee; WI; 1877; WI; 232D
Bodkin, Geo.; Gambling; Ballard; KY; 1855; KY; 438D
Boe, Chas. W.; Tramp; Schuylkill; PA; 1847; PA; 137A
Boehm, Albert; Tramp on public street; St. Clair; IL; 1841; Hesse
    D.; 484A
Boger, Robert; Tramp; Kankakee; IL; 1858; MS; 179D
Boileau, John; Vagrant; Muskingum; OH; 1842; PA; 284A
Boington, David; Gambler; Waupaca; WI; 1825; NY; 152B
Bois, George; Tramp; Belmont; OH; 1838; Ireland; 313C
Bolander, Thomas J.; Traveling with Circus; Fillmore; MN; 1862;
    PA; 335D
Boliver, Patsey; Vagrant; Leavenworth; KS; 1859; UT Terr.; 242A
Bolus, Charles C.; Canvas Boss of Circus; Wayne; OH; 1841; OH;
    397A
Bond, Ada L.; Medium; Franklin; MA; 1836; MA; 335A
Bond, John; Clog dancer; Bay; MI; 1858; NY; 335D
Bond, Thomas H.; Base ball player; Suffolk; MA; 1856; NY;
    341B
Bonefield, John; Gambler; Fulton; GA; 1848; GA; 243C
Boney, Andrew; Farming dead; Fairfield; SC; 1815; SC; 194B
Bonhess, John; Professer of magic; Seneca; OH; 1853; Elsase;
    345B
Bonner, Frank; Tramp on public street; St. Clair; IL; 1840;
    Austria; 482A
Bontelle, Susan A.; Clairvoyant; Suffolk; MA; 1830; NH; 292A
Booker, W.O.; Circus; Ohio; WV; 1846; OH; 448D
Boond, William; Gambler; Yavapai; AZ; 1854; CA; 415A
Booth, Amos; Base ball; Hamilton; OH; 1849; OH; 403B
Booth, Ebe; Dead; Walton; GA; 1877; GA; 564A
Booth, John E.; Magnectic Healer; Livingston; NY; 1818; NY;
    279A
Borden, A.A.; Tramp; Lancaster; NE; 1855; Canada; 173A
Borgain, C.; Tramp; Douglas; NE; 1852; OH; 291B
Bornman, Louisa; Dead; Adams; IL; 1879; IL; 483B
Bosley, Charles; Gambler; Deer Lodge; MT; 1837; NY; 127D
Boss, Lewis; Astronomer; Albany; NY; 1847; RI; 411C

Bosworth, George; Dead; Allegheny; PA; 1879; England; 235B

Bousher, Sarah A.; Dead; Fountain; IN; 1855; IN; 200D

Bowers, Edward; Tramp; Berkeley; WV; 1867; WV; 290A

Bowles, Tom; Gambler; Travis; TX; 1839; IA; 205C

Bowman, Max; Gambler; Sumner; KS; 1848; TX; 283A

Bowman, William; Dancer in theatre; St. Louis; MO; 1855; USA; 279B

Bowman, William; Song and dancer; St. Louis; MO; 1853; LA; 351B

Boyd, John; Gambler; Kinney; TX; 1845; VA; 296C

Boyd, Joseph; Agent for Circus; Scott; IA; 1828; PA; 666A

Boyd, William; Fire Eater in Circus; Morris; NJ; 1817; NJ; 170B

Boyle, John; Circus; Ohio; WV; 1834; NY; 449A

Boyle, William; Dead; Hamilton; OH; 1879; OH; 12D

Boynton, Mary P.; Clairvoyant; Cumberland; ME; 1835; ME; 24B

Bradac, John; Circus Canvas Man; St. Louis; MO; 1852; Bohemia; 632A

Bradberry, Susan M.; Dead; Panola; TX; 1837; GA; 201B

Braddon, John; Tramp on public street; St. Clair; IL; 1850; PA; 483C

Bradford, Edward; Dead; Orleans; LA; 1851; NY; 103A

Bradford, J.A.; Gambler; Deer Lodge; MT; 1853; OH; 126B

Bradley, Frank S.; Circus Employee; Windham; CT; 1852; CT; 598C

Bradley, George W.; Ball player; Providence; RI; 1851; PA; 375C

Bradley, James; Gambler; Bexar; TX; 1838; GA; 75B

Bradley, Nancy; Dead head; St. Landry; LA; 1825; MS; 335D

Bradley, Nancy; Dead; Tarrant; TX; 1844; IN; 129A

Brady, James; Tramp; New York; NY; 1857; NY; 581C

Brady, James; Tramp; New York; NY; 1830; Ireland; 288A

Brady, John; Vagrant Cook; Winnebago; WI; 1855; Ireland; 163A

Braggs, Tomas; Tramp on public street; St. Clair; IL; 1842; PA; 482A

Brak, Henry; Tramp on public street; St. Clair; IL; 1849; IL; 482B

Branchly, Thomas; Clown; New York; NY; 1835; England; 341A

Branden, Frank; Tramp; New York; NY; 1850; VA; 581D

Branly, Mary; Huckster in Carnival; Tompkins; NY; 1835; Italy; 214D

Brannon, James; Gambler; Montgomery; KS; 1841; OH; 244B
Branon, Willie; Tramp; Clinton; IA; 1867; NY; 380D
Branscomb, Bennet; Gambler; Bullock; AR; 1804; VA; 36A
Braun, John; Tramp on public street; St. Clair; IL; 1854; Prussia;
   483C
Bravoley, Babe; Dead; Caldwell; TX; 1880; TX; 190D
Bread, Lucy; Wild Indian; Oneida; NY; 1848; NY; 268D
Bredeck, Wm.; Dead; St. Louis; MO; 1879; MO; 502B
Breeden, D.; Gambler; Goliad; TX; 1850; TX; 311B
Breeding, Martha; Dead; Claiborne; TN; 1879; TN; 175D
Brennam, Queen Ann; Dead; Fairfield; SC; 1878; SC; 190B
Brennan, John; Healer; New York; NY; 1859; PA; 426B
Brenze, Albert; Deadbeat; Copiah; MS; 1830; MS; 42D
Bresnehan, Maurice; Baseball player; Suffolk; MA; 1857; MA;
   463A
Brett, Maggie; Vagrant; Knox; TN; 1865; TN; 118D
Brewer, Evan T.; Gambler; Sangamon; IL; 1856; KY; 220A
Brewer, Pinkie; Fortune Teller; La Fayette; AR; 1830; England;
   423D
Briand, King; Tramp on public street; St. Clair; IL; 1842; TN;
   483D
Bride, I.M.; Circus; Ohio; WV; 1844; KY; 448D
Bridenthall, Charles; Dead; Kosciusko; IN; 1872; IA; 143D
Bridenthall, Edith; Dead; Kosciusko; IN; 1873; IN; 143D
Bridenthall, Inabell; Dead; Kosciusko; IN; 1879; IN; 143D
Bridenthall, Lydia; Dead; Kosciusko; IN; 1870; IN; 143D
Bridges, George; Gambler; Grayson; TX; 1844; TN; 89A
Briggs, Geo. R.; Thief; Westchester; NY; 1856; MA; 96A
Brigham, B.; Circus; Ohio; WV; 1844; NY; 449B
Bright, Edith M.; Dead; Northumberland; PA; 1880; PA; 541B
Brighthart, Theresa; Vagrant; Seneca; NY; 1832; Germany; 121D
Brimeyer, Elisabeth; Dead; Dubuque; IA; 1876; IA; 343C
Brimeyer, Lewis; Dead; Dubuque; IA; 1880; IA; 342B
Brimeyer, Mary; Dead; Dubuque; IA; 1851; IA; 342A
Brinson, Jacob; Dead; Colleton; SC; 1838; SC; 240C
Britt, Amy; Dancer; New York; NY; 1860; NY; 165D
Brocker, Casper; Tramp; Mercer; NJ; 1839; Germany; 293A
Brolheis, Alex; Clog dancer; Cass; IL; 1864; IA; 719C

Broofield, Legon; Dead; Columbia; AR; 1880; AR; 244B

Brookfield, A.; Gambler; Baker; OR; 1857; CO; 3D

Brooks, Anthony; Farm hand (dead); Orleans; LA; 1840; MS; 311D

Brooks, Arnold D.; Gambler; Lamar; TX; 1835; NY; 209C

Brooks, Bradford; Gambler; Atchison; KS; 1856; MO; 257C

Brooks, Isaac; Gambler; Atchison; KS; 1852; MO; 257C

Brooks, Richard; With the Circus; Rock; WI; 1842; England; 225D

Brooks, William; Cricket player; Philadelphia; PA; 1850; England; 229C

Broom, Dawson; Dead; Fairfield; SC; 1876; SC; 193D

Broom, Edward; Dead; Fairfield; SC; 1878; SC; 193D

Broom, Margaret; Dead; Fairfield; SC; 1800; SC; 193D

Broom, Mary M.; Dead; Fairfield; SC; 1878; SC; 191C

Brothers, Charles J.; Lazy Laborer; Tyler; WV; 1863; OH; 99B

Brothers, John C.; Lazy Laborer; Tyler; WV; 1856; OH; 99B

Brougher, W.; Gambler; Nye; NV; 1855; PA; 13D

Brown, ---; Gambler; Lake; CO; 1854; NY; 358A

Brown, A.F.; Dead; Republic; KS; 1810; KS; 71A

Brown, Adison; Gambler; Lawrence; Dak. Terr.; 1829; Ireland; 292D

Brown, Andy; Gambler; McLennan; TX; 1858; LA; 2D

Brown, Charles; Gambler; Muscogee; GA; 1846; GA; 667A

Brown, Cora; Dead; Ellsworth; KS; 1879; KS; 485B

Brown, Dan A.; Clairvoyant; Worcester; MA; 1827; VT; 328B

Brown, Edward; Dead; Caldwell; TX; 1879; TX; 194C

Brown, Elick; Dead; Kemper; MS; 1866; MS; 142B

Brown, Frank; Magnetic Healer; Suffolk; MA; 1851; NY; 65D

Brown, George; Tramp; St. Johns; FL; 1852; GA; 145B

Brown, George; Laborer & Tramp; Randolph; MO; 1858; NJ; 71D

Brown, Harrison; Vagrant; Warren; GA; 1860; GA; 109B

Brown, Henry F.; Gambler; Pinal; AZ; 1824; Ireland; 398C

Brown, J.F.; Whorehouse pimp; Atchison; MO; 1852; NC; 380A

Brown, J.V.; Gambler; Grant; NM; 1850; TX; 347D

Brown, James; Gambler; Maverick; TX; 1834; VA; 55A

Brown, Jo; Dead; Woodruff; AR; 1879; AR; 246B

Brown, Joe; Tramp on public street; St. Clair; IL; 1846; LA; 483C

Brown, John; Gambler; Grant; NM; 1850; MO; 343D
Brown, John A.; Gambler; Storey; NV; 1838; PA; 119D
Brown, Johnson; Quack Doctor; Plymouth; MA; 1823; MA; 506C
Brown, Josephine; In the Circus Business; Philadelphia; PA; 1825; France; 132D
Brown, Laura; Dead; Ellsworth; KS; 1879; KS; 485B
Brown, Margaret; Clairvoyant; New York; NY; 1834; NY; 205C
Brown, Mrs.; Dead; Milwaukee; WI; 1838; England; 293C
Brown, Nancy; Dead; Pointe Coupee; LA; 1879; LA; 313C
Brown, Nathanel; Quack Doctor; Montgomery; NY; 1815; NH; 84C
Brown, Rob't; Magnetic Physician; Arapahoe; CO; 183; Canada; 53A
Brown, William; In the Circus Business; Philadelphia; PA; 1826; PA; 132D
Brubach, Charles; Dead; Allegheny; PA; 1873; PA; 237A
Bruce, Isaac T.; Magnetic Doctor; Worcester; MA; 1821; VT; 526B
Brumbaugh, George; Advance Agt. for Circus; Darke; OH; 1859; KS; 426B
Bruner, Joel; Lazy Cus; Linn; IA; 1832; OH; 202A
Brunish, Benj.; Gambler; Woodbury; IA; 1828; NY; 396D
Brunner, Thomas; Gambler; Onondaga; NY; 1833; NY; 394A
Bryal, David A.; Horse Thief; Montgomery; IN; 1857; NC; 325C
Bryan, James; Tramp; New York; NY; 1820; Ireland; 581D
Bryan, W.; Dead; Colleton; SC; 1848; SC; 240D
Bryant, David; Lazy; New York; NY; 1864; NY; 236C
Bryant, John; Dead; Union; NJ; 1806; NJ; 336C
Buchanan, Ansolon; Tramp; New York; NY; 1854; NY; 581D
Bucher, Edward; Dead; Hamilton; OH; 1879; KY; 18C
Buck, Henrietta E.; Fortune Teller; Lake; CO; 1826; Hamburg; 410A
Buck, Palmer; Circus Man; Manistee; MI; 1856; NY; 74A
Buckler, H.; Circus; Ohio; WV; 1829; PA; 449A
Buckner, Thos.; Gambler; Storey; NV; 1827; KY; 111C
Bucky, Benj. L.; Gambler; Buchanan; MO; 1850; PA; 222A
Buderson, David; Dead; Colleton; SC; 1830; SC; 251A
Buelna, Rudolph; Gambler; Santa Clara; CA; 1846; Mexico; 129C

Bulfinch, Amos; Wanderer - parcial pauper; Middlesex; MA; 1839; NH; 92D

Bulger, Elizabeth; Dead; Oswego; NY; 1793; Ireland; 458B

Bullock, De Witt C.; Gambler; Jasper; MO; 1839; KY; 558C

Bumpus, Flory B.; Dead; Jefferson; IL; 1879; IL; 549D

Bunch, George; Gambler; Arapahoe; CO; 1850; MO; 110C

Bunet, Edith; Dead; St. Louis; MO; 1878; MO; 497C

Bunnell, Edwrd; Gambler; Clinton; IN; 1854; IN; 223A

Bunnheiser, John; Gambler; Grant; NM; 1853; PA; 350B

Burdett, Thomas; Professional Thief; Mercer; NJ; 1828; PA; 293A

Burdock, John J.; Base ballist; Suffolk; MA; 1852; NY; 342C

Burk, Charles; Tramp on public street; St. Clair; IL; 1858; Scotland; 483D

Burke, James; Tramp; Douglas; NE; 1856; NY; 337D

Burke, John; Dead; Bristol; MA; 1879; MA; 408A

Burke, Mary; Vagrant; Leavenworth; KS; 1860; Ireland; 242A

Burke, Mich.; Baseball player; Rensselaer; NY; 1854; NY; 427A

Burke, Thomas; Tramp - Prisoner; Ashtabula; OH; 1858; Ireland; 467C

Burkner, Osborne; Vagrant; Leavenworth; KS; 1860; MO; 242A

Burner, J.F.; Tramp; White Pine; NV; 1842; VA; 356C

Burnett, Louis; Gambler; Grant; NM; 1843; CA; 350B

Burnham, John; Wandering round the land living in tents; Oxford; ME; 1806; Canada; 76C

Burns, Charles; Crook; Franklin; OH; 1861; OH; 478A

Burns, Clark; Gambler; Leavenworth; KS; 1844; KY; 336B

Burns, Michael; Dead; Oswego; NY; 1795; Ireland; 461D

Burns, Thomas; Tramp; Monroe; NY; 1845; Ireland; 387C

Burr, Charles; Tramp on public street; St. Clair; IL; 1862; OH; 483C

Burton, Jack; Dead - druggist; Adair; MO; 1858; IN; 90D

Burton, John; Tramp; Oneida; NY; 1845; PA; 306A

Burton, Walter; For murder; Parker; TX; 1856; KY; 321D

Burton, William; Gambler; Graves; KY; 1862; TN; 187D

Burton, William; For murder; Parker; TX; 1853; KY; 321D

Bush; (Stillborn) dead; Ross; OH; 1880; OH; 168C

Bush, Elizabeth; Dead; Clark; KY; 1836; KY; 427D

Bush, Joe; Tramp; Davidson; TN; 1861; TN; 111D

Bush, Mary; Clairvoyant; Onondaga; NY; 1826; Ireland; 516A
Bushee, Louis; Circus Actor; New Haven; CT; 1858; France; 74A
Bushnell, Lewis; Magnetic Physician; Cook; IL; 1826; NY; 7B
Bushong, Albert; Baseball player; Worcester; MA; 1857; PA; 22B
Bustin, F.; Circus; Ohio; WV; 1845; NY; 449B
Butler, Henry; Gambler; Dinwiddie; VA; 1847; VA; 328C
Butler, Isaa; Dead; Autauga; AL; 1796; SC; 132D
Butler, Jas.; Circus; Ohio; WV; 1859; CT; 448D
Butler, Matilda; Dead; Greene; AL; 1855; AL; 38A
Butt, Chas.; Magnetic Physician; Jackson; MO; 1820; England;
    163D
Buvens, Isaac; Gambler; Galveston; TX; 1848; TX; 76A
Byers, B.; Gambler; Arapahoe; CO; 1841; OH; 45A
Byrne, John; Tramp; New York; NY; 1860; NY; 581D
Byrumn, Charles G.; Gambler; Deer Lodge; MT; 1853; MO; 116A
Bysell, Frank; Gambler; Lucas; OH; 1845; OH; 127D
Cable, John J.; Gambler; Deer Lodge; MT; 1850; OH; 137C
Cadett, T.A.; Drunk All Time; Beaufort; NC; 1840; NC; 172D
Cain, Mary A.F.; Clairvoyant; Suffolk; MA; 1818; SC; 81D
Cain, Zachariah; Tramp; Berrien; MI; 1852; MI; 148A
Calhoun, Ettie; Dead; Monroe; IN; 1855; MO; 82C
Callaghan, J.J.; Gambler; Grant; NM; 1851; Ireland; 343D
Callahan, Caroline; Dead; Blount; AL; 1879; AL; 458B
Callahan, James; Vagrant; Buchanan; MO; 1847; MO; 41B
Callahan, John; Thief; Westchester; NY; 1840; NY; 107D
Caloway, Bob; Gambler; Dallas; TX; 1851; TX; 23B
Cambell, Thomas; Tumbles in Circus; Passaic; NJ; 1861; NJ;
    478D
Cambridge, Chas.; Thief; Franklin; OH; 1843; LA; 481D
Camel, Nellie; Dead; Westmoreland; PA; 1877; PA; 143A
Cameron, Wm.; Thief would dignify him. ; Rio Grande; CO;
    1844; Canada; 324D
Cammel, J.; Tramp; Johnson; IL; 1812; TN; 591D
Campbell, Clements F.; Gambler; Cass; IN; 1833; IN; 321A
Campbell, John; Bummer; New York; NY; 1855; Scotland; 104A
Campbell, Juddie; Dead head; St. Landry; LA; 1790; LA; 335D
Campbell, Mary; Fortune Teller; Cook; IL; 1832; MA; 160C

Campbell, Rankin; invalid recorded dead; Vermillion; LA; 1829; LA; 91A

Campor, Francisco; Gambler; Las Animas; CO; 1855; NM Terr.; 74B

Candy, Nancy; Wanderer; Goochland; VA; 1820; VA; 277D

Cantrell, Theodoria; Dead; Fulton; GA; 1860; GA; 261D

Capori, Antonette; Ballet dancer; New York; NY; 1857; Italy; 658A

Cardenas, Jesus; Circus Actor; Atascosa; TX; 1862; Mexico; 322A

Carey, Peter; Gambler; Pottawattamie; IA; 1861; NY; 232A

Carington, Thomas; Thief; Ripley; IN; 1850; IN; 522D

Carleton, Mrs.; Clairvoyant; Suffolk; MA; 1834; MA; 316A

Carmicheal, Olive; Tramp; Coweta; GA; 1840; GA; 456A

Carney, Edith; Clair Voyant; New York; NY; 1858; Liberia; 190D

Carpenter, Ada; Magnetic Physician; York; ME; 1850; VT; 496A

Carpenter, George; Dead; Schenectady; NY; 1830; England; 132A

Carpenter, John; Gambler; Storey; NV; 1830; NY; 141D

Carpenter, Mr.; Baseball player; Hamilton; OH; 1852; NY; 101C

Carr, B.R.; Circus; Ohio; WV; 1850; KY; 448D

Carr, F.W.; Gambler; Storey; NV; 1834; NY; 114B

Carr, Mary; Dead; Sandusky; OH; 1872; OH; 156B

Carr, Patrick; Glass Blower dead; St. Louis; MO; 1847; Ireland; 357C

Carraway, J.H.; Gambler; Arapahoe; CO; 1835; OH; 98D

Carroll, James; Gambler; Galveston; TX; 1824; Ireland; 75D

Carroll, James; Gambler; Maverick; TX; 1859; NY; 45B

Carroll, Pelic R.; Tramp; Duplin; NC; 1815; NC; 569B

Carroll, S.; Circus; Ohio; WV; 1856; NY; 449B

Carroll, William; Circus Performer; New York; NY; 1849; MD; 74A

Carroll, William B.; Circus Actor; Westchester; NY; 1818; TN; 320C

Carson; Dead; Indiana; PA; ---; PA; 417B

Carter, Richard; Bummer; Philadelphia; PA; 1855; PA; 202A

Carter, W.F.; Gambler; Nevada; CA; 1834; MO; 31A

Carvon, Matheir; Base ball player; Hamilton; IA; 1858; IA; 164A

Cary, Eliza; Dead; McLennan; TX; 1850; TX; 267B

Case, John; Circus Performer; Hunterdon; NJ; 1840; NJ; 124D
Case, Marion; Gambler; San Bernardino; CA; 1855; CA; 480B
Casey, Angeline; Dead; Oswego; NY; 1861; NY; 461C
Cash, Virginia; Tramp; King George; VA; 1863; VA; 566D
Cashin, Jno.; Gambler; Conejos; CO; 1846; AL; 165C
Caskins, Eugene; Ball player; Rensselaer; NY; 1855; NY; 268A
Casler, Paul; Magestic Healer; Wapello; IA; 1821; IN; 118B
Casserly, Michael; Parents dead - laborer; Jo Daviess; IL; 1835; --
     -; 266B
Cassidy, John; Ball player; New York; NY; 1856; NY; 92B
Cassidy, John P.; Ball player; Rensselaer; NY; 1853; NY; 268A
Cassin, John J.; Gambling; Deer Lodge; MT; 1848; Canada; 110A
Castiano, Jaun; Gambler; Kinney; TX; 1816; Mexico; 296C
Castillo, Rey; Fortune Teller; San Francisco; CA; 1832; Peru;
     660C
Castleman, Phil; Tramp; Davidson; TN; 1825; TN; 110B
Castro, J.; Gambler; Pima; AZ; 1835; Equador; 302B
Caughey, George; With Circus; Allegheny; PA; 1860; PA; 145C
Caulan, Emile; Dead; Orleans; LA; 1876; LA; 108C
Cavinder; None (Tramp); Lamar; TX; 1850; AR; 247B
Cederstrom, Oliver, Sr.; Phrenologist; Utah; UT; 1834; Sweden;
     275C
Cerdella, Chas.; Circus Performer; New York; NY; 1856; IN;
     448B
Cerdella, Lizzie; Circus Performer; New York; NY; 1859; PA;
     448B
Cha, Ling; Gambler; Elko; NV; 1836; China; 56C
Chah, Lee; Gambler; Elko; NV; 1850; China; 56C
Chamberlan, Alvira; Raising Hell; Susquehanna; PA; 1826; PA;
     286C
Chambers; Gambler; Cherokee; KS; 1835; WI; 507D
Chambers, Ibeby; Dead; Kent; MD; 1805; MD; 163B
Chancellor, J.M.; Dead; Tarrant; TX; 1858; TX; 127B
Chandler, Alfred E.; Tramp; Susquehanna; PA; 1844; PA; 265C
Chandler, Ira; Quack Doctor; Plymouth; MA; 1826; MA; 546B
Chandler, Jim; Gambler; Bexar; TX; 1844; LA; 75B
Chapa, Dionicio; Vagrant; Hidalgo; TX; 1853; Mexico; 222C

Chapman, Alexander; Circus Driver; New York; NY; 1855; America; 65C

Chapman, Harry; Tramp; Stephenson; IL; 1861; NY; 63A

Chapman, Jno. C.; Baseball club; New York; NY; 1844; NY; 232C

Chapman, May; Phrenologist; Norfolk; MA; 1836; VT; 181C

Charley; Gambler; Ormsby; NV; 1840; CA; 88B

Charlottee, Wm.; Murderer; Franklin; OH; 1815; OH; 161A

Charlton, Mary; Vagrant; Davidson; TN; 1845; TN; 24D

Chase, Charles M.; Magician; Suffolk; MA; 1852; NH; 313C

Chase, Elizabeth S.; Medium; Cumberland; NJ; 1820; NJ; 282B

Chase, Esther C.; Dead; Blair; PA; 1867; PA; 88D

Chase, Rachael; Vagrant; Alexandria; VA; 1857; VA; 448C

Chat, Chu; Gambler; San Francisco; CA; 1842; Kwantung; 388D

Chaw, Kong; Gambler; Kern; CA; 1855; China; 586C

Chay, So; Gambler; Santa Clara; CA; 1851; China; 127C

Che, Hing; Gambler; Elko; NV; 1850; China; 56C

Chee, Lee; Gambler; Ada; ID; 1835; China; 19A

Chen, Sung; Gambler; Washoe; NV; 1842; China; 277A

Cheo; Gambler; Fresno; CA; 1820; China; 288D

Cheong, Chee; Gambler; San Francisco; CA; 1860; Sam Yap; 635D

Chesher, Amanda; Dead; Covington; AL; 1879; AL; 307B

Cheun, Wong; Gambler; San Francisco; CA; 1830; Kwantung; 392B

Cheung, Hi; Gambler; Washoe; NV; 1839; China; 277A

Cheval, Armand; Gambler; Orleans; LA; 1837; LA; 176A

Chew, Saw; Sell Opium; Placer; CA; 1847; China; 339A

Chi, Kin; Keeps Opium Den; Shasta; CA; 1840; China; 2D

Chin, Fong; Gambling House; Yuba; CA; 1816; Canton; 445A

Chin, Foo; Keeps Opium Den; Shasta; CA; 1846; China; 2D

Chin, Hoy; Gambler; Nevada; CA; 1830; Canton; 220B

Chin, Qua; Fortune Teller; San Francisco; CA; 1820; Kwantung; 385B

Ching; Gambler; Idaho; ID; 1851; Canton; 166C

Chinnis, H.J.; Dead; Colleton; SC; 1835; NC; 250C

Chip, Fong; Keeps Gambling House; Calaveras; CA; 1824; China; 345B

Cho, Kee; Opium Shop; Santa Clara; CA; 1820; China; 127C
Chock, Chuen; Gambler; Washoe; NV; 1850; China; 277A
Chon, Mann; Gambler; Boise; ID; 1845; China; 146B
Chong; Gambler; Butte; CA; 1855; China; 262C
Chong, Fai Mon; Opium Dealer; San Francisco; CA; 1827;
       Kwantun Sun Voi; 379A
Chong, Lung; Gambler; Eureka; NV; 1853; China; 212C
Chong, Tan; Gambler; San Francisco; CA; 1853; Kwantung; 391A
Choo, Wah; Gambler; San Francisco; CA; 1831; Qwantung; 609C
Chop, Lon; Gambler; Boise; ID; 1823; China; 118B
Chow; Selling Opium; Siskiyou; CA; 1840; China; 250A
Chow, Chu Chong; Gambler; Kern; CA; 1838; China; 586C
Chow, Guy; Keeps Gambling House; Calaveras; CA; 1816; China;
       345B
Chow, Wan; Gambler; San Francisco; CA; 1830; Qwantung; 609C
Christian, Sa--; Dead; Carroll; MS; 1879; MS; 139B
Christopher, C.; Gambler; Cooke; TX; 1842; Norway; 196D
Christopher, John; Dead; Tarrant; TX; 1876; MS; 131A
Chu, Fee; Gambler; Washoe; NV; 1844; China; 276D
Chu, See; Lawyer & Fortune Teller; San Francisco; CA; 1845;
       Sun Ning; 633C
Chu, Yong; Geisha House Keeper; El Dorado; CA; 1838; China;
       65B
Chuch, John; Dead; New York; NY; 1806; Germany; 46D
Chue, Long; Gambler; Santa Clara; CA; 1821; China; 126A
Chum, Gip; Gambler; Ada; ID; 1848; China; 19A
Chun, Gee Sum; Fortune Teller; San Francisco; CA; 1836;
       Kwantung; 382C
Chun, Sing; Pimp; San Francisco; CA; 1848; Kwontung; 375D
Chung, Gu; Opium Seller; El Dorado; CA; 1834; China; 65B
Chung, Hay; Opium Store; Santa Clara; CA; 1840; China; 126B
Chung, Hoo; Gambler; San Francisco; CA; 1850; Kwan Tung;
       630B
Chung, Kam; General Bummer; Leander; NV; 1850; China; 297A
Chung, Kee; Opium Shop; Santa Clara; CA; 1826; China; 127D
Chung, Ling; Gambler; Washoe; NV; 1810; China; 277A
Chung, Lo Man; Gambler; Kern; CA; 1845; China; 586C

Chung, Loy; Opium Dealer; San Francisco; CA; 1845; Sam Yap;
636A
Chung, Lung; China Gambling House; Storey; NV; 1842; China;
236B
Chung, Sing; Gambler; Deer Lodge; MT; 1856; China; 111C
Chung, Son; Gambler; Boise; ID; 1845; China; 118B
Chung, Ti; Gambler; San Francisco; CA; 1825; Qwantung; 609C
Chung, Yin; Gambler; San Francisco; CA; 1855; Qwantung; 609C
Church, Jo; Gambler; McLennan; TX; 1857; TX; 1A
Churchill, Jennie; Clairvoyant; Wayne; MI; 1846; NY; 141D
Chy, Ling; Gambler; Eureka; NV; 1839; China; 191B
Ci, Foo; Gambler; Amador; CA; 1854; Canton; 46D
Clagg, Paul; Dead; Webster; IA; 1878; IA; 575B
Claghhorn, James; Tramp from place to place; Paulding; GA;
1813; GA; 388D
Clapp, Dwight M.; Agent for Circus; Ashtabula; OH; 1848; OH;
648B
Clare, Tirus; Circus; Ohio; WV; 1864; Canada; 449B
Clark, Charles; Clog dancer; Ionia; MI; 1862; NY; 108D
Clark, Charles E.; Gambler; Eau Claire; WI; 1850; OH; 356A
Clark, Doe; Gambler; Lucas; OH; 1830; OH; 127D
Clark, George; Circus Actor; Philadelphia; PA; 1840; PA; 255B
Clark, Gilbert; Traveling with Circus; Chautauqua; NY; 1859;
NY; 350C
Clark, H., Mrs.; Clairvoyant; Suffolk; MA; 1832; MA; 553B
Clark, Jesse; Gambler; Deer Lodge; MT; 1844; MO; 111D
Clark, John; Gambler; Storey; NV; 1852; MA; 141D
Clark, John; Gambler; Sumner; KS; 1850; LA; 283A
Clark, Maria J.; Magnetic Healer; Erie; PA; 1820; Canada; 253B
Clark, Nicholas W.; Tramp; New York; NY; 1845; PA; 581D
Clark, Wm.; Tramp on public street; St. Clair; IL; 1857; Canada;
483D
Clarke, William; Circus Performer; Providence; RI; 1858; MA;
285C
Clemens, Joseph; Tramp; New York; NY; 1831; SC; 581C
Clems, Robt.; Gambler; Storey; NV; 1849; England; 141D
Clennon, Charles; Tramp; Yell; AR; 1853; AR; 361B
Cleveland, Peter; Dead; Crawford; GA; 1876; GA; 653C

Cliff, George; Gambler; Eau Claire; WI; 1850; NY; 352B

Clifford, John H.; Gambler; Salt Lake; UT; 1830; MO; 85D

Clifton, Florence C.; Clairvoyant; Essex; NJ; 1851; NJ; 28C

Clock, Henry W.; Phrenologist; Montcalm; MI; 1828; CT; 202B

Clogson, Nancy; Dead; Schenectady; NY; 1811; NY; 131D

Cloninger, Henry; Vagrant; Knox; TN; 1865; TN; 118D

Cloninger, Mary; Vagrant; Knox; TN; 1820; TN; 118D

Cloninger, Nancy; Vagrant; Knox; TN; 1865; TN; 118D

Coate, Samuel; Tramp; Hanson; Dak. Terr.; 1858; PA; 56C

Cobb, Pollock Willis; Performer Sells Bros. Circus; Clinton; OH; 1842; OH; 187B

Cochran, Rufus L.; Gambler; Butte; CA; 1857; CA ; 144A

Coffield, Winnie; Dead; Halifax; NC; 1812; NC; 662B

Cogall, Patrick; Gambler; Deer Lodge; MT; 1844; Ireland; 135D

Coggeswell, Edward; Ball player; Rensselaer; NY; 1856; OH; 268A

Coggswell, Edward; Base ball player; Worcester; MA; 1854; England; 537D

Cogsdale, Stephen D.; Drinks bad whiskey; Baker; OR; 1822; NY; 9A

Cohen, Simon; Astrologer; San Francisco; CA; 1831; Prussia; 693B

Coker, Nathan; Fire eater; Caroline; MD; 1820; MD; 257A

Cokey, Covington; Gambler; Baltimore; MD; 1818; MD; 175C

Cole, Charles; Gambler; San Bernardino; CA; 1845; USA; 508A

Cole, Edward; Tramp; Lapeer; MI; 1858; Canada; 315B

Cole, George W.; Quack Doctor; Oakland; MI; 1817; NY; 227B

Cole, H.; Gambler; Eureka; NV; 1847; NY; 160C

Cole, Harry; Tramp; Hennepin; MN; 1826; ME; 272A

Cole, T.E.; Gambler; St. Louis; MO; 1850; America; 225D

Coleman, A.; Gambler; Woodbury; IA; 1857; NY; 398B

Coleman, Larkin; Gambler; Worcester; MA; 1835; MA; 286B

Coleman, Sylvanus; Gambler; Worcester; MA; 1828; MA; 286B

Coleman, T.B.; Vagrant; Davidson; TN; 1850; TN; 20D

Collamore, Lucinda J.; Magnetic and Electric Physician; Suffolk; MA; 1843; ME; 396C

Collar, P.H.; Circus; Ohio; WV; 1862; MI; 449A

Collins, Annie; Dead; Allegheny; PA; 1879; PA; 249A

Collins, Henry; Gambler; King; WA; 1830; Ireland; 283A
Collins, Isaac; In Circus; Washtenaw; MI; 1858; Canada; 435D
Collins, James; Tramp; Hennepin; MN; 1860; MA; 272A
Collins, John; Dead; Lawrence; MS; 1880; MS; 237D
Collins, Julia; Keeping house & fortune telling; Champaign; OH;
      1847; OH; 392C
Collins, Lillie Sue; Dead; Giles; VA; 1880; VA; 55A
Collins, Mary; Dead; Lawrence; MS; 1880; MS; 237D
Collins, Oscar; Thief; Leavenworth; KS; 1868; KS; 242A
Collins, Pat; Circus; Ohio; WV; 1858; IN; 449A
Collins, Rich.; Tramp on public street; St. Clair; IL; 1857; Wales;
      484A
Collins, Thos.; Tramp; Mercer; NJ; ---; NJ; 11A
Collins, Wyatt; Dead; Nevada; AR; ---; AR; 504B
Collmer, Jacob; Dead; St. Joseph; IN; 1830; Wurttemberg; 416B
Coltier, Benj.; Circus Performer; Franklin; OH; 1861; OH; 305D
Colwell, John H.; Travels with Circus; Middlesex; NJ; 1852; NJ;
      126B
Comet, M.; Circus; Ohio; WV; 1857; IN; 449A
Comfield, Noel; Tramp; Albany; WY; 1863; Turkey; 47D
Comfort, George; Gambler; Orleans; LA; 1856; LA; 267B
Comosh, John; Circus Informer; Tioga; PA; 1856; NY; 474A
Comosh, John; Tumbler; Steuben; NY; 1855; NY; 141B
Comstock, George C.; Asst. Astronomer; Washtenaw; MI; 1855;
      WI; 75B
Comstock, William; Tramp; Ogle; IL; 1863; IL; 167D
Conal, D.O.; Circus; Ohio; WV; 1863; IL; 449B
Conallin, Martin; Gambler & Speculator; Bourbon; KS; 1839;
      Ireland; 188B
Conant, J.P.; Tramp; McLean; IL; 1820; ---; 187D
Concinus, Frank; Dead; Dakota; MN; 1817; Luxemburg; 259D
Condon, John; Gambler; Cass; IN; 1853; IN; 320D
Condor, Margaret; Dead; Breckinridge; KY; 1810; KY; 87C
Cone, Ambrose; Dead; Van Buren; MI; 1858; MI; 431B
Confoy, John; Professional Thief; Mahoning; OH; 1858; OH; 76B
Conghlin, John; Gambler; New Haven; CT; 1843; Ireland; 302D
Conglin, George; Tramp on public street; St. Clair; IL; 1841; OH;
      482A

Conkling, Peter; Clown in Circus; Brown; OH; 1844; NY; 301A
Conley, Wm.; Tramp on public street; St. Clair; IL; 1848; Ireland;
    483D
Conly, Needham; Tramp; Marengo; AL; 1859; MS; 703D
Conly, T.; Gambler; Orleans; LA; 1854; New Orleans, LA; 72C
Connallin, John; Gambler; Bourbon; KS; 1835; Ireland; 223B
Connel, Edward; Tramp on public street; St. Clair; IL; 1856; NY;
    483C
Connel, Mic'l; Circus Actor; Lucas; OH; 1860; OH; 223C
Connelly, Thomas; Thief; Pettis; MO; 1853; NY; 248D
Conner, Morris; Jig dancer; Jefferson; KY; 1864; LA; 234B
Connors, John; Tramp on public street; St. Clair; IL; 1854; PA;
    481D
Connover, Murphy; Tramp; Utah; UT; 1853; NY; 186A
Conrad, F.; Circus; Ohio; WV; 1859; OH; 448D
Considine, James; Dead; Dubuque; IA; 1866; IA; 354A
Conway, Arthur; Dead; Karnes; TX; 1879; TX; 5B
Conway, Charles; Gambler; Deer Lodge; MT; 1857; NY; 123C
Conway, Wm.; Tramp on public street; St. Clair; IL; 1838;
    Ireland; 481D
Conyers; Wife - dead; Hart; KY; 1844; KY; 333A
Cook, Ellen; Circus Performer; New York; NY; 1854; England;
    74A
Cook, Henry; Tramp; New York; NY; 1820; NY; 581C
Cook, Henry; Tramp; Jackson; MO; 1851; IA; 370B
Cook, Jack; Gambler; McLennan; TX; 1857; TX; 1A
Cook, James; Circus Performer; Allegheny; PA; 1850; PA; 64A
Cook, John; Tramp; New York; NY; 1836; Germany; 581C
Cook, Joseph E.; Gambler; Deer Lodge; MT; 1835; NY; 107D
Cook, Samuel; Gambler; Storey; NV; 1845; NH; 137D
Cook, Seth; Gambler; Broome; NY; 1843; NY; 189B
Cooke, Chas. J.C.; Gambler; St. Louis; MO; 1852; NY; 132B
Cooley, Esra; Tramp; Jefferson; WI; 1820; VT; 167C
Coon; Gambling House; Boise; ID; 1842; China; 136A
Coon, Yun; Geisha House; El Dorado; CA; 1820; China; 64D
Cooper, Charles; Vagabond; Penobscot; ME; 1858; Germany;
    197C
Cooper, J.W.; Circus Actor; St. Louis; MO; 1845; NY; 176C

Cooper, Jacob; Watches Jewish dead; Hamilton; OH; 1814; Germany; 325C

Cooper, Mary; Circus Actor; St. Louis; MO; 1844; NY; 176C

Cope, Charles; Tramp; McKean; PA; 1862; PA; 477C

Copeland, Eveline; Vagrant; Putnam; GA; 1830; GA; 474D

Copeland, Wm.; Supposed to be a Gambler; Davidson; TN; 1850; TN; 131D

Copin, Chapman; Farmer dead; Kanawha; WV; 1822; WV; 228D

Copp, Byron; Criminal; Carroll; NH; 1832; NH; 297C

Copper, Marietta; Fortune Teller; Nodaway; MO; 1850; IA; 178D

Corbin, C.A.; Circus; Ohio; WV; 1834; NY; 449B

Corcoran, Lawrence; Ball player; New York; NY; 1861; NY; 401D

Cording, J.; On death list; Vermillion; IN; 1853; OH; 24D

Corelle, Mayhew A.; Prof. of magic; Middlesex; MA; 1828; MA; 122B

Corey, Alfred; B. ball player; Worcester; MA; 1850; NJ; 182D

Corey, Fred H.; Baseball player; Providence; RI; 1856; RI; 317D

Corey, Henry H.; Baseball player; Providence; RI; 1859; RI; 313C

Corey, Sam.; Gambler; Shelby; TN; 1846; MO; 44B

Correy, John; Tramp on public street; St. Clair; IL; 1852; IL; 481D

Corrigen, S.J.; Astronomer; Ramsey; MN; 1852; NY; 366D

Cosgrove, James; Tramp; Lancaster; NE; 1857; NJ; 173A

Cosgrove, Thos.; Tramp; Lancaster; NE; 1854; PA; 173A

Cott, Elizabeth; Dead; Orleans; LA; 1817; GA; 103B

Cottom, Thomas; County Vagrant; Pemiscot; MO; 1845; TN; 582A

Cotton, Frank; Gambler; Travis; TX; 1833; KY; 204B

Coulter, Frank; Gambler; Cooke; TX; 1848; TX; 196D

Coulter, John; Harlot pimp; Marinette; WI; 1857; WI; 456B

Coultre, Martin; Tramp; Green; WI; 1817; OH; 200D

Couly, Franker; Tramp; Lawrence; IN; 1823; TN; 548C

Counel, John; Tramp; Buchanan; MO; 1853; OH; 41A

Country, Lewis; Tramp; St. Clair; MI; 1866; MI; 197D

Coups, Mrs.; Circus Wife; Ohio; WV; 1830; MA; 449B

Coups, W.C.; Circus; Ohio; WV; 1830; MA; 449B

Courtney, William; Gambler; Deer Lodge; MT; 1846; England; 129C

Cove, Singleton; Gambler; Jersey; IL; 1837; KY; 79A

Covell, John S.; Phrenologist; Nez Perce; ID; 1829; VT; 259A

Covington, Ethyl; Dead; Owen; KY; 1876; KY; 170A

Covington, Lotta; Dead; Owen; KY; 1874; KY; 170A

Cow, Sum; Gambler; Eureka; NV; 1855; China; 191A

Cowart, Emil H.; Dead; Lawrence; MS; 1880; MS; 237D

Cox, D.B.; Gambler; Dinwiddie; VA; 1845; VA; 341B

Cox, Daniel; Dead; Parke; IN; 1840; IN; 484B

Cox, Emma; Tramp; Coweta; GA; 1851; GA; 456B

Cox, Peyton; Vagrant; Shawnee; KS; 1845; MO; 36A

Coy, John S.; Circus Agent; Uinta; WY; 1842; RI; 337D

Coyle, David; Dead; Blair; PA; 1799; Ireland; 80D

Coyle, John; Circus Performer; Jones; IA; 1860; IA; 298A

Coyne, Chas.; Gambler; Storey; NV; 1830; Ireland; 115D

Craddock, Thos.; Gambler; Sedgwick; KS; 1838; KY; 253A

Craig, Charles; Traveling with Circus; Kenton; KY; 1858; KY; 291D

Craig, P.; Gambler; Bexar; TX; 1858; TX; 104C

Cramer, Katie; Dead; Pulaski; IN; 1874; IN; 241D

Cramer, P.; Tramp; Lawrence; AR; 1859; MO; 492C

Crane, Sam'l N.; Base ball player; Hampden; MA; 1854; MA; 26B

Craoker, Anna; Magnatic Healer; Cook; IL; 1821; MA; 299D

Crauly, Henry; Quack; Knox; TN; 1864; DE; 165B

Crawford, Fanne; Dead; New York; NY; 1876; ---; 245B

Crawford, George Rice; Quack Doctor; Ascension; LA; 1841; MD; 82C

Crawford, Mary; Dead; St. Louis; MO; 1879; MS; 500B

Crawford, William; Gambler; Mobile; AL; 1834; GA; 214A

Crawford, William; Tramp; Wayne; MI; 1845; PA; 302C

Crawford, Wm.; Thief; Philadelphia; PA; 1831; PA; 291D

Creamer, Alfred; B. ball player; Worcester; MA; 1849; IL; 182D

Crego, Myron; Clairvoyant; Oneida; NY; 1846; NY; 55D

Crenshaw, Martha J.; Outcast; Marshall; KY; 1852; KY; 201C

Crenshaw, Nina; Dead; Fulton; GA; 1872; GA; 261C

Cressman, Elijah; Dead; Warren; NJ; 1850; NJ; 515D

Crill, Walt. H.; Attache of Circus; Miami; KS; 1852; NY; 443B

Crisol, Isac; Bummer; Clear Creek; CO; 1820; PA; 121B
Crittenden, Charles; Tramp; Jackson; MO; 1844; IA; 368B
Crocker, Jno.; Gambler; Dinwiddie; VA; 1849; VA; 327A
Crofoot, Henry; Tramp; Douglas; NE; 1861; OH; 337D
Crofoot, Shorty; Tramp; Douglas; NE; 1850; OH; 337D
Cromley, Annie; Dead; Allegheny; PA; 1874; PA; 239A
Cronan, Daniel; Base ballist; Middlesex; MA; 1859; MA; 308A
Cronin, John; Gambler; Deer Lodge; MT; 1855; NY; 121C
Cronin, John A.; Gambler; Deer Lodge; MT; 1855; NY; 127D
Cross, Alexander; Dead; Adair; MO; 1804; VA; 96C
Cross, Maria; Dead; Caldwell; TX; 1857; AL; 200C
Cross, Sophia; Magnetic Healer; Essex; MA; 1815; VT; 645A
Crotty, Joseph; Base ballist; Hamilton; OH; 1862; OH; 82C
Crouse, Lewis; Dead; Northumberland; PA; 1879; PA; 539A
Crowl, Reuben; Dead; Sandusky; OH; 1867; OH; 159D
Crowley, Jennie; Vagabond; Graves; KY; 1853; KY; 149C
Crowley, William; Baseball player; Camden; NJ; 1855; PA; 546A
Crown, James; Gambler; Arapahoe; CO; 1860; NY; 98D
Crull, Chas.; Tramp; Linn; IA; 1861; IL; 96C
Crumbaken, Kay; Dead; Meigs; OH; 1808; VA; 4A
Cu, Chan; Geisha House Keeper; El Dorado; CA; 1831; China;
    65B
Cullam, Patric; Tramp on public street; St. Clair; IL; 1859; IL;
    481D
Cullen, George; Tramp; Westmorland; PA; 1843; PA; 425C
Cullen, John; Circus Bus.; Middlesex; MA; 1852; Canada; 76D
Cummings, F.J.; Gambler; Buchanan; MO; 1853; LA; 211C
Cunningham, Henry; Trav. with Circus; St. Louis; MO; 1855; AR;
    229C
Cunningham, Henry; Circus Man; St. Louis; MO; 1859; NY;
    561D
Cunningham, Jas.; Gambler; Storey; NV; 1854; NY; 141D
Curley, John; Pick Pocket; Pettis; MO; 1855; NY; 248D
Curn, John; Gambler; Summt; UT; 1845; WI; 37D
Curran, Henry; Travels with Circus Confectioner; Jackson; MO;
    1858; NY; 330A
Curry, Lizzie; Death; New York; NY; 1860; NY; 300B
Curry, Thomas; Gambling; Grant; NM; 1826; VA; 343D

Curtis, Daniel; Gambler; Deer Lodge; MT; 1848; Ireland; 125C

Curtis, Sarah; Magnetic Physician; Lake; IL; 1810; NY; 559A

Curtis, William; Agt. for Circus; Wayne; MI; 1859; MI; 432B

Cut, Chun; Opium Dealer; San Francisco; CA; 1847; Kwantung; 391B

Cutting, E.A.; Magnetic Healer; Suffolk; MA; 1839; VT; 420A

Dahm, Charles; Teacher of Astrology; San Francisco; CA; 1827; Holstein; 112D

Dailey, Peter; Tramp on public street; St. Clair; IL; 1855; WI; 482A

Daily, John M.; Gambler; Kalamazoo; MI; 1844; NY; 195A

Daindree, L.R.; Magician; Orleans; LA; 1841; West Indies; 224C

Daker, Chas.; Circus Performer; Crawford; PA; 1864; PA; 265D

Dale, Harry; Gambler; Cass; IN; 1852; IN; 319A

Daley, Hugh; Pitcher of baseball club; Baltimore; MD; 1848; Ireland; 87C

Dalton, Thomas S.; Dead; Rutherford; NC; 1879; NC; 579D

Daly, James E.; No trade, Lazy; Washington; ME; 1858; ME; 58B

Daly, John; Tramp; New York; NY; 1850; NY; 581C

Daly, John; Baseball player; New York; NY; 1854; NY; 110C

Daly, Thomas; Tramp; Defiance; OH; 1856; OH; 102D

Damon, Chs.; Tramp; Orleans; LA; 1815; Germany; 151A

Danforth, George F.; Healer; Essex; MA; 1845; MA; 260A

Daniel, Racheal; Dead; Adair; MO; 1832; VA; 91B

Daniels, John; Gambler; Storey; NV; 1840; KY; 121D

Danlin, John; Dead; Blair; PA; 1815; Ireland; 76D

Dans, Nathaniel; Gambler; Laramie; WY; 1847; IL; 161B

Darhr, John B.; Dead; Dubuque; IA; 1824; Prussia; 347C

Darlot, Amand; Billiard player; New York; NY; 1854; France; 73D

Darrah, Joseph W.; Student of Medium; Belmont; OH; 1858; OH; 187B

Darro, Erastus; Tramp (Poet); Fulton; AR; 1818; CT; 42B

Dassett, Ida May; Dead; McLean; KY; 1879; KY; 271B

Daugherty, John; Pimp; Delta; MI; 1856; Ireland; 653A

Daugherty, Mary; Gypsy; Clark; OH; 1819; Ireland; 391A

Daugherty, Theodore; Circus Performer; Wayne; MI; 1848; Canada; 58B

Daugherty, Thos.; Gambler; Sacramento; CA; 1829; Ireland; 39B

Daven, Kate; Dead; Hamilton; OH; 1874; OH; 27A

Davenport, John L.; Circus Performer; Lucas; OH; 1840; VA; 188B

Davis, A.O.; Medium; San Francisco; CA; 1823; NY; 195C

Davis, Anna; Dead; Graves; KY; 1879; KY; 303D

Davis, Benj.; Tramp; Hamilton; OH; 1840; MD; 559B

Davis, Ebenezer; Wanderer; Washington; IL; 1842; IL; 432D

Davis, Emma; Prize fighter; Orleans; LA; 1850; OH; 246D

Davis, Frances; Dead; Fairfield; SC; 1878; SC; 192B

Davis, Geo.; Circus; Ohio; WV; 1828; MD; 448D

Davis, George; Tramp - Prisoner; Tippecanoe; IN; 1854; ---; 237C

Davis, Jack; Tramp on public street; St. Clair; IL; 1858; OH; 483C

Davis, Robert; Farmer dead; Washington; IL; 1825; KY; 363A

Davis, S. Mary; Dead; Marion; IA; 1870; IA; 644D

Davis, Sallie; Dead; Wilcox; AL; 1862; AL; 204A

Davis, Sarah; Dead; Paulding; GA; 1797; NC; 445C

Davis, Thomas; Tramp; St. Louis; MO; 1855; PA; 498A

Dawson, Samuel; Dead; Adair; MO; 1879; MO; 84D

Day, Charles H.; Agent for Foupaugh Circus; New Haven; CT; 1843; NY; 457C

Day, Florence K.C.; Magnetic Physician; Providence; RI; 1835; England; 335C

Day, Thomas; Dead; St. Louis; MO; 1867; MO; 308C

Day, William A.; Tramp; Jackson; MO; 1847; IA; 370B

De Fonest, Rich'd; Gambler; Franklin; OH; 1850; OH; 134D

De Forest, John; Gambler; Oneida; NY; 1858; NY; 79A

De Freye, B.C.; Quack Physician; Eureka; NV; 1835; Belgium; 193B

De Knevett, Laura; Clairvoyant; St. Louis; MO; 1822; NH; 47B

De La France, Frank; Gambler; Mobile; AL; 1830; AL; 222A

Deament, Arthur L.; Dead; Indiana; PA; 1877; PA; 374B

Dean, Alexander; Tramp; Jackson; AL; 1856; AL; 261B

Dean, Belle; Hurdy dancer; Deer Lodge; MT; 1856; England; 136B

Dean, S.L.; Pimp; Benton; MO; 1850; OH; 312A

Deaner, J.; Tramp; Defiance; OH; 1850; ---; 79B

Debardelabue, John; Dead; Autauga; AL; 1831; AL; 66C

Decamp, Zak.; Gambler; Sangamon; IL; 1847; IL; 147C

Decken, Frank; Tramp on public street; St. Clair; IL; 1850; Holstein; 482B

Deen, Francis; Dead; Wilcox; AL; 1880; AL; 185C

Deforest, Frank; Tramp; Nemaha; NE; 1846; NY; 134A

Degnan, Hanna; Ballet dancer; New York; NY; 1859; NY; 337C

Degner, August; Ball player; Hudson; NJ; 1854; NJ; 405B

Degrosse, Celia; Magnetic Healer; Cook; IL; 1828; KY; 160B

Dehoney, Martin H.; Tramp; Jackson; MO; 1847; NY; 371C

Deimer, Christana; Dead; Northumberland; PA; 1794; PA; 535A

Delamus; Dead; Autauga; AL; 1880; AL; 67B

Delf, Matilda; Dead; Ellsworth; KS; 1862; IN; 488C

Dell, Carolline; Fortune Teller; Hamilton; OH; 1841; Baden; 458D

Delong, William; Vagrant; Winnebago; WI; 1845; Ireland; 164C

Demott, James; Away with Circus; Philadelphia; PA; 1840; NY; 137B

Demott, Josephine; Away with Circus; Philadelphia; PA; 1840; NY; 137B

Demott, Josephine; Away with Circus; Philadelphia; PA; 1869; NY; 137B

Demott, Willie; Away with Circus; Philadelphia; PA; 1867; NY; 137B

Dempsey, Walton; Dead; Owen; KY; 1874; KY; 163D

Denell, Marianna; Phrenologist; Marshall; IA; 1840; Nova Scotia; 141C

Denison, Livinia; Dead; Taney; MO; 1874; MO; 255B

Dennie, John; Deadbeat; Fulton; NY; 1824; NY; 47D

Denning, Frank; Gambler; Mercer; NJ; 1848; VA; 293A

Depew, Joseph; Gambler; Hamilton; OH; 1856; OH; 524C

Dequasie, Laura; Crossed off - dead; Fillmore; NE; 1879; NE; 476C

Deramus, W.; Dead; Autauga; AL; 1856; AL; 129A

Derby, D.G.; Phrenologist; Moniteau; MO; 1818; NY; 432D

Derby, George B.; Baseball player; Washington; D.C.; 1856; NY; 378B

Derphey, John; Tramp; Lapeer; MI; 1853; Ireland; 315B

Desmuelin, F.; Prisoner Vagrant 90-days; Brown; WI; 1840;
    Holland; 149B
Devall, Will; Thief; Lancaster; NE; 1860; NY; 173A
Devall, Will; Thief; Lancaster; NE; 1860; NY; 173A
Dever, James H.; Circus Man; Suffolk; MA; 1861; MA; 115A
Devine, Manuel; Dead; Orleans; LA; 1879; LA; 105B
Devine, Michael; Tramp; Defiance; OH; 1855; OH; 102D
Devlin, William; Tramp; Douglas; NE; 1863; NY; 337D
Dewitt, Joachim; Vagrant; Ulster; NY; 1839; NY; 72A
Dexter, C.; Circus; Ohio; WV; 1853; OH; 449A
Dexter, Fannie C.; Clairvoyant Physician; Suffolk; MA; 1826; VT;
    396D
Dherer, Wm.; Laborer & Tramp; Decatur; IA; 1851; OH; 246D
Dick; Tramp; Fayette; TX; 1861; TX; 33C
Dickelman, Charles; Tramp; Kane; IL; 1862; KS; 69C
Dickenson, James; Tramp on public street; St. Clair; IL; 1857;
    MO; 482B
Dickerson, Chas.; Tramp on public street; St. Clair; IL; 1854; PA;
    481D
Dickerson, Lewis P.; Professional baseball player; Baltimore; MD;
    1858; MD; 506D
Dickerson, Louis; Ball player; Rensselaer; NY; 1854; MA; 268A
Dickman, Mary; Hurdy dancer; Deer Lodge; MT; 1856; England;
    136B
Dickson, Susan; Wanderer; Kent; DE; 1840; DE; 76C
Dicson, Catherine; Wandering Vagrant; Kent; DE; 1850; DE;
    341D
Dielking, Mary; Keeping House dead; St. Louis; MO; 1842; Hesse
    Darmstdt; 352B
Dietrich, Teodore; Tramp on public street; St. Clair; IL; 1841;
    Baden; 482B
Dietrichs, B.J.; Tramp; Douglas; NE; 1861; NY; 260D
Dignan, Steven E.; Ball player; Suffolk; MA; 1861; MA; 84D
Dill; Dead; Washington; IL; 1880; IL; 360D
Dillohanly, Mary Julia; Dead; Sevier; AR; ---; AR; 57A
Dillon, George; Vagrant; Westchester; NY; 1815; Ireland; 345D
Dillon, Owen; Professional dancer; Suffolk; MA; 1852; NY; 500C
Dillon, Rebecca; Omit - dead; Davidson; TN; 1842; TN; 282B

Dilvinie, Francis; Traveling with Circus; Chittenden; VT; 1860; VT; 14C

Dilvinie, Henry; Traveling with Circus; Chittenden; VT; 1862; VT; 14C

Dilvinie, Joseph; Traveling with Circus; Chittenden; VT; 1855; VT; 14C

Ding, Yit Tong; Gambler; San Francisco; CA; 1843; Qwantung; 608B

Dingmar, Janes; Vagrant; Bates; MO; 1858; IA; 250C

Dingmar, May; Vagrant; Bates; MO; 1851; OH; 250C

Dio, Low; Gambler; Deer Lodge; MT; 1851; China; 110A

Disney, Rosanna; Layer out of the dead; Philadelphia; PA; 1839; Philadelphia, PA; 15A

Dix, John; Tramp; Clay; MO; 1859; PA; 355C

Dixon, Charles; Gambler; Cook; IL; 1853; VA; 217A

Dixon, Dock; Gambler; Cook; IL; 1852; VA; 217A

Dixon, Isabella; Dead; Parke; IN; 1817; Scotland; 486B

Dixon, Moses; Vagrant; Putnam; NY; 1864; NY; 163C

Dixon, Wm.; Tramp lying under a tree; Hendricks; IN; 1830; England; 633B

Doakins; Dead; Fairfield; SC; 1879; SC; 195C

Dobbs, J.; Gambler; Pima; AZ; 1847; KY; 302B

Dobson, Richard; Gambler; Pottawattamie; IA; 1852; NY; 368B

Doc, Sin; Gambler; Idaho; ID; 1838; Canton; 166C

Dodd, Fannie A.; Magnetic Physician; Suffolk; MA; 1843; MA; 460C

Dodge, Stephen S.; Tramp; Cass; Dak. Terr.; 1857; NY; 277B

Dodson, Ben; Trav. agent of Circus; Macon; IL; 1858; IA; 379B

Dodson, Frederick; Gambler; Santa Fe; NM; 1836; CT; 83C

Dodson, Patsy A.; Tramp; Hawkins; TN; 1839; TN; 194A

Dody, Daniel; Tramp - Prisoner; Lawrence; IN; 1840; OH; 550D

Dolan, T.; Circus; Ohio; WV; 1858; PA; 449A

Dolan, Thomas; Baseball player; Erie; NY; 1855; NY; 297C

Dolan, Thos.; Base ball player; San Francisco; CA; 1854; NY; 132A

Dolan, Tom; Tramp on public street; St. Clair; IL; 1861; NY; 483C

Name; Occupation; County; State; Birth; Birth place; Page 43

Dolittle, John; Tramp on public street; St. Clair; IL; 1858; NY; 484A
Doll, Byron; Dead; Sandusky; OH; 1861; OH; 167C
Doll, Geo. M.; Gambler; Deer Lodge; MT; 1847; Bavaria; 124B
Dollahite, J.M.; Gambler; Travis; TX; 1829; TN; 98D
Dollmann, Blasius; Tramp on public street; St. Clair; IL; 1811; Switzerland; 482A
Donaldson, A.; Tramp; Hennepin; MN; 1859; Canada; 395B
Donnelly, Jane; Since dead; Philadelphia; PA; 1878; PA; 292B
Dorathy, Patrick; Tramp; Hanson; Dak. Terr.; 1850; MO; 56C
Dorfs, Charles; Tramp on public street; St. Clair; IL; 1824; Mecklanberg; 484A
Dorgan, Michael C.; Baseball player; Providence; RI; 1854; CT; 320C
Dormer, Nicholas; Gambler; Storey; NV; 1848; NY; 113D
Dormer, Wm.; Gambler; Storey; NV; 1845; WI; 118A
Dormstatter, Frank; Tramp on public street; St. Clair; IL; 1847; Hesse D.; 483C
Doronceau, Vincent; Pimp; Delta; MI; 1855; Italy; 653A
Dororan, Timothy; Base ballist; Middlesex; MA; 1856; MA; 308A
Dorsey, Michael; Base ball player; Summit; OH; 1856; Canada; 444C
Dorsey, Patrick; Vagrant; Winnebago; WI; 1851; Ireland; 162C
Dorvae, Helena M.; Clairvoyant; Suffolk; MA; 1843; France; 454D
Doscher, Herman; Baseball player; Rensselaer; NY; 1852; Prussia; 562D
Dotson, James; Quack Doctor; Roane; TN; 1838; TN; 387B
Doty, Anna; Electro Healer; Ontario; NY; 1830; NY; 86C
Doty, Fred; Gambler; Deer Lodge; MT; 1848; Canada; 125C
Doty, H.O.; Circus Performer; Preble; OH; 1848; OH; 25C
Dougherty, John; Vagrant; Richmond; NY; 1827; At Sea; 304C
Doughty, J.M.; Gambler; Refugio; TX; 1849; MS; 349B
Downie, John; Gambler; Tarrant; TX; 1837; Scotland; 72A
Downs, John; Magician; New London; CT; 1830; ME; 84A
Doyle, Ann; Showman Circus; Schuyler; IL; 1847; Germany; 460D
Doyle, David; Showman Circus; Schuyler; IL; 1842; PA; 460D

Doyle, John; Gambler; El Paso; TX; 1847; NY; 587A
Doyle, Michael; Tramp; New York; NY; 1835; Ireland; 421C
Doyle, Minerva; Clairvoyant; Oneida; NY; 1840; NY; 55D
Doyle, Patsy; Clog dancer; Chenango; NY; 1864; Canada; 259A
Drake, Dock A.; Horse Thief; Christian; KY; 1850; KY; 201B
Drakeke, Charles; Farmer dead; Oldham; KY; 1818; NY; 42A
Drew, C.; Circus; Ohio; WV; 1856; KY; 449A
Drew, James; Works for Circus Co.; Kent; MI; 1855; NY; 261C
Drew, William; Tramp; Marshall; MN; 1852; OH; 143D
Driscoll, James; Base ballist; Plymouth; MA; 1857; MA; 346A
Drulinger, Mity; Dead (Feby); St. Joseph; IN; 1865; IN; 430B
Drulinger, Thomas H.; Dead; St. Joseph; IN; 1867; IN; 430B
Dubois, Chas.; Gambler; Eureka; NV; 1853; NY; 198D
Dubois, Louisa; Dancer; Philadelphia; PA; 1867; PA; 1B
Ducket, William; Tramp; New York; NY; 1835; Washington,
    D.C.; 581C
Dugnan, Stephen; Base ballist; Middlesex; MA; 1859; MA; 308A
Duham, John; Tramp; Wayne; NY; 1831; NY; 367D
Duhr, Mary; Dead; Dubuque; IA; 1880; IA; 344B
Dunagan, Ora Retta; Dead crossed off; Fillmore; NE; 1880; NE;
    474D
Dunam, Joe; Gambler; Storey; NV; 1840; IL; 160B
Dunbar, Phillis; Dead; Fairfield; SC; 1837; SC; 192B
Duncan; Tramp; Buchanan; MO; 1851; IL; 41A
Duncan, Charity; Fortune Teller; Mercer; KY; 1840; KY; 67A
Duncan, Leander; Gambler; Deer Lodge; MT; 1847; OH; 125C
Duncan, Steven C.; Dead; Saline; IL; 1840; IL; 116C
Duncan, T.J.; Gambler; Storey; NV; 1843; IA; 111C
Dung, Yen; Gambler; Washoe; NV; 1852; China; 276C
Duniphan, James; Tramp on public street; St. Clair; IL; 144;
    Ireland; 482A
Dunlay, George A.; Dead June 7th; Suffolk; MA; 1879; MA;
    336A
Dunn, Barney; Gambler; Cherokee; KS; 1847; IL; 503C
Dunn, James; Gambler; Arapahoe; CO; 1844; KY; 98D
Dunn, John; Tramp; New York; NY; 1835; Ireland; 581D
Dunn, Mary; Dead; Hudson; NJ; 1868; NJ; 276C
Dunn, Maurice; Dead; Hudson; NJ; 1871; NJ; 276C

Dunn, William; Dead; Allegheny; PA; 1880; PA; 222C
Dunne, Luke; Gambler; San Francisco; CA; 1859; CA; 586C
Duphy, Mike; Tramp; Cuyahoga; OH; 1838; Ireland; 94B
Durain, Frank; Tramp on public street; St. Clair; IL; 1854; France;
      482A
Durant, Francis; Magician; San Francisco; CA; 1846; France;
      285A
Durell, Caroline; Dead; Orleans; LA; 1832; LA; 102D
Dutton, G.W.; Phrenologist; Page; IA; 1854; IA; 398A
Dutton, John; Bum; Cook; IL; 1863; MO; 370B
Dyke, Wesley; Quack Doctor; Chittenden; VT; 1831; VT; 354B
Eagenhead, Robert; Tramp; Franklin; OH; 1839; Baden; 479D
Eakin, George; Travels with Circus; Hamilton; OH; 1845; OH;
      241B
Earhart, Emrey B.; Dead; Adair; MO; 1875; MO; 87A
Earhart, George E.; Dead; Adair; MO; 1873; MO; 87A
Earl, Oriah; Dead; Taney; MO; 1856; MO; 285B
Eastbarn, A.; Magician; Philadelphia; PA; 1844; PA; 55C
Easten, George; Tramp on public street; St. Clair; IL; 1848;
      Scotland; 482B
Easter, James W.; Dead; Allegheny; PA; 1879; PA; 249A
Easterday, George; Magnetic Healer; Caldwell; MO; 1827; OH;
      277D
Eastwood, Mary; Dead; St. Joseph; IN; 1854; NY; 419D
Eatherine, William; Tramp; Buchanan; MO; 1843; OH; 41A
Eccentric refuses give name; Wanderer; Mille Lacs; MN; 1825;
      NY; 355A
Eckelbery, Jas.; Vagrant; Leavenworth; KS; 1868; KS; 242A
Ecker, Lucinda; Doctress (Clairvoyant); Crawford; KS; 1825; NY;
      51C
Eckhardt, Emily; Fortune Teller; New York; NY; 1829; Hanover;
      621A
Eckhart, John H.; Butcher & Tramp; Cass; NE; 1836; NY; 177A
Eckleburger, Rachael; Dead; Wabash; IN; 1810; PA; 348C
Eckles, Frank; Circus Agent; St. Louis; MO; 1844; IN; 63C
Edgerton, Freeman; Physician - Clairvoyant; Onondaga; NY;
      1830; NY; 457A

Edmunds, Mabel; Magnetic Physician; New York; NY; 1852;
     MA; 261C
Edstrom, C.H.; Gambler; Deer Lodge; MT; 1844; MA; 136B
Edward, E.; Gambler; Nevada; CA; 1838; MS; 32D
Edward, Matilde; Dead; Chenango; NY; 1828; NY; 105D
Edward, William; Gambler; Hamilton; OH; 1843; OH; 268D
Edwards, Charles; Base ball player; San Francisco; CA; 1855; WI;
     583B
Edwards, Charles W.; Dead; Coryell; TX; 1880; TX; 428C
Edwards, Clara; Fortune Teller; Cook; IL; 1842; Sweden; 439B
Edwards, G.F.; Gambler; Deer Lodge; MT; 1838; IL; 127D
Edwards, George; Gambler; Dauphin; PA; 1848; PA; 352D
Edwards, George; Tramp; New York; NY; 1851; England; 581D
Edwards, John; Tramp; New York; NY; 1854; NY; 581D
Edwards, Melton; Gambler; Shelby; AL; 1848; NY; 168C
Edwards, William; Prof. Thief; St. Louis; MO; 1858; MO; 103A
Egbert,Victor; Astronomer; Hamilton; OH; 1856; OH; 72D
Eggler, W. David; Base ballist; Erie; NY; 1849; NY; 260B
Eggleston, John; Magnetic Physician; Genesee; NY; 1831; NY;
     495C
Egleuch, Nicholas; Tramp; New York; NY; 1831; Germany; 581C
Eh, Ow; Gambler; Deer Lodge; MT; 1852; China; 111C
Eh, Sop; Gambler; Deer Lodge; MT; 1850; China; 111C
Ehrler, Hany; Dead; St. Louis; MO; 1879; MO; 289B
Ehrmann, George; Tramp on public street; St. Clair; IL; 1838;
     Saxonia; 482A
Eicles, Conelia; Fortune Teller; Orleans; LA; 1830; Mexico; 110C
Eldridge, Howlitt; Phrenologist; Los Angeles; CA; 1854; UT
     Terr.; 167A
Elkins, James; Vagrant; Richland; SC; 1840; SC; 158C
Elkins, Mary; Vagrant; Richland; SC; 1855; SC; 158C
Ellinwood, George R.; Dead; Jackson; MI; 1879; MI; 317B
Elliott, William B.; Phrenologist; Blair; PA; 1815; PA; 63B
Ellis, Abner; Gambler; Amador; CA; 1832; IL; 6C
Ellis, Frances; Phrenologist; Wayne; MI; 1834; England; 290C
Ellis, Frank; Tramp; Hennepin; MN; 1852; NY; 272A
Ellison, Ben; Farm hand (dead); Fairfield; SC; 1820; SC; 196A
Ellison, Dora; Dead; Caldwell; TX; 1878; TX; 179A

Ellison, Eliza; Not reported dead in June; St. Louis; MO; 1840;
    MO; 94B

Ellison, Henseley; Dead; Caldwell; TX; 1877; TX; 179A

Ellison, John; Gambler; Tarrant; TX; 1858; TN; 9B

Ellison, Minie; Dead; Caldwell; TX; 1879; TX; 179A

Ellison, William; Farm hand (dead); Fairfield; SC; 1871; SC;
    196A

Ellsworth, John; In Opium Factory; Hudson; NJ; 1859; NJ; 402C

Elsworth; Tramp; Bond; IL; 1867; IL; 260C

Elsworth, James; Tramp; Bond; IL; 1830; OH; 260C

Elwood, Charles; Keeps Horses in Circus; St. Louis; MO; 1838;
    England; 565A

Elwood, H.; Thief; Philadelphia; PA; 1851; PA; 289C

Emerson, B.; Gambler; Mono; CA; 1854; MI; 116D

Emerson, Edgar W.; Spiritualist M.D.; Hillsborough; NH; 1854;
    NH; 224B

Emerson, John L.; Magnetic Healer; Suffolk; MA; 1833; MA;
    218D

Emerson, Richard; Dead; Clark; KY; 1816; KY; 426B

Emery, Edward; Gambler; Fresno; CA; 1838; MO; 188D

Emory, Anne E.; Dead; Orange; VT; 1879; VT; 206B

Engles, Henry; Tramp on public street; St. Clair; IL; 1841;
    Hanover; 482B

English, Ann; Quack Doctor; Marquette; WI; 1832; NY; 590C

Enos, George E.; Phrenologist; Red Willow; NE; 1848; OH; 336A

Ephraim, Thos.; Tramp; Marengo; AL; 1860; AL; 477B

Epperson, Thomas; Dead; Adair; MO; 1838; KY; 87B

Erb, Alexander; Tramp; Douglas; NE; 1848; Germany; 297B

Ertel, Ernistena; Dead; Dubuque; IA; 1846; IA; 345C

Esperas, Felipe; Circus Actor; Atascosa; TX; 1860; Mexico; 322A

Espinosa, Torevia; Gambler; Las Animas; CO; 1850; NM Terr.;
    65D

Etherton, John; Stealing; Bledsoe; TN; 1815; TN; 33D

Eticheson, Matilda; Fortune Teller; Sacramento; CA; 1833; West
    Indies; 83A

Evans, Abram; Wandering about; Brazoria; TX; 1870; TX; 128B

Evans, Ibby; Listed as Dead since June 1; Martin; KY; 1837; KY;
    279B

Evans, Ike; Gambler; Dubuque; IA; 1828; NY; 229A

Evans, Jacob; Ball player; Rensselaer; NY; 1857; OH; 268A

Evans, Lucy; Dead; Davis; IA; 1878; IA; 60C

Evans, Uriah L.; Baseball; Baltimore; MD; 1857; MD; 496D

Evens, John; Tramp; Hennepin; MN; 1859; MA; 272A

Everett, Demmice; Vagrant; Potter; PA; 1824; PA; 481B

Everhardt, James; Tramp on public street; St. Clair; IL; 1836; KY;
    483C

Everts, H.; Circus; Ohio; WV; 1835; CT; 449B

Evine, Lucky B.; Dead; Washington; AR; 1879; AR; 572A

Ewell, George W.; With Circus; Ashtabula; OH; 1843; OH; 651C

Ewing, Emily; Dead; Taney; MO; 1847; MO; 283A

Ewing, Julia; Tramp; Clay; MS; 1845; MS; 188B

Ewing, W.N.; Gambler; Waller; TX; 1851; VA; 374A

Fagan, Bridget; Dead; New York; NY; 1847; Ireland; 450C

Fair, Thomas; Tramp; Lancaster; NE; 1857; Ireland; 173A

Fairbanks, Edward; Phrenologist; Martin; KY; 1824; MD; 273A

Fairman, Daniel; Phrenologist; Genesee; NY; 1819; Canada; 271A

Fairman, Eugene; Phrenologist; New York; NY; 1858; Canada;
    271A

Fake, James; Tramp; Potter; PA; 1805; PA; 457C

Falahey, John; Vagrant; Crawford; WI; 1855; Canada; 116A

Falck, William; With Circus; Allegheny; PA; 1854; PA; 88A

Falin, George; Vagrant; Hudson; NJ; 1831; NY; 398D

Fammy, Walter; Gambler; Jackson; MO; 1850; NY; 144B

Fante, John J.; Magnetic Healer; Cook; IL; 1823; Holland; 450B

Farley, Benjamin; Tramp; Santa Clara; CA; 1836; England; 202A

Farley, E.; Circus; Ohio; WV; 1846; Ireland; 448D

Farley, Lucy S.N.; Clairvoyant; Worcester; MA; 1816; VT; 492C

Farney, John; Magician; New York; NY; 1852; NY; 243D

Farrall, John; Ball player; Hartford; CT; 1857; CT; 141C

Farrel, John; Ball player; Providence; RI; 1853; NJ; 375C

Farrel, Mary; In the Circus Business; Philadelphia; PA; 1860; PA;
    132D

Farrel, William; In the Circus Business; Philadelphia; PA; 1857;
    PA; 132D

Farrell, John; Tramp; Hennepin; MN; 1840; MA; 208C

Farrell, Jos.; Base ball player; Rensselaer; NY; 1858; NY; 427A

Farrett, James; Tramp; Allegheny; PA; 1840; Ireland; 429B

Fat, Some; Gambler; Boise; ID; 1838; China; 118B

Fat, Wen; Gambler; Lander; NV; 1850; China; 297A

Fat, Yea; Gambler; Lander; NV; 1840; China; 297A

Faurnier, George; Tramp on public street; St. Clair; IL; 1848; France; 483D

Fauson, Fred; Tramp on public street; St. Clair; IL; 1856; IA; 483D

Fawn, E.; Gambler; Santa Cruz; CA; 1847; China; 521C

Fee, Tchu; Gambler; Union; OR; 1839; China; 177C

Feeny, Phil; Tramp; Linn; IA; 1854; Ireland; 91B

Felshaw, John S.; Magnetic Physician; Lucas; IA; 1848; NY; 468A

Fenel, Mary; Tramp; Franklin; PA; 1817; PA; 213A

Fennell; Medium; San Francisco; CA; 1845; France; 143A

Fenner, Michael; Gambler; Boise; ID; 1852; MI; 131D

Fenno, Elisabeth S.; Magnetic Physician; Middlesex; MA; 1820; NH; 272B

Ferguson, Henry; Tramp on public street; St. Clair; IL; 1825; Ireland; 482B

Ferguson, Jas.; Thief; Philadelphia; PA; 1829; Ireland; 289C

Ferguson, John; Tramp on public street; St. Clair; IL; 1845; Canada; 483C

Ferguson, William; Gambler; Eureka; NV; 1842; NY; 199B

Ferguson, Wm.; Preparing death; Montgomery; TN; 1770; VA; 186A

Fernando, Juan; Tramp - Prisoner; Rockingham; NH; 1850; Sicily; 277D

Ferrill, J.; Ball player; Storey; NV; 1853; CT; 119D

Ferry, John; Tramp; Hennepin; MN; 1858; OH; 394D

Fettie, Antone; Dead; St. Louis; MO; ---; ---; 231D

Fichter, Adolph; Dead; St. Louis; MO; 1879; MO; 500B

Fidel, Annie; Fortune Teller; Tuscarawas; OH; 1828; Switzerland; 333D

Field, Joseph; Gambler; Jefferson; KY; 1857; IN; 140A

Fields,Chas. W.; Gambler; Franklin; OH; 1862; OH; 481C

Fife, Charles; Gambler; Warren; MS; 1848; OH; 359C

Figures, William H.; Gambler; Madison; AL; 1848; AL; 408B

Finch, John; Gambler; Kinney; TX; 1818; GA; 296C

Findley, Julian J.; Gambler; Montgomery; KS; 1834; NY; 235C

Fineghan, Margaret; Dead; Allegheny; PA; 1847; Ireland; 218D

Fink, Wm.; Thief; Westchester; NY; 1858; NY; 97D

Finlay, Andrew; Gambler; Jackson; MO; 1820; Ireland; 43B

Finlay, Edward; Gambler; Jackson; MO; 1856; NY; 43B

Finn, Richard; Stage dancer; New York; NY; 1855; Canada; 1B

Finney, Faniee; Dead head; St. Landry; LA; 1795; MS; 335D

Finney, William; Base ballist; Middlesex; MA; 1858; MA; 308A

Finnie, Robert; Dead; Benton; AR; 1867; AR; 461D

Finnigan, John; Travels with Circus; New York; NY; 1855; NY; 86D

Finnigan, Patrick; Gambler; Washington; MN; 1855; Ireland; 285C

Fischer, Charles; Tramp on public street; St. Clair; IL; 1834; Saxonia; 482A

Fischer, Henry; Tramp on public street; St. Clair; IL; 1841; Prussia; 482B

Fish, Chas. W.; Circus Rider; Franklin; VT; 1850; PA; 240D

Fish, E.B.; Magnetic Doctor; New York; NY; 1815; NY; 366D

Fish, H.A.; Gambler; Storey; NV; 1841; NY; 96B

Fish, John; Vagrant; Berrien; MI; 1840; NY; 395D

Fish, L.; Magiztic Healer; San Francisco; CA; 1832; KY; 276A

Fisher, B.R.; Professional dancer; Williamson; IL; 1848; IN; 434A

Fisher, Charles J.; Dead; Northumberland; PA; 1879; PA; 532C

Fisher, Hy; Gambler; Orleans; LA; 1838; Ireland; 453C

Fisher, Julia; Tramp; Noble; IN; 1858; PA; 354D

Fisher, Robert; Gypsy; Dane; WI; 1830; England; 404A

Fisher, Vie; Gypsy; Dane; WI; 1832; England; 404A

Fitspatrick, John; Gambler; Hennepin; MN; 1855; MN; 314A

Fitz Patrick, John; Tramp; New York; NY; 1844; NY; 581C

Fitzgarald, Michail; Circus Actor; Bucks; PA; 1831; Ireland; 80A

Fitzgerald, -- J.; Gambler; Arapahoe; CO; 1846; KY; 98D

Fitzgerald, John W.; Dead; Owen; KY; 1879; KY; 189C

Fitzgerald, William; Tramp; New York; NY; 1846; Ireland; 431C

Fitziminy, George; Gambler; Bexar; TX; 1850; TX; 75B

Fitzmoriss, John; Dead; St. Louis; MO; 1840; Ireland; 146B

Fitzpatrick, James; Dead; New York; NY; 1832; Ireland; 512D

Fitzwilliam, James; Tramp on public street; St. Clair; IL; 1855; Ireland; 481D

Flanagan, Isabella; Dead; Bristol; MA; 1879; MA; 402A

Flanagan, Sarah; Dead; Bristol; MA; 1852; MA; 402A

Flanagan, Susan; Dead; Lapeer; MI; 1828; PA; 220B

Flanty, Thomas; Tramp; Stephenson; IL; 1840; OH; 63A

Flare; Dead; Adams; IL; ---; IL; 472C

Flarrity, Wm.; Gambler; Storey; NV; 1842; Ireland; 122A

Fleath, Patric; Tramp on public street; St. Clair; IL; 1860; OH; 482A

Fleming, Annie; Dead; Philadelphia; PA; 1837; PA; 359D

Fletcher, Elizabeth; Clairvoyant; Middlesex; MA; 1830; ME; 8C

Flinn, William; Vagrant; Buchanan; MO; 1834; MO; 41B

Flint, Frank; Baseball player; Cook; IL; 1835; PA; 316B

Flint, James; Dead; St. Louis; MO; 1802; England; 500A

Florence, George; Tramp; Buchanan; MO; 1841; KY; 41A

Floris, Antonio; Gambler; Santa Clara; CA; 1832; CA; 113B

Flowers, Ammie; Tramp; Screven; GA; 1853; GA; 229B

Floyd, Sarah; Dead; Dubuque; IA; 1811; KY; 69D

Floyd, Winnie; Vagrant; Spartanburg; SC; 1865; SC; 223B

Flynn, Fred; Gambler; Pulaski; AR; 1854; IA; 337D

Fogg, Miranda; Magnetic Physician; Suffolk; MA; 1831; ME; 481C

Foley, Charles; Bass ball player; Suffolk; MA; 1856; MA; 93A

Foley, John; Tramp; New York; NY; 1838; Ireland; 581D

Foley, Larry; Tramp; Union; IL; 1861; Germany; 144A

Folkner, Henry; Tramp; Buchanan; MO; 1854; MO; 41A

Followell, Thomas; Dead; Sullivan; IN; 1867; IN; 416A

Folly, Daglin; Dead; Sandusky; OH; 1873; Ireland; 165D

Folsom, Abbie; Dead; Adams; IL; 1845; ---; 475A

Fonar, Cyrus S.; Electric Healer; Cook; IL; 1830; NH; 566B

Fong, Chou; Phrenologist; Storey; NV; 1858; China; 236B

Fong, Chun; Gambler; San Francisco; CA; 1830; Kwantung; 387B

Fong, Fu; Keeps Opium Den; Shasta; CA; 1838; China; 2D

Fong, King Shuck; Opium Dealer; Sacramento; CA; 1838; China; 4C

Fong, Ling; Gambler; Sacramento; CA; 1852; China; 12C

Fong, Lung; Gambler; Nevada; CA; 1841; Canton; 220B

Fong, Mow; Opium Dealer; San Francisco; CA; 1841; Qwantung; 608B

Fong, On Yong; Physician & Fortune Teller; San Francisco; CA; 1830; Sam Yap; 632A

Fong, Say; Opium House; Ormsby; NV; 1851; China; 71A

Fong, Sing; Opium Dealer; San Francisco; CA; 1833; Qwantung; 608B

Fong, Yuk Lou; Fortune Teller; San Francisco; CA; 1820; Kwantung; 393B

Foo, Cau; Gambler; Yuba; CA; 1843; China; 454C

Fook, King; Keeps Gambling House; Eureka; NV; 1827; China; 191B

Fook, King; Keeps Gambling House; Eureka; NV; 1827; China; 191B

Fook, Tom; Gambler; Ada; ID; 1840; China; 19A

For, Chin; Gambler; San Francisco; CA; 1843; Kwantung; 392B

Forbes, Marth M.; Dead; Parke; IN; 1854; IN; 485C

Forbes, Pet.; Tramp; Douglas; NE; 1859; TN; 260D

Force, David W.; Base ballist; Erie; NY; 1849; NY; 269D

Ford, Canady; Wanderer; Yazoo; MS; 1825; MS; 454A

Ford, William; Gambler; St. Louis; MO; 1835; England; 356A

Ford, William; Dead; Jefferson; GA; 1820; NC; 144D

Ford, Wm.; Gambler; St. Louis; MO; 1840; NY; 250B

Foreback, George; Dead; Grundy; IL; 1840; Germany; 323C

Forest, Lofe; Circus; Ohio; WV; 1858; NY; 449B

Forguson, W.H.; Gambler; Deer Lodge; MT; 1854; MO; 125C

Formhales, Jacob; Dead; Allegheny; PA; 1876; PA; 252D

Formhales, Julia; Dead; Allegheny; PA; 1857; PA; 252D

Forrest, Edgar; Gambler; Shackelford; TX; 1852; GA; 466C

Forster, Emma; Clairvoyant & Keeping House; New York; NY; 1835; England; 280C

Forster, Thomas; Tramp on public street; St. Clair; IL; 1856; PA; 482B

Foster, Augusta; Clair Voince Dr.; Santa Cruz; CA; 1843; MA; 446D

Foster, Eveline; Clairvoyant Physician; Bradford; PA; 1833; NY; 418B

Foster, George B.; Gambler; Grayson; TX; 1845; TN; 40D

Foster, J.H.B.; Gambler; Deer Lodge; MT; 1832; England; 124B
Foster, Joe; Gambler; Bexar; TX; 1840; FL; 189A
Foster, Mary; Tramp; Christian; KY; 1868; KY; 298A
Fouck, Sam; Gambler; Deer Lodge; MT; 1835; China; 137D
Fountain, Geo.; Gambler; St. Louis; MO; 1850; PA; 257C
Fox, Carrie; Clairvoyant; Suffolk; MA; 1838; ME; 418A
Fox, Hugh; Tramp; Douglas; NE; 1850; NY; 337D
Fox, J.P.; Baseball professional; Huron; OH; 1860; NY; 332C
Fox, John; State Pauper & Tramp; Hampshire; MA; 1824; Baden;
        62A
Fox, Owen; Tramp; Hendricks; IN; 1859; Ireland; 635A
Fragle, William; Tramp; Baltimore; MD; 1822; Germany; 395D
Frame, James; Gambler; Jackson; MO; 1840; MO; 317C
Franci, Eliza; Clairvoyant; Albany; NY; 1821; NY; 324B
Francini, Frank; Gambler; Storey; NV; 1850; France; 138B
Francis, Mary; Dead; Clark; WI; 1833; France; 425C
Francisa, Bene.; Gambler; Lawrence; Dak. Terr.; 1853; TX; 238D
Franklin, Ben; Tramp; St. Mary; LA; 1864; LA; 275A
Fraser, Sidney A.; Clairvoyant; Hamilton; OH; 1834; OH; 139C
Frazer, Frank; Dead head; Marshall; KS; 1857; IN; 193C
Frazier, T.W.; Gambler; Yavapai; AZ; 1853; IA; 415A
Freeman, Trav; Gambler; McLennan; TX; 1853; TX; 1A
Freer, Gabriel; Tramp; Lake; OH; 1820; NY; 402D
Freerichs, Derk; Dead; Grundy; IA; 1858; Hanover; 396B
Freeze, William A.; Gambler; Lawrence; Dak. Terr.; 1853; New
        Brunswick; 246C
Frens, Frank; Circus Clown; Luzerne; PA; 1853; PA; 611C
Frey, Christian; Tramp on public street; St. Clair; IL; 1850;
        Bavaria; 482A
Frick, Peter; Dead; Sheboygan; WI; 1815; Hesse D.; 160C
Frink, Cloan; Tramp; Horry; SC; 1825; NC; 336A
Frost, John M.; Gambler; Saratoga; NY; 1835; MA; 455C
Fryberger, G.W.; Circus; Ohio; WV; 1849; IN; 449A
Fryman, Robert; Gambler; Monterey; CA; 1861; CA; 178C
Fryman,Alonzo; Gambler; Monterey; CA; 1849; CA; 178C
Fuelner, John; Vagrant; Buchanan; MO; 1853; MO; 41B
Fugmann, Conrad; Quack Doctor; New York; NY; 1805; Bavaria;
        122B

Fuguay, James A.; Circus Manager; Philadelphia; PA; 1833; VA;
     385B
Fuller, Benjamin F.; Dead; Caldwell; TX; 1805; SC; 183A
Fuller, Elias; Deadbeat; McHenry; IL; 1862; OH; 235C
Fuller, Ezekil E.; Dead; Caldwell; TX; 1879; TX; 183A
Fuller, Mary M.; Dead; Caldwell; TX; 1821; AL; 183A
Fung, Tie; Gambler; San Francisco; CA; 1854; Kwang Chow;
     627D
Funk, Emanuel; Tramp; Holmes; OH; 1848; Wurttemberg; 346A
Furgison, Wm. H.; Tramp; York; SC; 1821; Scotland; 294C
Furry, Patrick; Tramp; Carbon; PA; 1851; Ireland; 339A
Gaddis, Johnny M.; Dead; Washington; AR; 1879; AR; 570B
Gaddy, Thomas; Dead; Grundy; IL; 1792; NC; 323C
Gaffield, William Wesley; Tramp; Osborne; KS; 1867; Canada;
     351C
Gage, Charles; Circus Actor; Tazewell; IL; 1856; NY; 624D
Gah, Ton; Gambler; Butte; CA; 1841; China; 148B
Gahan, James; Tramp; St. Louis; MO; 1850; Ireland; 601C
Gaines, James; Vagrant; Buchanan; MO; 1835; MO; 41B
Gaines, John; Dead; St. Louis; MO; 1830; VA; 165B
Gains, Mary J.; Dead; Owen; KY; 1877; KY; 171D
Gains, Tel F.; Dead; Owen; KY; 1879; KY; 163D
Galager, James; Baseball; St. Louis; MO; 1856; MO; 205A
Galbagh, Gus; Gambler; St. Louis; MO; 1840; MO; 94B
Galindo, Tirso; Gambler; Dona Ana; NM; 1859; NM Terr.; 298C
Gallagher, John P.; Dead; St. Louis; MO; 1876; MO; 286C
Gallagher, Joseph; Circus Performer; Broome; NY; 1848; NY;
     187B
Gallagher, Michael; Dead; Cuyahoga; OH; 1821; Ireland; 350C
Gallagher, Thos.; Gambler Professional; Orleans; LA; 1858; KY;
     246D
Gamage, Lucinda; Clairvoyant Physician; Middlesex; MA; 1825;
     MA; 329B
Gamble, A.J.; Gambler; San Francisco; CA; 1815; TN; 77D
Gambrel, Daniel M.; Now dead; Putnam; TN; 1859; TN; 195B
Gamel, Josiah; Gambler; Fulton; GA; 1846; GA; 244A
Gandolfo, Jane; Dead; Hamilton; OH; 1813; Wales; 7A
Gang, Too; Gambler; Butte; CA; 1839; China; 150B

Ganner, Margeret; Ballet dancer; New York; NY; 1858; NY; 352B

Gannon, James; Circus Side Show; New York; NY; 1844; RI; 90B

Gannon, Wm.; Gambler; Eureka; NV; 1850; NY; 193B

Garcia, Juan; Rustler; Bernalillo; NM; 1840; NM Terr.; 26A

Garcia, Migel; Vagabond; Huerfano; CO; 1831; NM Terr.; 232A

Garcir, Frank; Bummer; Amador; CA; 1861; Spain; 5B

Garden, Joseph; Tramp; Venango; PA; 1841; MD; 95A

Gardner, Dick; Gambler; Dyer; TN; 1840; TN; 71C

Gardner, Frank W.; Professional ball player; Middlesex; MA;
    1859; MA; 117A

Gardner, S.M.; Gambler; Obion; TN; 1834; TN; 216B

Garitee, Mary J.; Dead; Jones; IA; 1857; IA; 337C

Garivay, Sostenes; Proffessional Thief; Zapata; TX; 1839;
    Mexico; 453A

Garner; Dead; Fairfield; SC; 1880; ---; 176C

Garrett, J.; Tramp; Crawford; AR; 1855; GA; 520D

Garrison, Riley; Gambler; Tarrant; TX; 1850; TX; 87C

Garvin, John Henry; Travelling with Circus; Dutchess; NY; 1852;
    NY; 361A

Garza, Lazaro; Gambler; Webb; TX; 1853; Mexico; 316D

Garza, Segundo; Gambler; Webb; TX; 1850; Mexico; 323D

Gaskins, Ann; Fortune Teller; Sumter; GA; 1830; GA; 107C

Gate, Fate; Gambler; Lafayette; LA; 1827; LA; 439A

Gauberal, Engel; Tramp not following any work; Berks; PA; 1822;
    Oldenburg; 94C

Gaus, Mary; Dead; Allegheny; PA; 1865; Wurttemberg; 252D

Gause, Elva P.; Phrenologist; Wayne; NC; 1842; NC; 619B

Gaylord, J.B.; Agt. for Circus; Buchanan; IA; 1842; OH; 485A

Ge, Ching; Gambler; Siskiyou; CA; 1845; Nin Young; 211A

Gedney, John; Traveling with a Circus; New York; NY; 1858;
    NY; 180B

Gee, Chung; Gambling House; Owyhee; ID; 1833; China; 353C

Gee, Haw; Gambler; Madison; MT; 1820; China; 386B

Gee, Lem; Gambler; Storey; NV; 1809; China; 147C

Gee, Sing; Gambler; Butte; CA; 1842; China; 200D

Gee, Won; Opium Dealer; New York; NY; 1858; China; 165D

Geise, Reuben; Gambler; Washoe; NV; 1838; PA; 267A

Gellespie, Peter; Ball player; Rensselaer; NY; 1855; IL; 268A

Georg, Thomas; Tramp on public street; St. Clair; IL; 1856; OH; 483C

George, Alfred; Tramp; New York; NY; 1842; Germany; 581C

George, William; Tramp on public street; St. Clair; IL; 1852; PA; 482B

Gephart, Phillip; Gambler; Montgomery; KS; 1845; OH; 245D

Gerard, Edward; Circus; Passaic; NJ; 1860; NJ; 253B

German, Frederick; Dead; New York; NY; ---; ---; 201A

German, P.T.; Gambler; Jefferson; KY; 1839; KY; 334A

Germani, Louis; Circus Business; Philadelphia; PA; 1820; Italy; 480C

Gernhart, Charles W.; Dead; Allegheny; PA; 1879; PA; 243A

Gessley, Edward; Sells Candy for Circus; Pickaway; OH; 1856; PA; 559D

Gessley, Rudolph; Traveling with Circus; Pickaway; OH; 1854; NY; 562B

Getkin, Franklin; Dead; Northumberland; PA; 1879; PA; 540D

Geyer, Albert; Circus Actor; Lafayette; MO; 1861; NJ; 206B

Geyer, Chas.; Thief; Philadelphia; PA; 1854; PA; 288B

Gheens, Hugh; Gambler; St. Louis; MO; 1814; KY; 261A

Gibbons, Patrick; Traveling with Circus; Walworth; WI; 1843; Ireland; 190A

Gibens, Thomas; Gambler; McLennan; TX; 1858; NC; 2D

Gibson, Benjamin; Tramp; Putnam; IL; 1857; NH; 266B

Gibson, Daniel D.; Gambler; Linn; MO; 1850; NY; 433D

Gifford, D.J.; Murdered by mother; Warren; NY; 1879; NY; 261C

Gifford, Frank; Dead; Onondaga; NY; 1850; ---; 259A

Gifford, James H.; Baseball player; Franklin; OH; 1847; NY; 475C

Gifford, Sarah; In jail for murder; Warren; NY; 1857; NY; 261C

Gilbert, Henry; Dancer; New York; NY; 1845; TX; 223B

Gilbert, Mary; Dead; Parker; TX; 1830; AL; 457C

Gilbs, Charles; Tramp on public street; St. Clair; IL; 1841; IA; 481D

Giles, George W.; With Circus; Madison; IL; 1849; MO; 97B

Gilham, Richard B.; Gambler; Washington; D.C.; 1840; VA; 205D

Gillam, Jas. A.; Tramp; Bertie; NC; 1849; NC; 288A

Gillen, Lewis; Gambler; Vermilion; IL; 1840; Scotland; 334B

Gillespie, Patrick; Baseball player; Lackawanna; PA; 1855; PA; 33B

Gillet, Peter; Tramp on public street; St. Clair; IL; 1845; MO; 481D

Gilliam, Asberry; Tramp; Newberry; SC; 1825; SC; 118C

Gilligan, Bernard; Base ball player; Middlesex; MA; 1858; MA; 10D

Gillis, James; Dead 2 years; Providence; RI; 1872; RI; 356C

Gim, Chung; Gambler; Storey; NV; 1840; China; 237C

Gin, Ark Chu; Fortune Teller; Nevada; NV; 1815; China; 84B

Gin, Lee; Gambler; Eureka; NV; 1840; China; 191A

Gin, Sin; Gambler; Sweetwater; WY; 1849; China; 275A

Ginn, Moses; Tramp; Hampton; SC; 1825; SC; 27B

Gip, Yok; Keeper Opium Den; Sacramento; CA; 1855; China; 2C

Gipson, Beckey A.; Fortune Telling; Shelby; IA; 1825; NY; 10C

Giroud, Ninny; Dead; Marion; IN; 1865; IN; 501A

Gise, H.; Circus; Ohio; WV; 1836; PA; 448D

Gise, Wm.; Circus; Ohio; WV; 1860; PA; 449A

Glackin, William; Circus Performer; New Castle; DE; 1863; DE; 371B

Glann, John; Circus Actor; Mercer; NJ; 1834; NJ; 297B

Gleason, Hattea; Dead; Republic; KS; 1879; KS; 70D

Gleason, Michael; Tramp; Hennepin; MN; 1856; Ireland; 394D

Gleason, Wm.; Thief; Lancaster; NE; 1866; Ireland; 173A

Gleason, Wm.; Thief; Lancaster; NE; 1866; Ireland; 173A

Glen, Burton; Tramp; Chester; SC; 1845; NC; 168D

Glidden, Irving W.; Magnetic Physician; Essex; MA; 1856; NH; 825B

Glilaspy, Thom; Tramp on public street; St. Clair; IL; 1857; Ireland; 483C

Gloria, Francesca; Fortune Teller; Monroe; NY; 1840; Italy; 18C

Glover, Mary; Dead; Adams; IL; 1811; Baden; 480D

Gnuse, Annie; Dead; Adams; IL; 1825; Hanover; 471B

Gobble, D.H.; Gambler; Macoupin; IL; 1839; IL; 196D

Godwin, James; Gambler; Kinney; TX; 1848; AL; 295A

Godwin, John; Tramp; Box Elder; UT; 1862; PA; 119D

Goetz, Lorenz; Tramp on public street; St. Clair; IL; 1837;
     Bavaria; 482B

Goffney, W.A.; Circus; Ohio; WV; 1857; IA; 449A

Golden, David; Tramp; Hennepin; MN; 1855; NY; 394D

Gonin, Louis; Gambler; Deer Lodge; MT; 1831; Canada; 136B

Gonzales, Jesus; Gambler; Maverick; TX; 1830; Mexico; 43B

Gonzales, Manuel; Gambler; Bernalillo; NM; 1851; NM Terr.; 7B

Gonzales, Peo; Clown; San Bernardino; CA; 1851; Mexico; 443C

Gooch, Deforest; Tramp; Eaton; MI; 1847; IN; 98A

Goode, Martela; Tramp; Barbour; AL; 1853; AL; 278D

Gooden, C.; Circus; Ohio; WV; 1858; NY; 449B

Goodman, Amelia; Milliner & Fortune Teller; Washoe; NV; 1833;
     Saxony; 273B

Goodman, Miles; Gambler; Storey; NV; 1821; KY; 102A

Goodrich, J.E.; Tramp; Nemaha; NE; 1861; NE ; 141D

Goodwater, W.S.; Tramp; Clay; IA; 1861; MN; 219C

Goodwin; Dead; Autauga; AL; 1880; AL; 131A

Goodwin, Chas.; Tramp; Androscoggin; ME; 1850; ME; 46C

Goodwin, Elizabeth; Fortune Teller; Albany; NY; 1834; MA;
     310A

Goodyard, Enoch; Gambler; Conejos; CO; 1843; Ireland; 158B

Gooey, Tow; Opium Dealer; San Francisco; CA; 1851; See Yap;
     635D

Googen, John; Tramp; Saunders; NE; 1857; Canada; 336B

Gooker, A.W.; Circus; Ohio; WV; 1853; MA; 448D

Goose, Jim; Dr. & Magician; Polk; WI; 1835; WI; 315A

Goosman, Wm.; Tramp; Defiance; OH; 1835; OH; 77B

Gorden, Frank; Tramp; De Kalb; IL; 1867; IL; 114C

Gordon, Ike; Tramp; Maury; TN; 1861; TN; 53D

Gormly, James; Ball player; New York; NY; 1859; NY; 102A

Gorrell, Thos.; Circus; Ohio; WV; 1859; GA; 448D

Gorsman, James; Tramp; Stephenson; IL; 1860; ---; 63A

Gould, George H.; Phrenologist; Suffolk; MA; 1831; ME; 285D

Gould, Jennie T.H.; Clairvoyant; New York; NY; 1857; NY; 25B

Gouse, R.; Circus; Ohio; WV; 1844; MD; 449B

Govin, Joseph; Gambler; Storey; NV; 1851; NY; 111D

Gower, Richard; Ball player; Cumberland; ME; 1852; ME; 553D

Gowns, Patrick; Tramp on public street; St. Clair; IL; 1854;
    Ireland; 483D
Gr(?), W.C.; Retired Gambler; Sacramento; CA; 1843; MO; 39B
Graboras, Carl; Dead; Brown; WI; 1832; Prussia; 300D
Grace, Michael; Tramp; Windham; VT; 1859; VT; 341A
Grady, Pat; Vagrant; Hudson; NJ; 1847; England; 398D
Graef, Lillie; Dead; St. Louis; MO; 1878; MD; 341B
Graham, Lidy; Dead; Colleton; SC; 1832; SC; 250D
Graham, Robert; Gambler; Beaverhead; MT; 1860; MT Terr.; 21C
Graham, Theodore H.; Magnetic Physician; Ingham; MI; 1815;
    NY; 366A
Grammar, Tom; Gambler; Van Zandt; TX; 1849; TN; 71C
Granger, Kitty C.; Dead; Susquehanna; PA; 1875; PA; 362C
Granly, Jacob; Tramp on public street; St. Clair; IL; 1848; Ireland;
    483C
Grans, Wash; Theft; Parker; TX; 1862; GA; 321D
Grant, E.B.R.; Gambler; St. Louis; MO; 1847; TN; 484B
Grant, John M.; Tramp; New York; NY; 1838; West Indies; 581D
Grant, Louis; Dead; Peoria; IL; 1880; IL; 400A
Grant, Mary Ann; Dead; Peoria; IL; 1850; England; 400A
Grant, Pigeon; Dead; Colleton; SC; 1879; SC; 240C
Grary, William; Tramp; New York; NY; 1855; RI; 581D
Graves, Andy; Dead; Essex; NY; 1877; NY; 281C
Graves, John; Gambler; Multnomah; OR; 1835; NY; 252B
Graves, Margret; Dead; Paulding; IN; 1831; OH; 251C
Graw, Henry H.; Deadbeat; McKean; PA; 1855; Canada; 105A
Gray, Benj. F.; Dead; Newport; RI; ---; ---; 85C
Gray, Eli; Tramp; Franklin; NY; 1844; Canada; 599B
Gray, Mr.; Gambler; Ramsey; MN; 1852; ---; 149D
Gray, Mrs.; Gambler; Ramsey; MN; 1855; ---; 149D
Gray, Robert; Criminal; Carroll; NH; 1846; ME; 297C
Gray, Sarah, Mrs.; Clairvoyant; Cuyahoga; OH; 1847; NY; 209B
Gray, Stephen; Tramp; Buchanan; MO; 1853; NH; 41A
Gray, Thomas; Dead; New York; NY; 1880; NY; 615C
Grayson, James; Tramp; Washington; IN; 1850; TN; 386D
Greathouse, John; Gambler; Oldham; TX; 1848; AR; 2C
Greeg, John; Tramp on public street; St. Clair; IL; 1859; AL;
    483D

Green; Fortune Teller; McKean; PA; 1820; Ireland; 190A
Green, Charles; Dead; Cook; IL; 1866; MA; 144B
Green, D.R.; Gambler; Vermilion; IL; 1839; KY; 362D
Green, Emma; Dancer; Tarrant; TX; 1862; NY; 17B
Green, Frank; Gambler; St. Louis; MO; 1860; KY; 264D
Green, Howard; Gimnasts in Circus; McLean; IL; 1865; IL; 255C
Green, J.; Base ball; McKean; PA; 1857; PA; 113B
Green, James; Tramp; Marshall; MN; 1850; IL; 143D
Green, John; Vagrant; Knox; TN; 1862; TN; 118D
Green, Josephine A.; Fortune Teller; San Francisco; CA; 1853;
     CA; 309C
Green, Kate; Dead; Colleton; SC; 1835; SC; 251A
Green, Samuel; Gambler; Cook; IL; 1833; IL; 218C
Green, Thomas; Gambler; Storey; NV; 1832; NY; 130B
Green, Thomas; Tramp; Lapeer; MI; 1802; NY; 315B
Greenwood, Alex; Circus Performer; Gallia; OH; 1843; OH; 292A
Greenwood, John; For murder; Parker; TX; 1863; TX; 321D
Gregerson, Leva; Dead; Racine; WI; 1820; Norway; 532D
Greggs, Geo.; Astrologer; New York; NY; 1850; MA; 540D
Grely; Gambling; Del Norte; CA; 1862; CA; 24C
Grier, Richard; Gambler; Eau Claire; WI; 1852; NY; 356A
Griffin, Edy Jane; Dead; Baldwin; AL; 1861; AL; 179D
Griffin, Henry; Tramp on public street; St. Clair; IL; 1837; PA;
     483D
Griffith, Richard; Tramp on public street; St. Clair; IL; 1852; OH;
     483C
Grims, Charlie; Gambler; Mahaska; IA; 1850; ---; 327C
Groeninger, Theresa; Dead; St. Louis; MO; 1879; MO; 497C
Groh, Christine; Dead; St. Louis; MO; 1795; Germany; 496A
Gross, Emil M.; Ball player; Providence; RI; 1856; MI; 375C
Gross, Rosa; Fortune Teller; Storey; NV; 1850; Hungary; 146A
Gross, Thos.; Circus; Ohio; WV; 1831; NY; 449A
Grosvenor, Mary F.; Magnetic Physician; Suffolk; MA; 1811;
     MA; 61D
Grote, Anna; Dead Sept.; Washington; IL; 1878; IL; 378B
Grubb, Anna; Tramp; Grayson; VA; 1798; NC; 370A
Gshwinder, John; Dead; Allegheny; PA; 1874; Prussia; 240D
Gudy, Harry; Gambler; St. Louis; MO; 1855; MO; 8C

Guise, Henry; Works in Circus; Tioga; PA; 1837; PA; 242A
Guise, William; Works in Circus; Tioga; PA; 1860; PA; 242A
Gulley, Nat; Dead 2 yrs; Wilcox; AL; ---; ---; 184B
Gully, P.H.; Farmer; assasin or murderer; Kemper; MS; 1821; NC;
    75A
Gum, Chum; Gambler; Trinity; CA; 1860; China; 570C
Gunar, Richard; Dead; Milwaukee; WI; 1878; WI; 295D
Gunar, Samuel; Dead; Milwaukee; WI; 1875; WI; 295D
Gunderson, Gunder; Tramp; Winnebago; IA; 1863; Norway; 601C
Gunderson, Leive; Tramp; Winnebago; IA; 1856; Norway; 601D
Gunnels, Martha E.; Dead; Fairfield; SC; 1851; SC; 196A
Gunther, Thomas; Deadbeat; Greenbrier; WV; 1856; VA; 385B
Gurnee, Charles P.; Gambler; Passaic; NJ; 1841; NJ; 369C
Gurula, Jesus; Rustler; Bernalillo; NM; 1835; NM Terr.; 19C
Gut, Lee; Gambler; Ada; ID; 1850; China; 19A
Guthrie, Thomas; Circus Rider; New Castle; DE; 1857; DE; 21B
Gutwein, John; Tramp on public street; St. Clair; IL; 1853; IL;
    482A
Guyon, Mary; Fortune Teller & Astrologist; Marion; IN; 1835;
    OH; 495B
Gwynn, Elizabeth; Wanderer; Johnson; TN; 1862; TN; 67A
H (?), Moi; Gambler; Nevada; CA; 1848; Canton; 220B
Ha, Woc; Gambler; Butte; CA; 1845; China; 149C
Haas, Jacob; Magician; Northampton; PA; 1834; PA; 446A
Hackel, Fanney; Dead; Allegheny; PA; 1876; PA; 247A
Hadley, Samuel; Tramp; Parke; IN; 1816; NC; 413D
Haedel, Herman; Healer; Allegheny; PA; 1848; PA; 128B
Haeslentine, Ira; Gambler; Clarion; PA; 1852; Canada; 14D
Haff, Abram; Gambler; Pike; MO; 1843; MO; 493B
Hagar, W.D.; Circus; Ohio; WV; 1848; NY; 449B
Haggard, Shirley; Dead; Clark; KY; ---; KY; 423D
Haight, Jennie; Dead; Jo Daviess; IL; 1847; IL; 403B
Haigood, J.C.; Farmer dead; Fairfield; SC; 1818; SC; 194A
Haines, William; Gambler; Deer Lodge; MT; 1825; NJ; 127D
Halbert, Daniel; Tramp on public street; St. Clair; IL; 1841;
    Bavaria; 482A
Halden, Lina; Fortune Teller; St. Louis; MO; 1859; Prussia; 256A
Hale, Davidson; Dead; Wilcox; AL; 1810; SC; 200A

Hale, Jane P.; Clairvoyant Physician; Worcester; MA; 1828; Canada; 604C

Hale, Nathaniel; Vagrant; Clinton; OH; 1828; OH; 201B

Haley, John; Tramp on public street; St. Clair; IL; 1857; MA; 482B

Hall, Anna; Fortune Teller; San Francisco; CA; 1824; NH; 256B

Hall, Deborah; Dead; Van Buren; MI; 1817; MA; 430D

Hall, Henry; Tramp; Lancaster; NE; 1857; NY; 173A

Hall, John; Tramp; Buchanan; MO; 1858; IN; 41A

Hall, Julia; Clairvoyant; Macon; IL; 1834; OH; 366C

Hall, Kate; Tramp; Madison; NC; 1849; NC; 56B

Hall, Mary T.; Dead; Caldwell; TX; 1827; TN; 194D

Hall, Rhoda; Tramp; Madison; NC; 1800; NC; 56B

Hall, S. Myra; Magnetic Physician; New York; NY; 1835; CT; 261C

Hall, Sarah P.; Clairvoyant; Androscoggin; ME; 1828; ME; 215B

Hallerman, Th.; Tramp on public street; St. Clair; IL; 1827; IL; 483D

Halpin, Sylvester; Tramp; New York; NY; 1842; Ireland; 581D

Halsinger, M.S.; Farmer dead; Fremont; IA; 1834; PA; 127D

Halstead, H.L.; Gambler; Albany; WY; 1852; PA; 30D

Halt, George; Gambler; Cook; IL; 1828; NY; 180B

Haly, Martin J.; With a Circus; Rensselaer; NY; 1856; NY; 419A

Hamer, Savania; Dead; Allegheny; PA; 1831; Baden; 7A

Hamilton, Barnabas; Deadbeat; Henry; IN; 1833; IN; 131D

Hamilton, Dot; Dancer; Lake; CO; 1863; NJ; 393B

Hamilton, Elwood; Propr. Circus; Ashtabula; OH; 1832; OH; 651C

Hamilton, Jas. B.; Tramp; Autauga; AL; 1856; LA; 39B

Hamilton, Richard; Travels with Circus; Washtenaw; MI; 1852; NC; 428B

Hamison, Charles; Tramp; Defiance; OH; 1860; OH; 102D

Hammel, Polly; Wanderer; Clayton; AL; 1820; GA; 47A

Handley, Andree F.; Dead; Crenshaw; AL; 1858; AL; 460A

Handsel, Wm.; Dead; Fairfield; SC; 1818; SC; 196A

Hanerstadt, John; Tramp; New York; NY; 1840; Germany; 581C

Hang, See; Gambler; Eureka; NV; 1853; China; 192C

Hanley, Addison; Gambler; Broome; NY; 1835; NY; 221A

Name; Occupation; County; State; Birth; Birth place; Page   63

Hanley, James; Tramp; Chautauqua; NY; 1809; Ireland; 142D
Hanley, Joseph; Tramp on public street; St. Clair; IL; 1852; OH;
483D
Hanlon, Edward; Base ballist; Hartford; CT; 1858; CT; 310B
Hanly, Margaret A.; Dist. Relation, mother dead, rasing child;
Essex; NJ; 1879; NJ; 162D
Hann, Theodore; Tramp; Philadelphia; PA; 1838; Germany; 275A
Hanna, Franklin; Vagrant; Morgan; IN; 1863; KY; 139A
Hannan, Ellen; Witch ; St. Louis; MO; 1820; Ireland; 587A
Hannison, Chas.; Tramp; Defiance; OH; 1852; NY; 78C
Hannond, Chas.; Circus Performer; Allegheny; PA; 1843; PA; 4D
Hanson, Gorge; Tramp; Marshall; IL; 1857; Denmark; 342D
Hanson, John M.; Gambler; Wayne; OH; 1821; PA; 377B
Hanson, Joseph A.; Dead; Columbia; AR; 1870; AR; 245C
Hanson, Nickless; Dead; Jones; IA; 1812; Germany; 342A
Hanson, Peter; Gambler; Travis; TX; 1853; Norway; 176A
Harbidge, William A.; Professional base ball player; Philadelphia;
PA; 1855; PA; 148C
Harbige, Wm.; Ball player; Rensselaer; NY; 1856; MA; 268A
Harbrook, Phebe; Dead - crossed out; Schenectady; NY; 1789;
NY; 132A
Hard, Charles; Tramp on public street; St. Clair; IL; 1848; MO;
482B
Harden, George S.; Gambler; Boise; ID; 1833; SC; 130A
Harden, Wm. E.; Foot racer (champion); Harlan; Ne; 1851; IN;
416D
Hardin, Daniel C.; Gambler; Lawrence; Dak. Terr.; 1848; KY;
238D
Hardin, Emory W.; Foot racer; Red Willow; NE; 1851; IN; 338A
Harding, Charles H.; Clairvoyant; Essex; MA; 1850; MA; 639B
Hardy, James A.; Dead; Henry; MO; 1839; IL; 263A
Hare, George; Phrenologist; Montgomery; PA; 1835; PA; 430D
Hargrove, Alfred; Astrologer; Providence; RI; 1851; England; 88B
Harkey, James; Tramp on public street; St. Clair; IL; 1850; IL;
482B
Harlan, Anders G.; Gambler; Buchanan; MO; 1856; VA; 243D
Harmon, John; Tramp; Rowan; KY; 1850; KY; 421B
Harper, William; Gambler; Greene; OH; 1854; OH; 465D

Harrigan, Henry; Ball player; Kalamazoo; MI; 1857; MI; 146D
Harrington, Daniel; Tramp; New York; NY; 1845; England; 581D
Harrington, Joanna; Dead; Oswego; NY; 132; Ireland; 465C
Harrington, Joseph; Tramp on public street; St. Clair; IL; 1850;
    Ireland; 483D
Harrington, Mark W.; Astronomer; Washtenaw; MI; 1849; IL;
    76C
Harris, Berry; Vagrant; Mobile; AL; 1863; AL; 329B
Harris, Geo.; Gambler; Franklin; OH; 1830; OH; 134D
Harris, George; Tramp; Defiance; OH; 1850; OH; 102D
Harris, Jack; Vagrant; Walton; GA; 1857; GA; 451A
Harris, Jacob; Dead; Cook; IL; 1823; France; 147C
Harris, Jesse; Gambler; Montgomery; AL; 1831; GA; 143D
Harrison, Elizabeth; Dead; Ray; MO; 1845; VA; 411D
Harrison, Mathew; Dead; Wilcox; AL; 1879; AL; 190B
Harry; Gambler; Eureka; NV; 1858; NV; 148B
Hart, Henry T.; Phrenologist; Philadelphia; PA; 1842; Nova
    Scotia; 324A
Hart, John; Dead; Benton; AR; 1879; AR; 467C
Hart, Maggie; Wanderer; Bergen; NJ; 1825; NJ; 256A
Hartley, James; Thief; Franklin; OH; 1858; OH; 481C
Hartley, Lavigon; Dead; Wilcox; AL; 1880; ---; 189D
Hartman, Phillipina; Dead a few days; Marion; IN; `850; IN; 502D
Hartnett, Thomas; Circus Rider; Philadelphia; PA; 1859; England;
    195C
Hartons, Charles; Tramp on public street; St. Clair; IL; 1836; NY;
    483C
Hartranft, Anna R.; Layer out of the dead; Philadelphia; PA; 1820;
    PA; 570D
Harvey, H.H.; Gambler; Washington; MS; 1841; OH; 127C
Harvey, John; Gambler; Montgomery; IA; 1845; KS; 323A
Hasting, Albert; Stealing; Sandusky; OH; 1857; OH; 174A
Hatcher, Joseph; Wks in Circus; New York; NY; 1831; VA; 623A
Haubry, Chas.; Gambler; Tarrant; TX; 1838; MO; 26D
Haughem, Frank; Gambler; Calhoun; MI; 1855; IN; 335A
Haughton, Eliza; Dead; New York; NY; 1846; NY; 23B
Haupt, Hellen; Dead; Northumberland; PA; 1847; PA; 535A

Hauser, Casper; Tramp on public street; St. Clair; IL; 1841; Switzerland; 481D

Havelin, Edward; Gambler; Galveston; TX; 1857; TX; 79D

Hawarth, Catharine; Dead; Blair; PA; 1832; Ireland; 79A

Hawkins, Jas.; Gambler; Gunnison; CO; 1856; OH; 100A

Hawkins, Myrtie; Dead; Knox; IL; 1880; IL; 211A

Hawley, Arthur; Dead; Kane; IL; 1879; KS; 424C

Hawley, Elizabeth; Magnetic Physician; Providence; RI; 1848; RI; 40D

Hawley, Janey; Dead; Kane; IL; 1879; KS; 424C

Hawood, Andrew J.; Teamster Gambler; Cherokee; KS; 1820; TN; 507C

Hayden, Ona T.; Dead; Grant; IN; 1879; OH; 420B

Hayes, Frank; Gambler; Marathon; WI; 1857; WI; 453C

Hays, Henry F.; Quack Dr.; Montgomery; PA; 1827; DE; 428A

Hazel, Frank; Tramp; Hennepin; MN; 1860; IL; 394D

Heap, William H.; Magician; Bristol; MA; 1850; England; 36D

Hearley, Cornelia; Dead; Benton; AR; 1872; TX; 464A

Heath, Charles; Dead; Grundy; IL; 1862; Canada; 319D

Heath, Henry W.; Gambler; Barry; MI; 1848; NY; 112B

Heaton, Will L.; Gambler; Baker; OR; 1845; IL; 6C

Hecker, Phillip J.; Dead; Orleans; LA; 1879; LA; 107B

Heckle, Benedict; Dead; Adams; IL; 1847; Baden; 477A

Hefflinger, Emma; Dead; Sandusky; OH; 1869; OH; 163C

Hefs, Conrad; Quack Doctor; Orleans; LA; 1820; Germany; 488D

Heidenburg, Chapman; Circus Actor; Cook; IL; 1853; MI; 254C

Heinig, Louisa; Dead; Milwaukee; WI; 1879; WI; 219A

Heitz, Minnie; Dead; St. Louis; MO; 1844; Germany; 314B

Hellyn, George; Magician; New York; NY; 1829; England; 683D

Hemelright, Joseph; In jail stealing chickens; Chester; PA; 1843; PA; 159C

Hemer, Peter; Gambler; Clarion; PA; 1850; PA; 20C

Hender, Mary J.; Electro Magnetic Phys.; San Francisco; CA; 1818; ME; 440A

Hendricks, Carson; Tramp on public street; St. Clair; IL; 1862; IN; 482B

Hendricks, J. Thomas; Tramp Farmer; Knox; IL; 1855; IL; 328C

Hendricks, James L.; Laborer; dead; McLean; KY; 1836; KY; 271B

Hendrickson, John; Drunkard; Meeker; MN; 1838; Sweden; 314A

Hendrics, Lee; Tramp on public street; St. Clair; IL; 1849; IL; 481D

Hendriks, Benj.; Tramp on public street; St. Clair; IL; 1857; IN; 482B

Hendrill, H.G.; Gambler; Sacramento; CA; 1820; ME ; 39B

Henley, James; Vagrant; Clayton; MS; 1850; MS; 256B

Henn, Tong; Gambler; Boise; ID; 1837; China; 146B

Hennessey, Michael; Professional dancer; Worcester; MA; 1855; MA; 606D

Hennig, Chs.; Tramp on public street; St. Clair; IL; 1848; Prussia; 484A

Henninger, Charles G.; Crook in whole sale; St. Louis; MO; 1851; PA; 11B

Henon, John; Tramp; Hanson; Dak. Terr.; 1852; MO; 56C

Henrich, Fred; Tramp on public street; St. Clair; IL; 1845; Bavaria; 482A

Henry, Ann; Tramp; Cumberland; NJ; 1857; Ireland; 183C

Henry, Edward; Dealer in death finding; New York; NY; 1836; Ireland; 468D

Henry, John; Gambler; Multnomah; OR; 1855; France; 251D

Henry, John; Tramp; New York; NY; 1840; Ireland; 581C

Henry, M.L.; Gambler; Collin; TX; 1854; TX; 37C

Henry, Stewart; Tramp; Sullivan; IN; 1857; VA; 595A

Henshaw, William; Travels with Circus; Fairfield; CT; 1840; CT; 35B

Henshaw, William; Travels with Circus; Fairfield; CT; 1840; CT; 37A

Herrick, Lucy; Dead; Adair; MO; 1841; MO; 84C

Herrick, Semantha; Magnetic Doctor; Chautauqua; NY; 1831; PA; 318A

Herrmann, Alex; Magician; New York; NY; 1845; France; 567C

Herst, Annie; Tramp; Elliott; KY; 1845; KY; 640A

Herst, Peter; Tramp; Elliott; KY; 1867; KY; 640A

Hertig, Ulyses; Phrenologist; Washington; PA; 1841; PA; 113A

Hertzell, Chas. M.; Dead; St. Joseph; IN; 1870; IN; 421C

Herzog, Mary; Dead Jan 12; Washington; IL; 1876; IN; 359B

Hess, Julius; Tramp; New York; NY; 1849; Germany; 581C

Hesse, Frank; Tramp on public street; St. Clair; IL; 1849; NY;
    484A

Hesse, William; Tramp on public street; St. Clair; IL; 1844;
    Prussia; 481D

Hesselman, Henery; Dead; Allegheny; PA; 1878; PA; 236D

Hester, Frank; Gambler; Cherokee; AL; 1844; GA; 294D

Hettinger, George; Gambler; Nevada; CA; 1834; Baden; 65C

Hewen, Loring; Dead; Susquehanna; PA; 1818; PA; 363A

Hey, Loy; Fortune Teller; San Francisco; CA; 1846; Kwan Tung;
    685A

Hi, Long; Gambler; Nevada; CA; 1843; Canton; 38C

Hibbard, George; Tramp; New York; NY; 1821; Germany; 581D

Hickey, Patrick; With Circus; McHenry; IL; 1862; IL; 137B

Hickman, Callie; Vagrant; Davidson; TN; 1855; TN; 21A

Hicks, Charles; Gambler; Morgan; IL; 1855; IL; 154D

Hienrich, Mina; Dead; St. Louis; MO; 1879; Carondelet [MO];
    380D

Higby, Nathan; Gambler; Lake; CO; 1857; PA; 347D

Higgins, Mike; Tramp on public street; St. Clair; IL; 1845;
    Ireland; 483D

Higgins, Thos.; Tramp; Rio Grande; CO; 1842; Ireland; 329A

Higgins, William; Gambler; Madison; AL; 1830; AL; 409D

Higman, Susan; Dead; Hamilton; OH; 1824; England; 17A

Hilderbrand, F.D.; Circus; Ohio; WV; 1858; Ireland; 449A

Hill, Aaron; Running wild; Union; TN; 1848; TN; 150D

Hill, George W.; Gambler; Henrico; VA; 1841; VA; 322A

Hill, Jacob; Gambler; Berks; PA; 1848; PA; 210B

Hill, Pleasant; Miner and Gambler; Santa Fe; NM; 1840; ME; 60A

Hill, Thomas; Gambler; Bexar; TX; 1852; MA; 115D

Hill, Thomas; Vagrant; Buchanan; MO; 1852; MO; 41B

Hill, W.H.; Circus; Ohio; WV; 1859; England; 449A

Hill, William; Circus Riding; Rio Grande; CO; 1858; IA; 327A

Hilliard, Mary; Tramp; Cumberland; NJ; 1855; OH; 183C

Hillman, Patience C.; Clairvoyant Physician; Providence; RI;
    1830; RI; 396B

Hills, Ira; Magnetic Healing; Green; WI; 1824; NY; 19B

Hin, Bin; Gambler; Elko; NV; 1863; China; 55B
Hinckley, John; Tramp - Prisoner; Ashtabula; OH; 1861; OH;
    467C
Hinckley, Josephine; Tramp; Essex; MA; 1839; MA; 32A
Hine, Florence; Dead; St. Joseph; IN; 1870; IN; 425D
Hines, George; Dead; St. Louis; MO; 1879; MO; 502B
Hines, Mary; Fortune Teller; Lake; CO; 1854; MO; 452A
Hines, Paul; Baseball player; Washington; D.C.; 1855; VA; 450B
Hines, Paul; Ball player; Washington; D.C.; 1853; Washington
    D.C.; 375C
Hines, Ruffus; Gambling; Pulaski; AR; 1860; AR; 256A
Hinks, Clara; At home - dead; Republic; KS; 1880; KS; 70D
Hinn, Chung; Opium Shop; Santa Clara; CA; 1846; China; 127C
Hiss, J.W.; Vagrant; Leavenworth; KS; 1850; MO; 242A
Hix, Charles; Gambler; Pettis; MO; 1844; MO; 196C
Ho(?), John; Dead; Blair; PA; 1819; Ireland; 77B
Ho, Way; Gambler; San Francisco; CA; 1836; Qwantung; 608B
Hoar, Annie; Tramp; Buchanan; MO; 1851; PA; 41A
Hoar, Mary; Tramp; Buchanan; MO; 1829; MS; 41A
Hobdy, Samuel; Dead; Wilcox; AL; 1879; ---; 209C
Hockensmith, John; Gambler; Amador; CA; 1832; KY; 8A
Hockter, John; Tramp - Prisoner; Tippecanoe; IN; 1862; NY;
    237C
Hodge, Susan; Tramp; King George; VA; 1857; VA; 565A
Hoffman, Annie; Dead; Allegheny; PA; 1879; PA; 239A
Hoffman, Eliza; Clairvoyant; Philadelphia; PA; 1843; NY; 184D
Hoffman, Henery; Dead; Allegheny; PA; 1873; PA; 239A
Hoffman, Joseph; Dead; Allegheny; PA; 1875; PA; 252C
Hoffmann, George; Tramp on public street; St. Clair; IL; 1845;
    Prussia; 482B
Hofgesang, August; Profl. Tramp; Jefferson; KY; 1860; Bavaria;
    43B
Hogadoo; Magician; Eureka; NV; 1820; NV; 205A
Hogan, Chas. H.; Gambler; Montgomery; KS; 1839; OH; 244A
Hogan, James; Tramp; Hennepin; MN; 1859; ---; 272A
Hogan, Richard; Tramp on public street; St. Clair; IL; 1855; IN;
    483D
Hoggat, Addison; Farmer dead; Grant; IN; 1829; IN; 490D

Holbert, William H.; Ball player; Rensselaer; NY; 1854; MD; 81A

Holbrook, Delila; Tramp; Elliott; KY; 1842; KY; 647A

Holbrook, Martha; Tramp; Elliott; KY; 1848; KY; 647A

Holcomb, Lizabeth; Dead; Warren; TN; 1826; TN; 398A

Holden, Edward S.; Astronomer; Washington; D.C.; 1847; MO; 18D

Holden, George; Tramp; New York; NY; 1835; England; 581C

Holland, Edward; Circus Performer; Walworth; WI; 1855; WI; 20A

Holland, George; Circus Rider; Walworth; WI; 1850; WI; 20A

Holland, H.; Circus; Ohio; WV; 1864; NY; 449B

Holland, Kate; Circus Rider; Walworth; WI; 1857; England; 20A

Holleren, Henry; Tumbler in Circus; Chemung; NY; 1866; NY; 378A

Holliday, Ida M.A.; Dead?; Adams; MS; 1872; MS; 138A

Hollister, Edward; Tramp on public street; St. Clair; IL; 1845; OH; 482A

Holly, Sarah; Dead; St. Louis; MO; 1856; MO; 486A

Holman, George L.; Dead; Morgan; MO; ---; ---; 203A

Holmes, James; Circus; New York; NY; 1854; NY; 394B

Holmes, Malinda; Dead; Colleton; SC; 1848; SC; 240D

Holmes, Mary E.; Dead; McLean; KY; 1871; KY; 262B

Holmes, Sarah; Vagrant; Tensas; LA; 1800; ---; 29C

Holt, Peter; Dead; Redwood; MN; 1833; Sweden; 55D

Hon, Chung; Gambler; Trinity; CA; 1845; China; 570C

Hong, Chin; Opium Dealer; San Francisco; CA; 1855; See Yup; 627C

Hoo, Kan Chin; Opium Dealer; San Francisco; CA; 1832; Kwantung; 379B

Hoo, Kun Son; Gambler; San Francisco; CA; 1840; Qwantung; 609C

Hoo, Yon Kim; Gambler; San Francisco; CA; 1835; Qwantung; 608B

Hook; Gambler; Trinity; CA; 1852; China; 570C

Hop, Shue; Opium Dealer; Grant; OR; 1820; China; 30C

Hope, James E.; Circus Ticket Clerk; Cook; IL; 1864; Canada; 540D

Hopkins, Charles; Gambler; Jackson; MO; 1859; NY; 42D
Hopper, Maurice; Gambler; Deer Lodge; MT; 1853; IL; 137C
Hornung, Joseph; Ball player; Oneida; NY; 1858; NY; 197B
Horre, Lewis; Dead; New York; NY; 1810; Germany; 45B
Horton, George; Orphan Tramp; Lee; IL; 1873; IL; 412C
Horton, Isaac L.; Dead; Miller; MO; 1877; IN; 162A
Horton, Orin; Tramp; Ionia; MI; 1863; NY; 108D
Hosack, Robert B.; Dead; Indiana; PA; 1876; PA; 376B
Hoskins, C.P.; Circus; Ohio; WV; 1852; MA; 449B
Hossatt, John; Saloon Gambler; Lake; CO; 1834; OH; 435D
Hotailing, Peter; Ball player; Herkimer; NY; 1858; NY; 117B
Hotley, John; Drunkard; Baraga; MI; 1850; MI; 624C
Houchi, Geo. S.; Gambler; Boise; ID; 1828; CT; 130B
Hough, George; Astronomer; Cook; IL; 1837; NY; 4D
Houser, Louisa; Dead; Autauga; AL; 1821; AL; 67A
Houser, Nancy M.; Magnetic Healer; McLean; IL; 1831; IL; 138B
Houston, Hugh; Gambler; McLennan; TX; 1846; TX; 2D
Houston, King; Vagrant; Randolph; MO; 1835; VA; 197C
How, Et; Gambling; Yuba; CA; 1829; Canton; 427A
Howard, Alamand; Laborer Tramp; Floyd; KY; 1850; KY; 95A
Howard, Capt. F.; Dead; Colleton; SC; 1847; SC; 240C
Howard, Charles; Thief; Franklin; OH; 1854; PA; 480B
Howard, Frank; Pick Pocket; Cook; IL; 1868; IL; 638B
Howard, Jacob; Dead; Wilcox; AL; 1874; AL; 210A
Howard, James; Tramp; Lincoln; GA; 1828; GA; 122B
Howard, James; Tramp; Hennepin; MN; 1856; ---; 272A
Howard, James B.; Gambler; Deer Lodge; MT; 1853; PA; 116A
Howard, Jessee; Dead; Autauga; AL; 1878; AL; 49A
Howard, Lee; Dead; Autauga; AL; 1879; AL; 59A
Howard, Margaret; Dead; Clay; KY; 1878; KY; 563B
Howard, Mark; Dead; Autauga; AL; 1850; AL; 59B
Howard, William; Gambler; Yolo; CA; 1840; IN; 372B
Howe, P.; Circus Man; Cook; IL; 1832; NY; 178D
Howell, James; Performer in Circus; Wayne; MI; 1845; Canada;
      172B
Howell, Margarett; Dead; Newton; IN; 1843; IN; 230B
Hoy, Chun; Opium Dealer; San Francisco; CA; 1848; Sam Yap;
      439B

Hoy, Lan; Opium Dealer; San Francisco; CA; 1841; Sam Yap;
635D

Hoyt, Bell K.; Clairvoyant; Providence; RI; 1835; MA; 160C

Hoyt, Earnest; Traveling with Circus; Chautauqua; NY; 1854;
NY; 332C

Huapes, R.; Dead; St. Louis; MO; 1809; PA; 180B

Hubbard, Andrew; Dead; Clay; KY; 1810; KY; 567A

Hubbard, H.; Gambler; La Crosse; WI; 1850; USA; 495B

Hubbell, Alonzo H.; Circus Employee; Hamilton; OH; 1838; NY;
558D

Huckstep, David; Quack Doctor; Campbell; VA; 1837; VA; 244C

Hudson, Dolla; Fortune Teller; Warren; TN; 1805; VA; 418B

Hudson, Edward; Gambler; Galveston; TX; 1847; MA; 79D

Hudson, Eliza J.; Dead; Owen; KY; 1877; KY; 166A

Hudson, Jake; Tramp; Kalamazoo; MI; 1855; OH; 357C

Hues, Thos.; Traveling Circus; New Haven; CT; 1855; CT; 130D

Huggins, L.E.; Phrenologist; Berks; PA; 1844; OH; 290B

Hugh, Kelley; Tramp; Lackawanna; PA; 1830; PA; 226D

Hugh, Kelley; Tramp; Lackawanna; PA; 1861; PA; 226D

Hughes, Anna; Layer out of the dead; Philadelphia; PA; 1846; PA;
525C

Hughes, Isaiah H.; Magician; Erie; NY; 1827; England; 47B

Hughes, John; Thief; Westchester; NY; 1845; NY; 109C

Hughes, T.W.; Gambler; Conejos; CO; 1846; TN; 180D

Hull, Carrie; Dead; Webster; IA; 1876; IA; 577B

Hull, John; Tramp; New York; NY; 1838; NY; 581D

Hull, Louisa; Crossed out on census (dead); Hamilton; OH; 1880;
OH; 16D

Humes, Jane; Dead; Grundy; IL; 1800; England; 318A

Hummel, Lee; Phrenologist; Lawrence; PA; 1855; PA; 114B

Humphrey, Lewis; Dead; St. Joseph; IN; 1817; OH; 406B

Hunderson, J.A.; Circus Rider; Philadelphia; PA; 1846; PA; 306B

Hung, Chan; Gambler; San Francisco; CA; 1856; Kwan Tung;
630B

Hung, Yun; Opium Dealer; San Francisco; CA; 1845; Hap Wa;
434D

Hungerman, Bernhard; Dead; Allegheny; PA; 1878; PA; 236D

Hunison, Minnie; Dead; Adams; IL; 1875; IL; 467A

Hunly, Nathan; Laborer & Thief; Johnson; MO; 1853; MO; 327A

Hunsicker, Jacob; Landlord - dead; Northumberland; PA; 1828; PA; 535A

Hunt, Amos; Clairvoyant; New Haven; CT; 1829; CT; 401D

Hunt, John; Tramp on public street; St. Clair; IL; 1840; Ireland; 484A

Hunter, Arthur; Dead; Owen; KY; 1879; KY; 168A

Hunter, George; Tramp on public street; St. Clair; IL; 1846; MN; 481D

Hunter, John T.; Gambler; Custer; CO; 1850; IA; 302B

Hunter, Julia; Fortune Teller; Pulaski; AR; 1828; NC; 587D

Hunter, Willis; Tramp; Noxubee; MS; 1854; AL; 83D

Hunting, Robb; Circus Clown; Lawrence; PA; 1842; Ireland; 90A

Hurd, Harry; Dead; Cook; IL; 1878; IL; 143C

Hurly, Charles; Dead; Bristol; MA; 1875; MA; 403D

Hurtet, William; Ball player; Erie; NY; 1863; NY; 367C

Huse, Asa H.; Seer (Medium); Suffolk; MA; 1821; ME; 454D

Huseman, Edith; Dead; Adams; IL; 1877; IL; 472C

Hussey, Leona; Circus Performer; St. Lawrence; NY; 1854; NY; 327A

Hutcheson, John C.; Gambler; Lawrence; Dak. Terr.; 1821; MO; 195A

Hutchings, Henry; Gambler; Sullivan; IN; 1846; IL; 532C

Hutchins, A.; Vagrant; Warren; MS; 1849; MS; 443C

Hutchinson, Pheba; Dead; Benton; AR; 1830; TN; 463C

Hutchison,Chs.; Tramp on public street; St. Clair; IL; 1861; MA; 483C

Hyam, David; Magician; Erie; NY; 1845; England; 35A

Hyde, Cooper; Tramp; Davidson; TN; 1863; TN; 122A

Ia, Quin; Gambling House; Storey; NV; 1848; China; 237D

Ia, Won; Gambler; Madison; MT; 1834; China; 386B

Ieller, Catharine; Dead - crossed out; Schenectady; NY; 1789; NY; 131D

Ilschy, Jack; Circus; Ohio; WV; 1835; Canada; 449B

Ilschy, M.; Circus; Ohio; WV; 1835; Canada; 449B

Ing; Keeps Opium Den; Shasta; CA; 1852; China; 2D

Ingles, Loclose; Circus; Ohio; WV; 1846; Canada; 449B

Ingles, M.; Circus; Ohio; WV; 1856; Canada; 449B

Ingles, Maxium; Circus; Ohio; WV; 1816; Canada; 449B

Irving, Minnie W.; Clairvoyant Physician; Susquehanna; PA;
        1839; CT; 402A

Irwin, Arthur A.; Baseball player; Worcester; MA; 1858; Canada;
        22B

Isaacs, Rosa; Dead; Hamilton; OH; 1870; OH; 13A

Isom, Matthew; Gambler; Richland; SC; 1847; SC; 277A

Ivins, John; Vagrant; Mercer; NJ; 1864; China; 257A

Jack, James M.; Gambler; Hamilton; OH; 1827; NY; 114B

Jack, Sam; Ball player; Shasta; CA; 1862; CA; 47A

Jackel, Stanley; Circus Performer; Alexander; IL; 1864; IL; 112C

Jackson, A.A.; Fortune Teller; Suffolk; MA; 1828; MA; 247D

Jackson, Andrew; Vagrant; Chester; SC; 1842; SC; 154A

Jackson, Berry; Tramp; Buchanan; MO; 1842; VT; 41A

Jackson, Dan; Gambler; McLennan; TX; 1859; TX; 3A

Jackson, Greene; Run Away Vagrant; Morgan; GA; 1840; GA;
        278A

Jackson, Henry S.; Tramp; Jackson; MO; 1851; PA; 371C

Jackson, J.G.; Gambler; Arapahoe; CO; 1842; KY; 98D

Jackson, J.J.; Test Medium; Alameda; CA; 1845; England; 214D

Jackson, John; Gambler; Charleston; SC; 1832; SC; 365C

Jackson, Liney; Circus Prop.; St. Louis; MO; 1848; MO; 500D

Jackson, London; Farmer dead; Fairfield; SC; 1830; SC; 195D

Jackson, Mary; Tramp; Monroe; KY; 1864; KY; 291B

Jackson, S.G.; Tramp; St. Landry; LA; 1837; IL; 491C

Jackson, Thomas; Tramp; New York; NY; 1854; VT; 581C

Jackson, William; Tramp; Monroe; KY; 1859; KY; 291B

Jackson, William; Tramp; Buchanan; MO; 1837; MS; 41A

Jackvil, Simon; Tramp; St. Landry; LA; 1832; MD; 495D

Jacobs, R.P; Saloon Keeper and Gambler; Sacramento; CA; 1810;
        VA; 39B

Jacomani, Joseph; Gambler; Monterey; CA; 1849; Switzerland;
        176D

Jagger, L.R.; Gambler; Jackson; MO; 1851; NY; 152A

Jaggers, James W.; Gambler; Lemhi; ID; 1854; IL; 206C

James, John; Tramp on public street; St. Clair; IL; 1845; PA;
        482A

James, Sarah; Fortune Teller; Barbour; AL; 1835; SC; 95B

James, Thowston; Dead; Clayton; GA; 1814; GA; 490D

James, Walter; Thief; Westchester; NY; 1849; NY; 108B

James, William; Gambler; Arapahoe; CO; 1853; CT; 110C

Jamison, Marguirette; Medium; Jackson; MO; 1838; Austria;
        232A

Jansen, Frederick; Tramp; Monroe; IL; 1850; IL; 118D

Jaurique, Jesus; Gambler; Grant; NM; 1820; Chihuahua; 336B

Jefferson, Giles; Tramp; Sharkey; MS; 1845; MS; 143D

Jenkins, Augustus; Vagrant; Crawford; WI; 1863; IL; 118A

Jenkins, Edward; Vagrant; Crawford; WI; 1858; IL; 118A

Jenkins, Peter; Tramp; Randolph; GA; 1868; GA; 189B

Jenkins, S.G.; Circus; Franklin; OH; 1863; PA; 130C

Jenkins, Solomon; Tramp on public street; St. Clair; IL; 1855; IL;
        481D

Jenks, Albert L.; Magnetic Healer; Volusia; FL; 1837; NY; 384A

Jim; Gambler; San Bernardino; CA; 1860; CA; 537A

Jim; Gambler; Sierra; CA; 1838; China; 148D

Jim ; Gambler; Ormsby; NV; 1850; NV; 77A

Jim, Lee; Gambler; Deer Lodge; MT; 1848; China; 110A

Jim, Wing Ti; Gambler; Lander; NV; 1855; China; 297A

Jimmie; Gambler; Ormsby; NV; 1840; NV; 77B

Jiner, Rena; Vagrant; Lafayette; MS; 1800; VA; 327B

Jinkins, George A.; Clogg dancer; Hamilton; OH; 1861; PA; 191D

Jnowle, Clabe; Gambler; Conejos; CO; 1848; MO; 180D

Jo, Chuen; Opium Dealer; San Francisco; CA; 1844; See Yup;
        627C

John; Gambler; Eureka; NV; 1860; NV; 148B

John; Gambler; Ormsby; NV; 1860; NV; 77A

John, Jack; Vagrant; Meigs; OH; 1860; WV; 46C

John, Sam; Gambler; Nevada; CA; 1841; China; 175B

John, Tong; Gambler; Madison; MT; 1835; China; 386B

Johnes, Thomas; Tramp; Jackson; MO; 1852; MO; 368B

Johnsen, William; Tramp; Pike; MO; 1847; OH; 582C

Johnson, Absalom; Stroler wanderer; Jackson; TN; 1835; TN;
        285D

Johnson, Andrew; Tramp on public street; St. Clair; IL; 1848;
        Sweden; 481D

Johnson, Anna; Clairvoyant; San Francisco; CA; 1850; NY; 585B

Johnson, Caroline; Tramp; W. Baton Rouge; LA; 1862; LA; 341D
Johnson, Cecelia; Dead; Loudoun; VA; 1866; VA; 425C
Johnson, Charles; Dead; Adams; IL; 1879; IL; 470C
Johnson, Debora; Fortune Telling; Surry; NC; 1820; NC; 129B
Johnson, Diana; Dead; Colleton; SC; 1864; SC; 245B
Johnson, Edward; Dead; Crawford; GA; 1877; GA; 667A
Johnson, Gorgen; Dead; Lincoln; Dak. Terr.; 1879; Dak. Terr.;
     346C
Johnson, Janet; Dead; Pointe Coupee; LA; 1810; VA; 312B
Johnson, Jeff; Vagrant; Mercer; KY; 1865; KY; 149C
Johnson, Jesse; Thief; Westchester; NY; 1852; Washington, D.C.;
     107C
Johnson, Joanna; Dead; Wilcox; AL; 1855; ---; 188A
Johnson, John; Quack Doc; Will; IL; 1840; VA; 154D
Johnson, John; Tramp on Road; Hancock; IN; 1840; OH; 88D
Johnson, John; Thief; Westchester; NY; 1830; NY; 109C
Johnson, John J.; Gambler; Atchison; KS; 1855; MO; 285D
Johnson, Joseph; Tramp; Lapeer; MI; 1811; NY; 315B
Johnson, Lily V.; Dead; Fillmore; NE; 1863; OH; 469B
Johnson, Mary; Tramp; Mobile; AL; 1864; AL; 454B
Johnson, Mary; Dead; Oswego; NY; 1820; Ireland; 459D
Johnson, Morris; Gambler; Multnomah; OR; 1855; MO; 257D
Johnson, Otto; Dancer; Milwaukee; WI; 1858; WI; 46A
Johnson, Ruth Ann; Dead; Harrison; IA; 1825; OH; 10A
Johnson, Sadie; Clairvoyant; Suffolk; MA; 1840; ME; 456D
Johnson, Sam; Tramp on public street; St. Clair; IL; 1855; PA;
     483D
Johnson, Simpson; Dead; Clay; KY; 1858; KY; 567B
Johnson, Thomas; Tramp; New York; NY; 1827; Scotland; 581C
Johnson, William; Gambler; Montgomery; KS; 1840; KY; 238B
Johnston, Aleck; Vagrant; Person; NC; 1842; NC; 122A
Johnston, Andrew; Crossed out. Dead clergy; Schenectady; NY;
     1809; Scotland; 132A
Johnston, Ezra B.; Gambler; Butte; CA; 1844; MI; 140A
Johnston, Jessey; Vagrant; Surry; NC; 1832; NC; 68C
Johnston, M.M.; Dead; Cook; IL; 1821; OH; 145D
Johnston, Moris; Tramp; New York; NY; 1853; NY; 581D
Johnston, Rob't; Circus; Ohio; WV; 1848; Ireland; 449A

Johnston, William; Vagrant; Person; NC; 1865; NC; 122A

Joiner, Elizabeth; Vagrant; Lafayette; MS; 1840; MS; 327B

Joiner, Milly; Vagrant; Lafayette; MS; 1780; VA; 327B

Jok, Chan; Fortune Teller; San Francisco; CA; 1850; Quong Tong
    Nam Noi; 443B

Jokirk, Patrick John; Tramp; Spencer; KY; 1840; Ireland; 509A

Jolliff, Elizabeth; Dead Feb 1880; Washington; IL; 1830; IL; 362C

Jones, A.; Dead; Fairfield; SC; 1877; SC; 99D

Jones, Alice; Clairvoyant; Suffolk; MA; 1845; MA; 220D

Jones, Brandon; Dead; Clay; KY; 1878; KY; 533B

Jones, C.W.; Boston baseball; Suffolk; MA; 1842; MA; 521B

Jones, Eli; Circus Worker; Montgomery; IN; 1860; IN; 361C

Jones, Erma F.; Dead; Caldwell; TX; 1868; TX; 189A

Jones, George F.; Advertising Agent for Circus; Allegheny; PA;
    1830; NY; 51D

Jones, George F.; Dead; Blair; PA; 1853; England; 75A

Jones, J.P.; Gambler; Deer Lodge; MT; 1854; UT Terr.; 126B

Jones, Jane; Dead; Fairfax; VA; 1790; VA; 371B

Jones, John; Tramp - Prisoner; Tippecanoe; IN; 1856; ---; 237C

Jones, L.; Gambler; Ramsey; MN; 1853; USA; 147D

Jones, Lena; Dead; McKean; PA; 1874; PA; 17B

Jones, Levy; Quack; Henderson; NC; 1836; NC; 307D

Jones, Luther; Prisoner for murder; Randolph; GA; 1850; SC ;
    118C

Jones, Margaret; Fortune Teller; Franklin; OH; 1845; Wales;
    148A

Jones, Mathies; Dead; Clark; KY; 1862; KY; 428B

Jones, Phebe; Tramp; Buchanan; MO; 1841; MO; 41A

Jones, Sallie; Tramp; De Soto; LA; 1845; LA; 190A

Jones, W.M.; Tramp; Davidson; TN; 1824; TN; 130B

Jones, William; Tramp; York; ME; 1840; VT; 420A

Jonson, Patrick; Vagrant; Hamilton; TN; 1800; NC; 56A

Jordan, Jacob; Tramp; Putnam; IN; 1831; KY; 554C

Jordan, Loue; Circus Performer; Logan; OH; 1862; OH; 72A

Jordon, Charles; Gambler; Grayson; TX; 1839; VA; 184C

Jorgenson, Alex; Spiritual Medium; Orleans; LA; 1850; LA; 221C

Jorgenson, Bertha; Spiritual Medium; Orleans; LA; 1855; Sweden;
    221C

Joseph, Nancy; Vagrant; Bullock; AL; 1857; AL; 105C

Jourdan, James F.; Travels with Circus; Daviess; IN; 1842; IN;
458D

Joyner, Isabella; Dead; Fairfield; SC; 1820; SC; 193C

Juday, Emaly; Dead; Elkhart; IN; 1855; IN; 380C

Judd, William; Magician; New York; NY; 1841; England; 325D

Judge, Charles; Gambler; Storey; NV; 1840; MA; 141D

Judson, Royal; Lazy Laborer; New Haven; CT; 1812; CT; 242C

Julian, Chris; Gambler; Pottawattamie; IA; 1851; VT; 273D

Jun, Lee; Opium Shop; Santa Clara; CA; 1845; China; 126B

June, Lewis; Circus Agent; Fairfield; CT; 1825; CT; 254A

Jung, Tong; Gambler; Elko; NV; 1830; China; 55A

Junkins, Charles; Baseball player; Jackson; MO; 1859; VA; 401B

Juss, John; Tramp on public street; St. Clair; IL; 1854; Prussia;
484A

Juss, Martin; Tramp on public street; St. Clair; IL; 1852; Prussia;
484A

Justice, Richard; Gambler; Grant; NM; 1863; NM Terr.; 344A

Kael, George; Tramp; Northampton; PA; 1827; Bavaria; 285B

Kah, Ton; Gambler; Butte; CA; 1841; China; 147D

Kai, Wen; Gambler; San Francisco; CA; 1862; Kwan Tung; 630B

Kain, Harry; With Circus; Jefferson; OH; 1862; OH; 470C

Kaiser, Jacob; Carpenter dead; St. Louis; MO; 1819; Switzerland;
358B

Kaiser, Joseph; Wanderer; Seneca; OH; 1832; Luxemburg; 79B

Kammerich, Ch's; Gambler; Conejos; CO; 1852; Prussia; 180D

Kane, Thomas; Circus Labr.; Adams; IL; 1857; IL; 371B

Kannell, Joseph; Tramp; Stark; OH; 1817; OH; 446B

Kappes, William; Circus Traveler; Hudson; NJ; 1864; NJ; 360D

Karney, John; Tramp; New York; NY; 1840; Ireland; 581D

Karney, Michael; Tramp; New York; NY; 1828; NY; 581D

Kasanjack, Luther; Astronomer; New York; NY; 1843; South
Africa; 94C

Kase, Carrie M.; Dead; Northumberland; PA; 1876; PA; 541B

Kasl, Anna; Dead; Republic; KS; 1878; KS; 73B

Kastanie, Charles; Tramp on public street; St. Clair; IL; 1852;
Prussia; 481D

Kay, Samuel; Tramp; Tallahatchie; MS; 1842; England; 112C

Kearney, Anna; Dead; Albany; NY; 1832; Ireland; 367A

Keck, Agnes; Dead; Adams; IL; 1877; IL; 481A

Kee, Chow; Gambler; Yuba; CA; 1830; Canton; 428D

Kee, Gee; Gambler; Lander; NV; 1855; China; 298C

Kee, Long; Opium Dealer; San Francisco; CA; 1820; See Yup; 629C

Kee, Noun; Gambler; Santa Cruz; CA; 1845; China; 521C

Kee, Ten; Gambler; Trinity; CA; 1850; China; 570C

Keefner, George; Gambler; Peoria; IL; 1840; Bavaria; 84B

Keels, Jane; Dead; Sumter; SC; 1878; SC; 246B

Keenan, James; Ball player; New Haven; CT; 1856; CT; 40D

Keiser, Martha; Dead; Sandusky; OH; 1875; OH; 162B

Keith, Jas.; Tramp; Lancaster; NE; 1859; NJ; 173A

Kelley, Edward; Brass Moulder & Tramp; Greene; IL; 1859; PA; 191A

Kelley, John; Tramp - Prisoner; Ashtabula; OH; 1865; PA; 467C

Kelley, William; Tramp on public street; St. Clair; IL; 1840; Ireland; 482B

Kelly, Ann; Tramp; Cumberland; NJ; 1857; Ireland; 183C

Kelly, C.J.; Gambler; Storey; NV; 1835; KY; 160B

Kelly, Geo.; Tramp ; Harrison; IA; 1824; Ireland; 111C

Kelly, Honora; Dead; Hudson; NJ; 1880; NJ; 261A

Kelly, Honora; Dead; Allegheny; PA; 1870; PA; 219A

Kelly, James; Tramp - Prisoner; Tippecanoe; IN; 1850; ---; 237C

Kelly, John; Gambler; Storey; NV; 1820; IL; 122A

Kelly, John; Baseball player; San Francisco; CA; 1859; NJ; 113B

Kelly, John; Ball player; New York; NY; 1857; NY; 240B

Kelly, K.; Tramp; Hennepin; MN; 1854; MA; 272A

Kelly, Luke; Circus Actor; Philadelphia; PA; 1840; PA; 38D

Kelly, Thomas; Gambler; Dane; WI; 1856; NY; 123D

Kelly, W.F.; Tramp; Monroe; KY; 1852; KY; 308C

Kelly, William; Tramp; New York; NY; 1845; NY; 581D

Kelly, Wm. B.; Gambler; Calhoun; MI; 1851; MI; 335A

Kelsey, William F.; Quack Doctor; White; TN; 1852; TN; 422B

Kemp, Jule; Gambler; Muscogee; GA; 1843; GA; 665B

Kemph, Bet; Tramp; Davidson; TN; 1861; TN; 111C

Ken, Chun; Gambler; San Francisco; CA; 1851; Kwantung; 392B

Kenau, Edward; Tramp on public street; St. Clair; IL; 1862; OH; 482A

Kendall, Frank; Magnetic Physician; Lake; IL; 1835; VT; 559A

Keneday, Gus; Gambler; Duval; FL; 1846; GA; 523A

Kenneddy, James; Gambler; Steuben; NY; 1840; OH; 153B

Kennedy, Eliza; Kpg house dead; Fairfield; SC; 1854; SC; 194B

Kennedy, Hugh; Theater dancer; New York; NY; 1862; NY; 86A

Kennedy, Thomas; Tramp; New York; NY; 1840; Ireland; 581D

Kenney, Charles B.; Magnetic Physician; New York; NY; 1846; ME; 192B

Kenney, John; Cole's Circus; Douglas; NE; 1855; MA; 206C

Kenney, Patrick; Dead; Milwaukee; WI; 1856; WI; 232C

Kenny, Irene A.; Fortune Teller; St. Louis; MO; 1818; VT; 485D

Kenyon, Eliza; Clairvoyant Physician; Oneida; NY; 1825; NY; 82A

Kerlen, Graves; Tramp; Elbert; GA; 1835; GA; 443A

Kerley, Emmet J.; Dead; Claiborne; TN; 1879; TN; 180A

Kernell, Harry; Circus Performer; Philadelphia; PA; 1850; PA; 78C

Kernell, John; Circus Performer; Philadelphia; PA; 1860; PA; 78C

Kerr, James; With Forspaughs Circus; Armstrong; PA; 1857; PA; 33A

Kerr, M.J.; Dead; Indiana; PA; 1856; PA; 197D

Kesler, Henry; Professional ball player; New York; NY; 1847; NY; 60C

Kesler, Jessie M.; Quack Doctor; Portage; WI; 1817; NY; 33D

Kesler, Savalla; Vagrant; Oswego; NY; 1808; NY; 5B

Kessinger, Andrew H.; Parents dead; Perry; IN; 1867; IN; 163B

Ketchen, Alfred; Gambler; Pettis; MO; 1843; KY; 196C

Ketchin, Harry; Gambler; Solano; CA; 1859; CA; 496B

Kettler, George; Agt. Cooper, Bailey Circus; Wayne; OH; 1857; OH; 377B

Kewhoff, Jules; Tramp; New York; NY; 1843; Wurtemburg; 431D

Key, You; Gambler; Lander; NV; 1850; China; 298B

Ki, Poon; Gambler; San Francisco; CA; 1836; Kwantung; 391A

Kibber, Austin D.; Abortionist (Drunk); Putnam; IL; 1818; VT; 314D

Kiersky, Adolph; Gambler; Warren; MS; 1857; MS; 336B
Kiger, Joseph; Tramp; Morris; NJ; 1851; Ireland; 143B
Kilmall, Fransisgo; Dead; Orleans; LA; 1823; Baden; 103A
Kim, Hop; Gambler; Amador; CA; 1841; Canton; 46D
Kimball, Charles T.; Agent for Circus; Buchanan; IA; 1830; VT;
    577D
Kimball, Louise; Gambler; Salt Lake; UT; 1840; MA; 232C
Kimball, Myron; Bummer; Madison; NY; 1830; NY; 240D
Kimble, Jenny; Circus Rider; New York; NY; 1856; NY; 259A
Kin, Chim; Vag.; Nevada; CA; 1820; ---; 83D
Kin, Joe; Gambler; Madison; MT; 1832; China; 386B
Kindle, Paulina; Dead; Sandusky; OH; 1837; PA; 164A
Kiney, Thomas; Tramp on public street; St. Clair; IL; 1861; NJ;
    484A
King, Ada; Dead; Morgan; IN; 1878; NC; 17C
King, Frank; Teamster in a Circus; Lake; OH; 1861; OH; 412C
King, George; Tramp on public street; St. Clair; IL; 1852; NJ;
    484A
King, John E.; Tramp; New York; NY; 1832; PA; 581C
King, Major; Dead; Morgan; IN; 1873; NC; 17C
King, Nain; Gambler; Lewis and Clark; MT; 1849; China; 278A
King, Ny; Dealer in Opium; Sierra; CA; 1855; Canton; 177D
King, Peter; Gambler; Garland; AR; 1834; NY; 133D
King, Richard; Tramp; New York; NY; 1845; Germany; 581C
King, Robert; Tramp; New York; NY; 1822; Ireland; 581D
King, Samuel; Dead; Madison; KY; 1864; KY; 386A
King, T.; Circus; Ohio; WV; 1856; MA; 449A
King, Thomas; Gambler; Atchison; KS; 1853; Ireland; 257C
King, Wm. H.; Healing Medium; Sacramento; CA; 1826; ME;
    127B
Kinkaede, William; Dead; Jackson; MI; 1880; MI; 318C
Kinkner, Samuel; Driver in Circus; Philadelphia; PA; 1856; PA;
    61A
Kinman, Victor; Fortune Teller; Tom Green; TX; 1843; GA; 393C
Kinn, Chung; Gambler; Deer Lodge; MT; 1825; China; 111C
Kinnebrew, Henry; Gambler; Tarrant; TX; 1852; MO; 57A
Kipp; Dead; Adams; IL; ---; IL; 468D

Kirchhof, Peter; Tramp on public street; St. Clair; IL; 1836; Holstein; 482A

Kirchner, George; Tramp on public street; St. Clair; IL; 1847; Bavaria; 482A

Kirk, Alice; Layer out of the dead; Philadelphia; PA; 1827; England; 171D

Kirk, James; Vagrant; Mercer; IL; 1840; IL; 446B

Kirkin, David J.; Tramp; Wayne; IN; 1866; OH; 181D

Kirkland, Sarah; Dead; Washington; AR; 1815; AL; 571C

Kirkman, James T.; Gambler; Morgan; IL; 1845; IL; 196D

Kirkpatrick, Permelia; Dead; Cooper; MO; 1811; TN; 238B

Kirschner, Anna; Dead; Allegheny; PA; 1879; PA; 225B

Kirschner, Edger; Dead; Allegheny; PA; 1876; PA; 225B

Kissinger, W.N.; Dealer in Gambling; Lake; CO; 1841; Germany; 342A

Kister, Mary; Dead; Monroe; NY; 1880; NY; 265D

Kit, King; Gambler; Nevada; CA; 1840; Canton; 220B

Kit, Pong; Gambler; San Francisco; CA; 1842; Kwantung; 393B

Klein, Charles; Dead; Orleans; LA; 1874; LA; 107A

Kleinhag, John; Tramp on public street; St. Clair; IL; 1841; OH; 482B

Klinch, Jas.; Gambler; Clarion; PA; 1850; IL; 16C

Klock, Anderson; Traveling with Circus; Chautauqua; NY; 1859; NY; 344C

Klotz, Conrad; Baker Vagrant; Winnebago; WI; 1835; Germany; 162C

Knap, Bud; Gambler; Buchanan; MO; 1847; France; 148A

Knardt, Chiss; Dead; Milwaukee; WI; 1830; Germany; 290B

Knight, Catherine; Fortune Teller; Shelby; IN; 1820; IN; 314C

Knights, Longo; B. ball player; Worcester; MA; 1850; PA; 182D

Knorr, Ellen M.; Works for Circus John Abrien; Philadelphia; PA; 1848; PA; 136C

Knott, Millard; Dead; Blair; PA; 1875; PA; 77A

Knowles, Asa; Gambler; Custer; CO; 1839; IN; 326A

Knowles, James; Base ballist; Middlesex; MA; 1857; Canada; 308A

Knox, Charles B.; Magician; Suffolk; MA; 1846; MA; 323B

Knox, James C.; Gambler; Storey; NV; 1850; NY; 141D

Koeler, Chs.; Tramp on public street; St. Clair; IL; 1844; OH;
    484A

Kohn, Ben; Gambler; Dallas; TX; 1862; TX; 16D

Kohn, Laf; Gambler; Dallas; TX; 1864; TX; 16D

Kolb, Jacob; Tramp on public street; St. Clair; IL; 1854; Hanover;
    481D

Koring, Lydia; Dead; Adams; IL; 1878; IL; 484C

Kow, Tsun; Opium Dealer; San Francisco; CA; 1831; Kwantung;
    391B

Kramele, Charles; Tramp on public street; St. Clair; IL; 1832;
    Hesse D.; 483C

Kramer, Reinhard; Tramp; Sibley; MN; 1821; Prussia; 318B

Ku, Ping; Sell Opium; Placer; CA; 1851; China; 338D

Kuehne, Alexander; Works in plainning mill dead; St. Louis; MO;
    1832; Baden; 359C

Kuel, Fridrich; Tramp on public street; St. Clair; IL; 1848; Baden;
    482B

Kum, Vo; Gambler; Kern; CA; 1851; China; 586C

Kung, Leong; Gambler; San Francisco; CA; 1845; Kwantung;
    392B

Kung, Ling Kee; Opium Dealer; San Francisco; CA; 1861; Sam
    Yup; 634B

Kunz, Louis; Tramp on public street; St. Clair; IL; 1857; Prussia;
    482B

Kurtz, Adelbert; Baseball pitcher; Van Buren; MI; 1854; NY;
    430C

Kwah, Tie; Gambler; San Francisco; CA; 1858; Sun Ning; 627D

Kwong, Kit; Opium Dealer; San Francisco; CA; 1839; See Yap;
    635D

Kwong, Lee Ah Lum; Gambler; Nevada; CA; 1838; China; 84B

Labonte, Moses; Gambler; Sangamon; IL; 1833; NY; 212A

Lacey, Hennetta; Magnetic Physician; Monroe; NY; 1837; NY;
    261D

Lacy, Newton J.; Gambler; Dallas; TX; 1855; KY; 106A

Ladden, Michael; Circus Rider; Cook; IL; 1866; IL; 465C

Lafayett, Jeny M.; Farm hand (dead); Orleans; LA; 1869; LA;
    311D

Lai, Hong; Opium Dealer; San Francisco; CA; 1855; Yung Wo; 635D

Lakin, Sarah V.; Fortune Teller; St. Louis; MO; 1824; Canada; 262B

Laku, D.B.; Gambler; Eureka; NV; 1854; France; 206C

Lam, Yee; Gambler; San Francisco; CA; 1843; Kwantung; 388D

Lamar, John; Dead; Autauga; AL; 1878; AL; 62D

Lamar, Martha; Dead; Autauga; AL; 1861; AL; 62D

Lamont, Annie; Clairvoyant; Suffolk; MA; 1841; Atlantic Ocean; 105B

Lan, Gee; Gambler; Butte; CA; 1836; China; 147C

Lancer, John; Tramp on public street; St. Clair; IL; 1857; NY; 483C

Landers, Luther; At P. Goodnight Mother & Father Dead; Allen; KY; 1865; KY; 218B

Landers, Sophia; At P. Goodnight Mother & Father Dead; Allen; KY; 1870; KY; 218B

Landon, James; Tramp on public street; St. Clair; IL; 1848; TN; 483C

Landy, Hester; Tramp; Washington; OH; 1825; OH; 211C

Lane, Dutton; Tramp; Sullivan; TN; 1816; VA; 448A

Lane, F.W.; Tramp; Sullivan; TN; 1865; VA; 448A

Lane, John S.; Tramp; Sullivan; TN; 1870; KY; 448A

Lane, Mary L.; Tramp; Sullivan; TN; 1869; KY; 448A

Lane, S.J.; Tramp; Sullivan; TN; 1834; KY; 448A

Lane, W.C.; Thief; Pittsylvania; VA; 1835; VA; 92A

Lane, Winafred; Tramp; Sullivan; TN; 1857; VA; 448A

Lang, Julius; Laborer Vagrant; Winnebago; WI; 1844; Germany; 162D

Lang, Wah; Gambler; Washoe; NV; 1845; China; 277A

Langford, Henry W.; Gambler; Davidson; TN; 1834; TN; 147A

Lanier, Harriet; Dead; Washington; NC; 1845; NC; 264C

Lannagan, J.; Professional Thief; St. Louis; MO; 1854; MO; 103B

Lanspach, John; Dead; Dubuque; IA; 1841; Hesse D.; 352B

Lapalne, Leon A.; Gambler; Deer Lodge; MT; 1853; Canada; 136B

Lappart, Davis; Circus Performer; Alexander; IL; 1860; OH; 84D

Larkin, Frank; Ball player; Rensselaer; NY; 1857; NY; 268A

Larnche, Mat.; Gambler; Deer Lodge; MT; 1854; Canada; 135D
Larson, Godfrey; Tramp on public street; St. Clair; IL; 1853;
        Prussia; 482B
Larson, John; Confirmed Vagabond; Penobscot; ME; 1854; ME;
        197C
Lary, Alison; Dead; Wilcox; AL; 1879; AL; 210A
Laspel, Andrew; Tramp; Brunswick; NC; 1858; NC; 607C
Latham, J.E.; Gambler; Pima; AZ; 1852; TN; 245B
Latimer, P.E.; Gambler; Huron; OH; 1835; OH; 308B
Lauerance, John; Tramp; Douglas; NE; 1860; IN; 172A
Laurenz, Peter; Tramp on public street; St. Clair; IL; 1847;
        Denmark; 483D
Lauris, William; Gambler; Buchanan; MO; 1859; China; 230A
Lavardie, Madame; Fortune Teller; Suffolk; MA; 1838; NH; 106A
Laven, Peter; Gambler; Darke; OH; 1848; NY; 184D
Lavin, John; Ball player; Rensselaer; NY; 1856; NY; 200B
Lavin, Thos.; Cole's Circus; Douglas; NE; 1840; Ireland; 206D
Lawanda, Alexander; Circus Troupe; Philadelphia; PA; 1805;
        Brazil; 139B
Lawanda, Sig; Circus Man; Lake; CO; 1845; NY; 401B
Lawins, G.W.; Dead; St. Louis; MO; 1828; MA; 181D
Lawnner, Wm.; Tramp; Jackson; MO; 1841; CT; 368B
Lawrence, Ben; Gambler; Jefferson; KY; 1854; KY; 361C
Lawrence, Fred; Agent for Circus; Merrimack; NH; 1838; MA;
        367B
Lawrence, Mark; Tramp; Jackson; MO; 1849; NJ; 370B
Lawson, Charles; Tramp on public street; St. Clair; IL; 1850;
        Sweden; 481D
Lawson, Herman; Tramp; New York; NY; 1850; Sweden; 581C
Lawson, James; Tramp; Jackson; MO; 1849; IL; 368B
Lay, Mary E.; Dead; Sandusky; OH; 1814; OH; 161D
Lay, Yon; Gambler; Storey; NV; 1832; China; 237C
Laydin, C.P.; Gambler; Lake; CO; 1830; NY; 314D
Le, Gow; Dealer in Opium; Sierra; CA; 1844; Canton; 177C
Le, Joy; Gambler; Nevada; CA; 1839; Canton; 38C
Leach, Eugene; Circus Acter; Chemung; NY; 1844; NY; 349C
Leach, Eugene; Circus; Ohio; WV; 1844; NY; 449B
Leadford, William A.; Dead; Marshall; TN; 1864; TN; 331B

Leary, J.; Ball player; Storey; NV; 1850; CT; 119D
Leary, John; Prof. ball player; New Haven; CT; 1859; CT; 572B
Ledford, Stephen; Dead; Clay; KY; 1878; KY; 556C
Lee, Abey; Wandering Gypsy; Clayton; IA; 1877; ---; 473D
Lee, Alfonso; Gambler; Cuyahoga; OH; 1844; NY; 58B
Lee, Barda; Circus Performer; Orleans; LA; 1846; TX; 246D
Lee, Chung; Gambler; San Francisco; CA; 1832; Qwantung; 608B
Lee, Chung Yip; Opium; Sacramento; CA; 1818; China; 4C
Lee, Dantia; Wandering Gypsy; Clayton; IA; 1840; ---; 473D
Lee, Gee; Gambler; Storey; NV; 1839; China; 149D
Lee, Hip; Opium Dealer; San Francisco; CA; 1836; Kwang Chow;
    434D
Lee, Hook; Gambling House; Nevada; CA; 1827; China; 83D
Lee, Jane; Wandering Gypsy; Clayton; IA; 1850; ---; 473D
Lee, Jullia; Wandering Gypsy; Clayton; IA; 1876; ---; 473D
Lee, Kee; Gambler; Eureka; NV; 1835; China; 191B
Lee, Me; Gambler; Butte; CA; 1840; China; 261B
Lee, Moo; Opium Dealer; San Francisco; CA; 1840; Kwantung;
    380D
Lee, Omia; Wandering Gypsy; Clayton; IA; 1875; ---; 473D
Lee, Quong; Gambler; Yuba; CA; 1872; China; 481C
Lee, Sam; Gambler; Storey; NV; 1854; China; 149D
Lee, Shing; Opium Dealer; Grant; OR; 1848; China; 30C
Lee, Song; Gambler; Shasta; CA; 1852; Quong Tong; 95D
Lee, William; Wandering Gypsy; Clayton; IA; 1855; ---; 473D
Lee, Yep; Gambler; Eureka; NV; 1844; China; 213B
Lee, Ying; Gambler; Siskiyou; CA; 1840; China; 234C
Leed, James; Wandering Gypsy; Clayton; IA; 1845; Gt. Britain;
    473D
Leeland, Charles; Gambler; Shelby; TN; 1842; TN; 71C
Leffingwell, Catharine; Clairvoyant; Providence; RI; 1828; MA;
    394B
Leffler, Caterine; Dead; Allegheny; PA; 1878; PA; 222C
Lehan, Pat; Gambler; Wheeler; TX; 1854; Ireland; 99B
Leighton, Sam'l; Base ballist; Plymouth; MA; 1857; MA; 335D
Leindecker, Frank; Vagrant; Hamilton; OH; 1865; OH; 564D
Leist, Louis; Quack Doctor; Oneida; NY; 1846; Germany; 306A
Leister, Hattie; Dead; Sandusky; OH; 1880; OH; 166A

Leland, C. Emeline; Clairvoyant M.D.; Worcester; MA; 1827; MA; 269A

Lem, Wing; Opium Merchant; Baker; OR; 1850; China; 47A

Lemon, Geo. W.; Tramp; Mercer; NJ; 1830; NJ; 7A

Lenard, George; Clog dancer; Franklin; OH; 1860; OH; 188B

Lenard,Wm.; Circus; Ohio; WV; 1853; PA; 449A

Lenk, Carl J.; Tramp; Henry; IL; 1817; Sweden; 153C

Lenkner, Bertha; Fortune Teller; Cook; IL; 1844; Germany; 419B

Lent, Lewis B.; Circus Business; New York; NY; 1815; NY; 80A

Lent, Lewis B.; Circus Business; New York; NY; 1853; NY; 80A

Leon, A.; Clown Circus; Ohio; WV; 1858; England; 449A

Leonard, J.W.; Gambler; Santa Clara; CA; 1822; MO; 388D

Leonard, Stevens; Circus Agt.; Monroe; NY; 1816; MA; 97A

Leopold, George; Circus Performer; Strafford; NH; 1845; England; 122D

Leopold, Geraldine; Circus Performer; Strafford; NH; 1855; England; 122D

Leotard, Leon; Magician; Santa Cruz; CA; 1846; France; 501D

Lep, Gee; Opium Den; San Joaquin; CA; 1844; Canton; 11B

Lepper, Emily L.; Clairvoyant Phis; Anoka; MN; 1838; ME; 11B

Leptin, John; Tramp on public street; St. Clair; IL; 1836; Holstein; 482A

Lesandorsky, Leonard; Tramp on public street; St. Clair; IL; 1848; Poland; 482A

Leslie, F.H.; Circus Actor; St. Louis; MO; 1848; MO; 51D

Lessere, Alphonse; Gambler; Orleans; LA; 1857; LA; 184A

Lester, John; Circus Performer; Kenosha; WI; 1862; IL; 15C

Leung; Gambler; Elko; NV; 1840; China; 59D

Leung, Fook Ting; Fortune Teller; San Francisco; CA; 1841; Sam Yap; 595A

Levitt, William; Dancer; Ormsby; NV; 1857; MA; 46C

Levy, Julius; Gambler; Deer Lodge; MT; 1834; France; 120B

Lewis, Etta M.; Is lazy; New Haven; CT; 1864; CT; 225B

Lewis, Frederick; Baseball player; Oneida; NY; 1859; NY; 302A

Lewis, Henry; Gambler; Storey; NV; 1830; Sweden; 118A

Lewis, J.; Gambler; Orleans; LA; 1831; NY; 76C

Lewis, John; Bummer; New York; NY; 1853; England; 104A

Lewis, Shem; Vagabond; Portage; OH; 1825; England; 264A

Lewis, William; Tramp; Sharkey; MS; 1845; MS; 143D

Lewis, Wm. E.; Circus Rider; Providence; RI; 1835; RI; 120B

Leyton, George; Gambler; Caldwell; TX; 1845; AR; 249B

Li, Foy; Gambler; Nevada; CA; 1842; Canton; 38C

Liebert, Edward; Tramp on public street; St. Clair; IL; 1848;
    Wurtemburg; 481D

Liebguth, John; Tramp on public street; St. Clair; IL; 1840;
    France; 483D

Liebig, Julius; Dead; St. Joseph; IN; 1861; IL; 409C

Liles, R.L.; Gambler; Deer Lodge; MT; 1846; MO; 126B

Lilleston, Richard; Gambler; Franklin; OH; 1820; KY; 324B

Lillis, A.; Dead; Crenshaw; AL; 1880; AL; 477C

Lilly, Mary; Tramp; Marengo; AL; 1854; AL; 696B

Lim, Gow; Gambler; Siskiyou; CA; 1830; China; 234C

Limburg, Alen; Tramp on public street; St. Clair; IL; 1845;
    Sweden; 483C

Lin, Hoy; Keeping Opium Den; Sacramento; CA; 1823; China; 9B

Lin, Wo; Opium Den; Mono; CA; 1844; China; 126D

Lin, Yun; Gambler; Nevada; CA; 1840; Canton; 38C

Linch, J.; Circus; Ohio; WV; 1853; MA; 449A

Lincoln, Mirtie; Dead; Ellsworth; KS; 1879; KS; 485A

Lindes, S.; Death on Jul 1879; Polk; IA; 1867; IA; 524A

Lindsay, Dora; Dead; Cooper; MO; 1875; MO; 237C

Lindsay, George; Tramp on public street; St. Clair; IL; 1826; OH;
    482A

Ling, Ah Foo; Gambler; San Francisco; CA; 1855; Kwan Tung;
    630B

Ling, Huk; Gambler; Eureka; NV; 1850; China; 191A

Ling, Pan; Gambler; Placer; CA; 1830; China; 338C

Ling, Toi; Gambler; Union; OR; 1842; China; 177C

Link, Charly; Dead; Reno; KS; 1879; KS; 583A

Linton, F.; Clown Circus; Ohio; WV; 1858; Australia; 449A

Linton, John; Circus; Ohio; WV; 1857; Australia; 449A

Linzey, Mary Ann; Dead; Autauga; AL; 1846; AL; 131A

Lippott, Charles; Magician; Lancaster; PA; ---; NY; 31B

Lisle, Mary; Dead; Clark; KY; 1810; VA; 426A

Little Joe; Vagabond; Mendocino; CA; 1865; CA; 306A

Little Tom; Foot racer; Shasta; CA; 1845; CA; 47A

Little, Sookey; Vagrant; Putnam; GA; 1830; GA; 479A
Littler, Joseph W.; Gambler; St. Louis; MO; 1847; OH; 286A
Lively, Emma E.; Fortune Teller; Nodaway; MO; 1843; MD;
        195C
Livingson, Ed; Gambler; Lee; IA; 1855; MI; 176C
Locke, Calvin; Vagrant; Davidson; TN; 1845; GA; 21A
Locke, Ebenezer; Gypsy; Tehama; CA; 1860; CA; 475D
Locket, Ishmael; Laborer; dead; Taylor; GA; 1830; GA; 69B
Locket, Oney; Housekeeper; dead; Taylor; GA; 1812; GA; 69B
Lockridge, James; Gambler; Nez Perce; ID; 1838; KY; 260C
Logan, James; Gambler; Deer Lodge; MT; 1833; KY; 127D
Loi, Sai Chow; Opium Dealer; San Francisco; CA; 1845;
        Kwantung Shun Tuck; 380D
Lok, Yow; Gambling Hall Keeper; Santa Clara; CA; 1843; China;
        124A
Long, Clarence F.; Dead; Northumberland; PA; 1878; PA; 541B
Long, Edward; Tramp; Chautauqua; NY; 1864; NY; 34A
Long, Frank L.; Showman in Circus; Lenawee; MI; 1858; MI;
        247D
Long, J.; Circus; Ohio; WV; 1829; PA; 449A
Long, John; Gambler; Augusta; VA; 1852; VA; 19A
Long, Man; General Bummer; Leander; NV; 1850; China; 298B
Long, Toi; Gambler; Washoe; NV; 1845; China; 276D
Long, Wong; Gambler; Ada; ID; 1844; China; 19A
Longhand, Nath.; Tramp on public street; St. Clair; IL; 1850;
        Wales; 483C
Longshore, W.B.; Theif; Franklin; OH; 1857; Ireland; 479D
Longstreath, Nancy; Wanderer; Tippecanoe; IN; 1853; IN; 172B
Longstreath, William; Wanderer; Tippecanoe; IN; 1831; OH;
        172B
Loo, Gee; Gambler; San Francisco; CA; 1854; Qwantung; 608B
Look, Foy; Gambler; Ormsby; NV; 1847; China; 74C
Lop, Chair; Opium Dealer; San Francisco; CA; 1832; Kwantung;
        393A
Lopes, Antoino; Vagrant; Hidalgo; TX; 1854; Mexico; 222C
Lorberg, Frank; Circus Performer; St. Louis; MO; 1852; MO;
        467C
Lord, Eunice; Fortune Teller; Cumberland; ME; 1825; ME; 179C

Lord, Sarah A.; Magnetic Physician; Middlesex; MA; 1836; ME; 396B

Lorents, C.; Circus; Ohio; WV; 1849; NY; 449B

Lorenz, Emma; Death; Essex; NJ; 1880; NJ; 89A

Lorenz, Mary; Fortune Teller; New York; NY; 1830; Holstein; 422D

Lough, Pew; Keeps Gambling House; Calaveras; CA; 1820; China; 345B

Loughlin, David; Performer in Circus; Norfolk; VA; 1860; VA; 441B

Louis, George; Gambler; Presidio; TX; 1860; IA; 84D

Louis, J.B.; Gambler; Presidio; TX; 1812; KY; 84D

Low, Chang; Gambling House; Calaveras; CA; 1829; China; 343A

Low, Gee; Prepares Opium; San Francisco; CA; 1845; Canton Tong Koon; 377A

Low, He; Preparing Opium; San Francisco; CA; 1856; Canton Tong Koon; 377A

Low, Hong; Gambler; Butte; CA; 1835; China; 262C

Low, Kow; Keeps Gambling House; San Francisco; CA; 1845; Young Wo; 629C

Low, William; Tramp; New York; NY; 1828; England; 581C

Low, You; Preparing Opium; San Francisco; CA; 1835; Canton Tong Koon; 377A

Lowe, Charles; Vagrant; Shelby; TN; 1850; TN; 291D

Lowe, John W.; Phrenologist; Barry; MI; 1852; MI; 37B

Lowe, Louisa M.; Spirit Medium; Thurston; WA; 1848; IA; 106A

Lowe, Oscar; Gambler; St. Louis; MO; 1835; NY; 386A

Lowlow, John; Clown in Circus; Cuyahoga; OH; 1842; GA; 143B

Lowrey, Mary; Wanderer; Meigs; OH; 1824; PA; 157B

Loy, Chin; Gambler; San Francisco; CA; 1829; Kwantung; 393B

Loy, George H.; Gambler; Kern; CA; 1822; PA; 580D

Loy, Lung; Gambler; Kern; CA; 1840; China; 586C

Loyd, C.; Gambling House Clerk; Hamilton; OH; 1860; OH; 306A

Lu, Chow; Opium Shop; Santa Clara; CA; 1855; China; 125D

Lucas, Frank; Tramp; Buchanan; MO; 1862; ---; 41A

Lucas, George; Dead; Giles; VA; 1873; VA; 55B

Lucas, Mary Ann; Clairvoyant; St. Clair; IL; 1829; MO; 380B
Lucasie, Jsoeph R.; Cole's Circus; Douglas; NE; 1858; Hamberg; 205B
Lucero, Jose M.; Vagabond; Huerfano; CO; 1845; NM Terr.; 233D
Lue, Sum; Opium Shop; Santa Clara; CA; 1840; China; 125C
Lum, Kong; Gambler; Kern; CA; 1835; China; 586C
Lum, Sing; Opium Dealer; San Francisco; CA; 1847; See Yap China; 433A
Lumpkins, Nollie; Vagrant; Daviess; MO; 1861; WI; 1D
Lumsden, Thomas; Vagrant; Clare; MI; 1851; Ireland; 237B
Lunceford; Dead; Washington; IL; 1880; IL; 363A
Lunceford, Salem; Dead; Washington; IL; 1875; IL; 363A
Lund, Andrew E.; Dead; Redwood; MN; 1878; MN; 55D
Lund, Anton; Dead; Redwood; MN; 1875; MN; 55D
Lundey, William; Son dead; Hamilton; OH; 1858; OH; 14D
Lung ; Gambler; Idaho; ID; 1834; Canton; 166C
Lung, Ching; Gambler; Butte; CA; 1843; China; 148B
Lung, Ching; Gambler; San Francisco; CA; 1826; Kwantung; 393B
Lung, Chun; Gambler; San Francisco; CA; 1838; Kwantung; 392B
Lung, Tuny; Gambler; Boise; ID; 1853; China; 118B
Lung, Yin; Gambler; Washoe; NV; 1838; China; 276D
Lung, Yung; Opium Dealer; San Francisco; CA; 1832; Hoy Ping; 450D
Lunt, Mary S.; Magnetic & Clairvoyant Healer; Cumberland; ME; 1850; ME; 323A
Lusbie, B.; Treas. Circus; New York; NY; 1842; NY; 95C
Lut, Hun; Dealer in Opium; New York; NY; 1847; China; 172A
Lutz, George; Tramp on public street; St. Clair; IL; 1858; Bavaria; 482B
Lutz, George; Dead; New Haven; CT; 1851; Germany; 392C
Luy, Lucia; Dead; Carroll; IA; 1880; IA; 427B
Ly, Lay; Keep Opium Shop; Santa Clara; CA; 1820; China; 124B
Lyckberg, Peter; Farmer Vagrant; Winnebago; WI; 1840; Sweden; 162D
Lyles, Walter J.; Gambler; Lamar; TX; 1832; TN; 205D
Lyn, Wah; Gambler; Sacramento; CA; 1848; China; 332A

Name; Occupation; County; State; Birth; Birth place; Page 91

Lynch, Hannah; Dead; Tioga; NY; 1855; NY; 219C
Lynch, John; Tramp on Road; Lancaster; PA; 1853; Ireland; 604A
Lynch, John; Baseball player; Washington; D.C.; 1855; England;
102C
Lynch, Joseph; Tramp; New York; NY; 1839; Ireland; 287D
Lynch, Mary; Dead; Wayne; MI; 1845; Germany; 326B
Lyon, Charles; Gambler; Pettis; MO; 1844; NY; 200C
Lyons, Dixie; Gambler; Tarrant; TX; 1845; MO; 52C
Lyons, Frank; Tramp; New York; NY; 1848; England; 581D
Lyons, James M.; Tramp on public street; St. Clair; IL; 1847; IL;
482A
Lyunch, Eugene; Gambler; Davidson; TN; 1835; TN; 144D
M Creery ; Dead born; Indiana; PA; ---; PA; 374B
M Creery, Harry B.; Dead; Indiana; PA; 1879; PA; 374B
Maas, Theresa; Dead; Orleans; LA; 1879; LA; 104C
Mac Guire, Frank; Employed in a Circus; York; ME; 1860; ME;
117B
MacAllister, John M.; Magician; Arapahoe; CO; 1836; Scotland;
123C
MacCet, Thomas; Tramp; Calhoun; MI; 1813; England; 380A
MacDonald, Daniell; Base ball player; New York; NY; 1844; NY;
528C
MacKlen, Nore E.; Dead; Perry; IL; 1879; IL; 42C
Macon, Jackson; Dead; Hardeman; TN; 1879; TN; 462A
MacOussin, John; Tramp on public street; St. Clair; IL; 1858; IL;
482B
MacReady, William; Vagrant; New York; NY; 1841; England;
577A
Madden, Frank; Baseball player; Hampden; MA; 1860; MA; 5B
Madden, James; Tramp; New York; NY; 1845; Ireland; 581D
Madden, Winneford; Dead June 17th; Suffolk; MA; 1878; MA;
344B
Maddox, Hester Ann; Lined out dead, apparently childbirth; Allen;
IN; 1849; IN; 419B
Madigan, Edward; Circus Agent; Cuyahoga; OH; 1856; OH; 414D
Maers, Henry; Painter Tramp; Noble; IN; 1814; Germany; 363B
Maghee, Clifford; Dead; Crawford; GA; 1879; GA; 658B
Maginnis, Charles; Gambler; Billings; Dak. Terr.; 1842; PA; 59B

Maginnis, Chas.; Gambler R.R.; Billings; Dak. Terr.; 1842; PA;
    46C
Maguire, George; Waiting on death; Jefferson; MO; 1770; VA;
    46B
Mah, Yuk Mon; Opium Dealer; San Francisco; CA; 1845;
    Kwantung; 381A
Mahan, Fanny; Magnictic Healer; Cook; IL; 1840; IL; 561A
Mahar, Margaret; Dead; Albany; NY; ---; Ireland; 365A
Mahoney, Daniel; Bartender pimp; Manistee; MI; 1861; MI; 55A
Mahoney, Dennis; Dead; Bristol; MA; 1866; MA; 402B
Mahony, William; Tramp; Calumet; WI; 1846; Ireland; 73D
Mahora, M.; Gambler; Pima; AZ; 1830; Mexico; 307D
Mainard, William; Tramp; Henry; TN; 1845; TN; 203D
Mainor, F.; Circus; Ohio; WV; 1861; Scotland; 449A
Major, Thomas; Tramp; New York; NY; 1840; England; 431D
Maker, William; Tramp; Ionia; MI; 1862; NY; 108C
Malchi, Elizabeth; Dead; Solano; CA; 1849; MO; 401A
Malone, A.E.; Magician; Harrison; IN; 1851; ME; 272B
Maloon, Christ; Tramp on public street; St. Clair; IL; 1852; IL;
    482A
Man, Nap; Gambler; Ada; ID; 1840; China; 19A
Mang, Fung; Gambler; Eureka; NV; 1848; China; 206D
Manks, Lydia; Business Medium; Philadelphia; PA; 1841; NJ;
    293D
Manly, Thomas; Gambler; Deer Lodge; MT; 1840; OH; 137C
Mann, Alfred; Gambler; Yuba; CA; 1831; KY; 413B
Mann, E.; Healer; Pima; AZ; 1851; Wurttemburg; 288A
Mann, William; Gambler; Webb; TX; 1837; AL; 314D
Mannin, Jeptha; Quack Doctor; Pendleton; KY; 1834; KY; 503C
Manning, John E.; Base ballist; Suffolk; MA; 1855; MA; 342C
Manning, William R.; Magnetic Physician; Philadelphia; PA;
    1826; NY; 500B
Mans, Catharine; Dirty as Hell; St. Louis; MO; 1845; KY; 262A
Mansell, Thomas; Baseball player; Washington; D.C.; 1853; PA;
    378B
Marco, Geo. F.; Magician; Tuolumne; CA; 1849; MI; 137D
Marcum, Martha; Dead; Clay; KY; 1878; KY; 552D
Marien, Joseph; Gambler; Ramsey; MN; 1832; Canada; 278C

Mark, Gustav; Tramp on public street; St. Clair; IL; 1857;
      Wurtemburg; 482A
Marks, Benjamin; Gambler; Pottawattamie; IA; 1840; OH; 368B
Marks, Grant; Tramp; Dauphin; PA; 1850; England; 171C
Marks, M.; Gambler; Ormsby; NV; 1850; Poland; 88A
Marsh, Benj.; Quack Doctor; Roane; TN; 1805; TN; 377B
Marsh, Cyrus; Wandering lunatic; Boone; IN; 1840; IN; 71C
Marsh, Frank; Gambler; Shasta; CA; 1857; CA; 6C
Marsh, George; Gambler; Solano; CA; 1860; CA; 495D
Marsh, John; Gambler; Solano; CA; 1859; CA; 496B
Marsh, Wm.; Gambler; Conejos; CO; 1845; Canada; 180D
Marshall, Emma; Dead; Allegheny; PA; 1874; PA; 236D
Marshall, Frank A.; Baseball player; Baltimore; MD; 1859; MD;
      289A
Marshall, Fred; Supposed Gambler; Davidson; TN; 1830; TN;
      111C
Marshall, I.; Circus; Ohio; WV; 1862; VA; 448D
Marshall, W.H.; Dead; Marshall; TN; 1812; TN; 336C
Marston, George D.; Clairvoyant & Physician; Androscoggin;
      ME; 1834; ME; 400D
Marston, Ruell; Dead; Kenosha; WI; 1880; WI; 39A
Martin, ---; Infant wandering about with its mother; Russell; VA;
      1880; VA; 146C
Martin, Benjamin; Gambler; San Joaquin; CA; 1850; NY; 24B
Martin, Charles; Gypsies Fortune Teller & Trader; Fairfield; OH;
      1856; IN; 92B
Martin, George; Gypsies Fortune Teller & Trader; Fairfield; OH;
      1864; KY; 92B
Martin, Jane; Dresser of dead; Philadelphia; PA; 1825; Ireland;
      98B
Martin, John; Tramp; New York; NY; 1844; NY; 581C
Martin, John; Tramp on public street; St. Clair; IL; 1860; IL; 482A
Martin, John; Tramp on public street; St. Clair; IL; 1840;
      Scotland; 482B
Martin, John; Tramp; Lancaster; NE; 1853; Ireland; 173A
Martin, Jose; Gambler; Bernalillo; NM; 1845; NM Terr.; 2C
Martin, Katie; Gypsies Fortune Teller & Trader; Fairfield; OH;
      1862; NC; 92B

Martin, Mary; Vagrant; Leavenworth; KS; 1850; KS; 242A
Martin, Mary; Wandering about; Russell; VA; 1845; VA; 146C
Martin, Mary J.; Dead; Coryell; TX; 1854; AL; 429A
Martin, Rebecca; At home dead; Campbell; KY; 1819; KY; 311A
Martin, Samuel; Fortune Teller; Botetourt; VA; 1837; VA; 18C
Martin, Susan; Fortune Teller; Jackson; MO; 1835; Ireland; 294D
Martin, Thomas; Clog dancer; Essex; NJ; 1859; NY; 120D
Martin, Thomas W.; Dead; Grant; WV; 1879; WV; 224A
Martine, Pedro; Gambler; Las Animas; CO; 1850; NM Terr.; 62A
Martinez, John; Gambler; Orleans; LA; 1820; LA; 432D
Martinez, Luis; Gambler; Las Animas; CO; 1840; NM Terr.; 76A
Marvin, John; Mesmerie Healer; Whiteside; IL; 1836; OH; 279B
Marvin, John A.; Magnetic Physician; Milwaukee; WI; 1836; OH;
    243A
Mary, Joseph; Tramp; Cheshire; NH; 1829; England; 287B
Mason, John; Gambler; Deer Lodge; MT; 1854; NY; 125C
Mason, John; Tramp on public street; St. Clair; IL; 1832; OH;
    483D
Mason, N.; Circus; Ohio; WV; 1851; Prussia; 449A
Mason, William D.; Deadbeat; Livingston; IL; 1822; VA; 152B
Mass, Lydia; Gypsies Fortune Teller & Trader; Fairfield; OH;
    1866; NC; 92B
Massey, J.N.; Gambler; San Francisco; CA; 1835; NY; 128A
Massey, John; Dead; St. Joseph; IN; 1828; MD; 418A
Massey, Remald; Dead; Milwaukee; WI; 1872; WI; 175B
Matheney, Luke; Deadbeat; Obion; TN; 1841; TN; 40C
Matheny, William; Gambler; Champaign; IL; 1856; VA; 37D
Mathews, Geo; Tramp on public street; St. Clair; IL; 1859;
    Ireland; 483C
Mathews, Julia; Clairvoyant; Hillsborough; NH; 1836; England;
    453C
Mathias, Chas.; Tramp on public street; St. Clair; IL; 1852;
    Prussia; 481D
Mathis, Louisa; Dead; Northampton; NC; 1845; NC; 229D
Matteson, Antoinette; Clairvoyant; Erie; NY; 1848; Baden; 154D
Matthews, Aaron N.; Tramp; Johnson; AR; 1854; AR; 339A
Matthews, Robert; Baseball player; San Francisco; CA; 1854;
    MD; 113B

Mattison, Virginia; Astronomer; San Francisco; CA; 1845;
     Prussia; 95D
Mattson, S.P.; Dead; Allen; KS; 1842; Sweden; 41B
Maxwell, Benjamin E.; Farm Labor, Tramp; Knox; IL; 1857; IL;
     326D
Maxwell, T.G.; Magnetic Healer; Lancaster; NE; 1835; MA; 222A
Maxwell, Thomas; Deadbeat; Greenbrier; WV; 1839; VA; 377A
Mayberry, Elizabeth; Dead; Allegheny; PA; 1879; PA; 248D
Mayer, Emma J.; Medium; Sacramento; CA; 1846; NY; 71B
Mayer, Henry; Tramp on public street; St. Clair; IL; 1852; OH;
     483D
Mayer, Mary; Dead; Dubuque; IA; 1878; IA; 352B
Mayer, Regina; Dead; Milwaukee; WI; 1827; Baden; 221A
Mayers, Sam; Tramp on public street; St. Clair; IL; 1858; France;
     484A
Mayes, Elizabeth; Gypsies Fortune Teller & Trader; Fairfield;
     OH; 1854; NC; 92B
Mayes, Emaline; Gypsies Fortune Teller & Trader; Fairfield; OH;
     1833; NC; 92B
Mayes, Jane; Gypsies Fortune Teller & Trader; Fairfield; OH;
     1853; NC; 92B
Mayes, William; Gypsies Fortune Teller & Trader; Fairfield; OH;
     1855; NC; 92B
Maynard, V.M.; Spirit Medium; San Francisco; CA; 1821; OH;
     88C
Mayo, Clara E.; Spirit Trance Medium; San Francisco; CA; 1858;
     MA; 360A
Mayo, William; Thief; Franklin; OH; 1860; LA; 482B
Mayse, Jas.; Circus; Ohio; WV; 1860; NY; 448D
Mc Alister, Stephen H.; Gambler; Custer; CO; 1854; ME; 282C
Mc Bain, Dolph; Gambler; Pulaski; AR; 1846; IL; 330B
Mc Bride, John; Gambler; Deer Lodge; MT; 1830; Canada; 110A
Mc Call, Samuel H.; Gambler; Beaverhead; MT; 1858; MO; 20C
Mc Cauley, James; Gambler; Storey; NV; 1840; Ireland; 146B
Mc Corkle, Dick; Gambler; Hamilton; TN; 1835; DE; 143A
Mc Coy; Gambler; Storey; NV; 1835; NY; 116A
Mc Coy, Solomon A.; Gambler; Beaverhead; MT; 1859; MD; 20C
Mc Cullough, Charles; Gambler; Lake; CO; 1852; NY; 352B

Mc Donal, Lion; Gambler; Presidio; TX; 1846; KY; 86C
Mc Dowell, J.A.; Gambler; Jefferson; KY; 1850; KY; 336A
Mc Govern, James; Gambler; Deer Lodge; MT; 1842; NY; 137C
Mc Mahon, Peter; Gambler; Deer Lodge; MT; 1834; Ireland;
    125C
Mc Millen, John; Gambler; Grayson; TX; 1838; KY; 182D
Mc Neal, Frank; Gambler; Jefferson; KY; 1834; USA; 523A
Mc Taggart, Robert; Gambler; Deer Lodge; MT; 1846; Canada;
    124B
Mc---, Maggi; Mother dead; New York; NY; 1877; NY; 61C
McAdams, Rosa; Dead; Benton; AR; 1874; MO; 459C
McAfferty, John; Tramp on public street; St. Clair; IL; 1849; IN;
    481D
McAllister, Florence; Dead; St. Joseph; IN; 1880; IN; 409D
McAllister, I.M.; Magician; Erie; NY; 1839; PA; 62A
McAllister, J.W.; Magician; Custer; CO; 1837; ---; 308B
McBride, John B.; Traveling with Circus; Orange; VT; 1844; KY;
    148A
McBride, Martha; Magnetic Healer; Cook; IL; 1832; OH; 576A
McCammon, Blufort; Dead; Sullivan; IN; 1865; IN; 518A
McCammon, Monroe; Dead; Wilcox; AL; 1879; AL; 487B
McCandy, James; Tramp; Berrien; MI; 1847; NY; 148B
McCann, Dan'l; Gambler; Sacramento; CA; 1846; England; 10D
McCartha, John; Tramp; Lapeer; MI; 1861; NY; 315B
McCarthy, John; 1st class bummer; New York; NY; 1850; Ireland;
    104A
McCartney, Harry J.; Circus Treasurer; New York; NY; 1845;
    England; 329D
McCarty, Jeremiah; Dead; Bristol; MA; 1871; MA; 413C
McCarty, Thom; Tramp on public street; St. Clair; IL; 1848;
    Ireland; 482B
McCarty, William; Tramp on public street; St. Clair; IL; 1858;
    LA; 482B
McCarty, William; Tramp on public street; St. Clair; IL; 1833;
    Ireland; 483D
McCaulim; Tramp; Davidson; TN; 1857; TN; 113C
McCenter, James C.; Dead; New York; NY; 1880; NY; 625D
McClay, J.W.; Tramp; Defiance; OH; 1832; PA; 77B

McClellan, James; Baseball player; Washington; D.C.; 1857; IL; 378B

McClintice, Hugh; Phrenologist; Crawford; PA; 1843; PA; 294B

McClosky, Frank; Painter Tramp; Dallas; AR; 1792; Canada; 184C

McClung, Martha; Magnetic Healer; Monroe; NY; 1821; OH; 144B

McColester, Oscar; Dead; Benton; AR; 1875; MO; 463C

McCollough, John; Dead; Fairfield; SC; 1875; SC; 112A

McCollough, Lizzie; Dead; Fairfield; SC; 1877; SC; 112A

McColnaughy, Wm. H.; Gambler; Belmont; OH; 1840; OH; 410B

McConnell, F.; Circus; Ohio; WV; 1855; PA; 448D

McConoha, Wm.; Traveling with Circus; Wood; WV; 1857; OH; 374A

McCool, John; Emigrant or Tramp; Washington; PA; 1843; Ireland; 409A

McCormac, James; Tramp; New York; NY; 1845; Ireland; 581C

McCormick, P. Henry; Baseball player; Onondaga; NY; 1856; NY; 277C

McCorrey, John; Dead; Fairfield; SC; 1860; SC; 95C

McCrelly, James; Prisoner for theft; Isabella; MI; 1856; Scotland; 533A

McCrone, John; Tramp; Dauphin; PA; 1834; MD; 110D

McCullar, James; Baseball player; Suffolk; MA; 1858; Ireland; 108B

McCullom, Malcom; Circus Performer; Wayne; MI; 1835; NY; 45C

McCullough, James; Base ballist; Plymouth; MA; 1858; MA; 335D

McCullough, Sam; Dead since Jun 1; Davidson; TN; 1830; TN; 231D

McCurdy, James; Tramp; Jackson; MO; 1851; NY; 370B

McDermant, John; Gambler; Yuba; CA; 1848; OH; 402C

McDermott, James; Dead; Bristol; MA; 1810; Ireland; 403D

McDonald, Cath.; Dresses the dead; Philadelphia; PA; 1830; PA; 46A

McDonald, J.H.; Gambler; Marion; OR; 1835; VA; 46B

McDonald, James; Magician; Jackson; MO; 1844; MD; 468B

McDonald, Jane; Fortune Teller; Adams; IL; 1844; OH; 396C
McDonald, Maud L.; Dead; Blair; PA; 1875; PA; 79A
McDonald, Thomas; An outlaw; Pickaway; OH; 1846; KY; 530D
McDonel, Ned; Tramp on public street; St. Clair; IL; 1856; MO;
    482A
McDonnald, Mary; Dead; Hudson; NJ; 1879; ---; 274D
McDonnel, John; Tramp on public street; St. Clair; IL; 1857; OH;
    483C
McElligot, John; Ball player; New Haven; CT; 1857; Ireland;
    210A
McFalls, Bridget; Vagrant; Winnebago; WI; 1840; Foreign; 166C
McFarland, John; Tramp; New York; NY; 1815; Scotland; 581D
McGary, Michael; B. ball player; Philadelphia; PA; 1852; PA;
    298A
McGeary, Michael H.; Baseball player; Providence; RI; 1848; PA;
    375C
McGennis, John; Tramp on public street; St. Clair; IL; 1845;
    Ireland; 483C
McGinty, Abbie; Vagrant; Outagamie; WI; 1836; NY; 79D
McGonnigle, Wm.; Ball player; Erie; NY; 1855; Boston, MA;
    423B
McGowen, Carol; Dead; East Baton Rouge; LA; 1851; LA; 515A
McGTraw, Edw.; Tramp on public street; St. Clair; IL; 1854; OH;
    482A
McGue, Archibald; Vagrant; Laramie; WY; 1851; Scotland; 155B
McGuire, John; Tramp on public street; St. Clair; IL; 1845;
    Canada; 482A
McHatton, James E.; Dead; La Fayette; WI; 1880; WI; 212D
McHugh, Thomas; Tramp; Lackawanna; PA; 1865; PA; 165D
McIntire, John; Traveling Agent for Circus; Cook; IL; 1856; WI;
    334A
McIntosh, George D.; Circus Agt.; Summit; OH; 1848; OH; 9B
McIntosh, Jas.; With Circus; Ashtabula; OH; 1855; OH; 646B
McIntosh, Lucy; Tramp; Marengo; AL; 1866; AL; 703D
McIntosh, Martha; Tramp; Marengo; AL; 1845; AL; 703D
McIntyre, Ths. B.; W.W. Cole's Circus & Menagere; Douglas;
    NE; 1849; England; 205A
McIntyre, Wm.; Dead; Adams; IL; 1877; IL; 471A

McIver, Charles; Foot racer; Lapeer; MI; 1859; England; 102D
McKane, Alesel Z.; Boxing & trainer; Berkshire; MA; 1852; NY; 439D
McKee, Virgil; Tramp; Washington; KY; 1854; KY; 321D
McKeil, Claudie; Dead; Ellsworth; KS; 1880; KS; 485A
McKensey, W.; Quack Doctor; Rock; WI; 1820; NY; 367C
McKenzie, William; Tramp; Marshall; MN; 1856; MN; 143D
McKeyring, James; Tramp; Buchanan; MO; 1861; MO; 41A
McKinsey, Geo.; Stealing Horses; Montgomery; IN; 1852; KY; 325C
McKinzy, William; Tramp - Prisoner; Lawrence; IN; 1842; OH; 550D
McKnight, David; Tramp; Carlton; MN; 1854; Canada; 146C
McKnight, Emma C.; On death bed; Greenup; KY; 1851; OH; 170D
McLane, Charles; Tramp on public street; St. Clair; IL; 1858; NJ; 481D
McLane, James; Tramp on public street; St. Clair; IL; 1856; NY; 483D
McLany, Andrew; Tramp; Wayne; PA; 1805; Ireland; 55C
McLaughlin, Chas.; Tramp; Defiance; OH; 1853; PA; 102D
McLaughlin, Daniel; Wanderer - parcial pauper; Middlesex; MA; 1813; MA; 92D
McLaughlin, Thomas; Harlot pimp; Marinette; WI; 1854; Ontario; 456B
McLaughton, Frank; Base ballist; Middlesex; MA; 1858; Ireland; 308A
McLellan, Geo. W.; Magnetic Position; Suffolk; MA; 1825; ME; 255D
McMahan, Michael J.; Dead; Cook; IL; 1879; IL; 270C
McMahon, John; Circus Rider; Washtenaw; MI; 1853; MI; 314A
McMan, John; Tramp; New York; NY; 1852; NY; 581C
McMannes, John; Tramp; Hanson; Dak. Terr.; 1853; Ireland; 56C
McMannus, Albert; Deadbeat; Kennebec; ME; 1807; ME; 260B
McMichael, Dan; Vagrant; Montgomery; PA; 1835; Ireland; 224C
McMullen; Tramp; McPherson; KS; 1844; ---; 452C
McNalty, Robert; Tramp on public street; St. Clair; IL; 1860; IL; 482A

McNamara, John; Tramp; New York; NY; 1840; NY; 581D
McNeely, D.R.; Gambler; Allen; IN; 1845; Canada; 632C
McNemar, Thomas; Dead; Grant; WV; 1880; WV; 224B
McNerry, J.; Circus; Ohio; WV; 1859; TN; 448D
McNiel, Mary; Now dead since first; Oswego; NY; 1852; NY;
    479C
McNiel, Samuel A.; Deadbeat; Randolph; GA; 1838; GA; 109B
McNutt, John; Since dead; Vermilion; IL; 1856; KY; 250C
McPearson, Donald; Prisoner Vagrant; Westchester; NY; 1832;
    Scotland; 404C
McPearson, Rosannah; Prisoner Vagrant; Westchester; NY; 1830;
    Ireland; 404C
McPherson, Geo.; Gambler; Morgan; IN; 1835; NC; 51B
McPherson, Stephen J.; Quack Doctor; Montcalm; MI; 1830; OH;
    19B
McQuade, Ida M.; Dead; Allegheny; PA; 1879; PA; 250C
McQuarter; Dead; Fairfield; SC; 1879; SC; 198A
McQue, James; Tramp; New York; NY; 1855; PA; 581C
McQueen, Alexander; Gambler; Oakland; MI; 1833; Ireland;
    337A
McWilliams, Melviny; Dead; Wilcox; AL; 1845; AL; 213C
Meade, John; Gambler; Hamilton; OH; 1853; CT; 149C
Medora, A.L.; Thief in prison; Lenawee; MI; 1854; MI; 108C
Meek, Mary R.; Laying out dead; Dauphin; PA; 1818; PA; 216D
Meeller, Agnes; Dead; Milwaukee; WI; ---; WI; 233B
Mehan, Edward; Farmer dead; La Fayette; WI; 1822; Ireland;
    213A
Meir, Charles; Fortune Teller; St. Clair; MI; 1811; Prussia; 425C
Melia, John; Tramp; New York; NY; 1805; Ireland; 581C
Melkenur, John; Tramp; New York; NY; 1825; Prussia; 431C
Melone, T.J.; Base ball; McKean; PA; 1844; PA; 113B
Melton, Hampton; Vagrant; Rutherford; NC; 1807; NC; 501B
Melton, Sarah; Vagrant; Rutherford; NC; 1809; NC; 501B
Menan, James; Tramp on public street; St. Clair; IL; 1846; NY;
    482B
Mendelbaum, Louis; Billiard player; New York; NY; 1858; NY;
    178A
Menderhaus, J.T.; Circus Performer; McLean; IL; 1852; IN; 202A

Mengle, William H.; Gambler; Vermilion; IL; 1851; PA; 382D
Ments, M.G.; Circus; Ohio; WV; 1861; NY; 448D
Mericle, Mary Eliza; Tramp; Potter; PA; 1858; NY; 461D
Merino, Jose; Gambler; Grant; NM; 1843; Chihuahua; 332B
Merino, Jose; Gambler; Grant; NM; 1850; Chihuahua; 343C
Merrel, Matilda; Dead; Clinton; NY; 1839; Canada; 553B
Merryweather, May; Fortune Teller; Sacramento; CA; 1804; NY;
    158D
Mervery, Chas.; Tramp; Hennepin; MN; 1859; ---; 272A
Messer, Mary A.; Tramp; Hawkins; TN; 1860; TN; 194A
Metz, John; Tramp; Luzerne; PA; 1799; NY; 112D
Metz, John H.; Dead; Allegheny; PA; 1879; PA; 253A
Metzenger, J.; Circus Performer; Oneida; NY; 1849; NY; 416A
Metzher, Mary; Clairvoyant; New York; NY; 1836; Prussia; 167B
Metzler, Marcella; Abortionist; Mercer; NJ; 1836; France; 293A
Meyer, August; Tramp on public street; St. Clair; IL; 1853;
    Hessia; 482A
Meyer, Mead; Dead; Adams; IL; 1831; Holland; 496D
Meyers, Barbara; Dead; Allegheny; PA; 1872; PA; 238D
Meyers, Elizabeth; Dead; Allegheny; PA; 1876; PA; 238D
Meyers, Hiram; Quack Doctor; Oneida; NY; 1823; NY; 66A
Meynard, Mark; Showman Circus; Allegheny; PA; 1852; NY;
    362A
Micaco, Alfred; Circus Performer; New York; NY; 1844; NY;
    74A
Michals, H.; Base ball p.; Shawnee; KS; 1859; IL; 77D
Miera, Pantaleon; Rustler; Bernalillo; NM; 1840; NM Terr.; 22A
Mik, Harry; Gambler; Washoe; NV; 1856; TN; 296C
Miles, Anna; Fortune Telling; Gallia; OH; 1849; Ontario; 378B
Miles, Pat.; Circus Performer; Philadelphia; PA; 1824; NY; 455B
Millener, John; Tramp; Hennepin; MN; 1840; ---; 272A
Miller; Born dead; Scioto; OH; ---; OH; 319C
Miller; Dead; Fayette; IL; 1880; IL; 192D
Miller, A.E.; Circus; Ohio; WV; 1845; NY; 449A
Miller, Betsy; Tramp; Newton; GA; 1856; GA; 105C
Miller, Charles; Tramp on public street; St. Clair; IL; 1860; OH;
    483D
Miller, Charles; Dead; Campbell; KY; 1880; KY; 64D

Name; Occupation; County; State; Birth; Birth place; Page

Miller, Charles; Dead; St. Joseph; IN; 1878; PA; 416A
Miller, Henry; Tramp; New York; NY; 1839; England; 581D
Miller, Henry; Tramp on public street; St. Clair; IL; 1859; MO; 481D
Miller, Henry; Tramp on public street; St. Clair; IL; 1844; IL; 483C
Miller, Henry; Tramp on public street; St. Clair; IL; 1852; RI; 483D
Miller, Isah.; Circus; Ohio; WV; 1859; IN; 449B
Miller, J.; Tramp; Lawrence; AR; 1855; IL; 492C
Miller, J.H.; Gambler; Wake; NC; 1852; OH; 261D
Miller, J.W.; Circus; Ohio; WV; 1859; CT; 448D
Miller, James; Tramp; Bradford; PA; 1823; NJ; 457D
Miller, John; Gambler; Grant; NM; 1850; TX; 371B
Miller, John; Gambler; Vanderburgh; IN; 1842; KY; 324D
Miller, John; Tramp; Henry; IN; 1829; IL; 123D
Miller, John Peter; Magician; Allegheny; PA; 1844; Bayern; 419C
Miller, Korah; Dead; Fremont; IA; 1869; MO; 150B
Miller, Louis; Tramp; Placer; CA; 1850; Prussia; 365A
Miller, Lucy; Dead; Warren; TN; 1832; TN; 400B
Miller, Phillis; Dead; Choctaw; MS; 1837; SC; 449C
Miller, Samuel; Tramp; Polk; IA; 1854; PA; 237D
Millious, Hada; Dead; Sandusky; OH; 1879; OH; 170B
Mills, James P.; Quack Pills; New York; NY; 1850; PA; 290C
Milroy, Coon; Gambler; Pike; MO; 1842; MO; 497A
Milroy, Thos.; Gambler; Pike; MO; 1850; MO; 497A
Milroy, Wm.; Gambler; Pike; MO; 1859; MO; 497A
Milwall, Alfred; Tramp; New York; NY; 1839; England; 581D
Min, Sing; Opium Shop; Santa Clara; CA; 1835; China; 126B
Miner, John; Circus Performer; Westchester; NY; 1857; PA; 102B
Ming, Kai; Gambler; San Francisco; CA; 1854; Kwan Tung; 632A
Ming, King Pang; Fortune Teller; San Francisco; CA; 1836; China; 411A
Ming, Ng; Gambler; San Francisco; CA; 1849; Kwantung; 392B
Mingle, Lizzie; Clairvoyant; Philadelphia; PA; 1828; PA; 220B
Miquel, Louser Ann; Clairvoyant; New York; NY; 1835; England; 659D
Mise; Dead; Clay; KY; 1879; KY; 530C

Mitchell, James M.; Dead; Owen; KY; 1878; KY; 185C
Mix, Chas. B.; Circus Man; St. Louis; MO; 1843; KY; 107C
Mix, Elliot; Circus; Ohio; WV; 1851; NY; 448D
Mixer, Sarah C.; Magnetic Physician; Hillsborough; NH; 1828; NH; 375A
Moeler, Frank; Tramp on public street; St. Clair; IL; 1840; Wurtemburg; 484A
Mollere, Agabie; Tramp; Ascension; LA; 1846; LA; 75A
Mon, Yung; Gambler; Deer Lodge; MT; 1846; China; 110B
Moncays, Felsisitre; Circus Performer; Philadelphia; PA; 1860; Mexico; 102A
Moncays, Julian; Circus Performer; Philadelphia; PA; 1858; Mexico; 102A
Moncays, Sebastian; Circus Performer; Philadelphia; PA; 1856; Mexico; 102A
Moncays, Y. Sidro; Circus Performer; Philadelphia; PA; 1859; Mexico; 102A
Monk, George; Born dead; Claiborne; TN; 1879; TN; 180A
Monroe, Alex; Phrenologist; Saginaw; MI; 1840; England; 305C
Monroe, Jas.; Circus; Ohio; WV; 1860; NY; 448D
Monroe, Lizzie; Dead; Spotsylvania; VA; 1880; VA; 450B
Monskie, Anton; Dead; Milwaukee; WI; 1880; Milwaukee, WI; 287C
Montano, Manuela; Dancer; Santa Fe; NM; 1860; NM Terr.; 85A
Montero, Achelino; Gambler; Sierra; CA; 1847; Panama; 157B
Montgomery, Charity; Vagrant; Putnam; GA; 1863; GA; 474D
Montgomery, Joseph; Gambler; Cole; MO; 1837; NJ; 38B
Montgomery, Rachel L.; Dead; Allegheny; PA; 1879; PA; 244C
Montgomery, Robert M.; Dead; Allegheny; PA; 1877; PA; 244C
Montomery, Levi; Tramp; Stephenson; IL; 1855; NY; 63A
Montoya, Nestora; Dancer; Santa Fe; NM; 1856; NM Terr.; 85A
Moody; Dead; Switzerland; IN; ---; IN; 1A
Moon, James; Gambler; Arapahoe; CO; 1840; PA; 98D
Moon, Sing; Gambler; San Francisco; CA; 1847; Kwan Tung; 631C
Mooney, John; Tramp; Ulster; NY; 1852; NY; 312C
Moor, Charles; Laborer; Horse Thief; St. Clair; MI; 1844; ---; 209D

Moor, John; Horse Thief; St. Clair; MI; 1845; Canada; 204A
Moore, B.C.; Professional Gambler; Lake; CO; 1854; KY; 341C
Moore, Caleb B.; Magician; Clinton; IN; 1850; PA; 67A
Moore, Ellen B.; Dead; Limestone; AL; 1853; AL; 356C
Moore, Franklin; Spirit Medium Lecturer & Trance; Cape
    Girardeau; MO; 1855; MO; 148A
Moore, Jim; Vagrant; Leavenworth; KS; 1869; ---; 242A
Moore, Lilly Lee; Dead; Gonzales; TX; 1874; TX; 491B
Moore, Lottie; Clairvoyant; Suffolk; MA; 1843; ME; 227D
Moore, William; Gambler; Hays; TX; 1857; TX; 31C
Moore, William; Harlot pimp; Marinette; WI; 1854; Ontario;
    453D
Moorehouse, Isaac; Gambler; Deer Lodge; MT; 1849; MA; 112B
Moores, Linus H.; Barnum's Circus; Marion; IN; 1854; OH; 161A
Moorman, Laura; Dead; Fulton; GA; 1844; KY; 260B
Moran, John; Gambler; Steuben; NY; 1858; NY; 151A
Moran, Josephine; Dead; Blair; PA; 1864; PA; 86D
Morant; Dead born; Passaic; NJ; ---; NJ; 387D
Moranti, Joseph; Vagrant; San Francisco; CA; 1860; CA; 193C
Moranti, Manuel; Vagrant; San Francisco; CA; 1861; CA; 193C
More, Anna; Begger & Fortune Teller; Botetourt; VA; 1840; VA;
    125A
Morehouse, W.; Gambler; Sumner; KS; 1832; KS; 285B
Morely, William; Tramp; Wayne; IN; 1859; IN; 297A
Morgan, Geo.; Circus Rider; New York; NY; 1821; NY; 319A
Morgan, Geo. Q.; Tramp; Jackson; MO; 1852; ME; 368B
Morgan, James; Tramp; Stephenson; IL; 1859; NY; 63A
Morgan, John; Gambler; Calcasieu; LA; 1850; KY; 505A
Morgenstern, Louis; Magician; San Francisco; CA; 1859; CA;
    740B
Morison, Nellie; Tramp; Hawkins; TN; 1856; TN; 183C
Morison, William; Tramp on public street; St. Clair; IL; 1857;
    MS; 481D
Moriss, Edward; Tramp on public street; St. Clair; IL; 1858; PA;
    484A
Morkers, S.; Circus; Ohio; WV; 1830; Brazil; 449B
Morrell, William; Tramp on public street; St. Clair; IL; 1851; NY;
    483D

Morrill, Charles; Gambler; Lake; CO; 1840; ME; 352A
Morrill, John F.; Baseball player; Suffolk; MA; 1855; MA; 466C
Morris, Dan; Criminal; St. Louis; MO; 1848; MI; 226B
Morris, George; Phrenologist; Bay; MI; 1852; England; 452D
Morris, Henry; Vagrant; St. Louis; MO; 1864; GA; 252B
Morris, Hugh; Drunkard; New Haven; CT; 1824; Ireland; 240C
Morris, John; Circus Man; Hamilton; OH; 1842; England; 342B
Morris, John; Tramp; Grundy; IL; 1855; PA; 411A
Morrisey, John; Base ball player; Rensselaer; NY; 1853; WI;
    427A
Morrison, John; Harlot pimp; Marinette; WI; 1850; Ontario; 453D
Morrison, T.; Tramp; Hamilton; OH; 1861; IN; 424A
Morrissey, John; Baseball player; Rock; WI; 1858; WI; 202B
Morse, A.C.; Gambler; Bernalillo; NM; 1829; NH; 2D
Morse, Geo. W.; Tramp; Jackson; MO; 1853; PA; 368B
Morse, Jeff A.; Tramp; Montgomery; IA; 1861; IN; 321A
Mortin, Jack; Tramp; Buchanan; MO; 1858; KY; 41A
Morton, Eunice O.; Spiritual Medium; San Francisco; CA; 1830;
    ME; 266A
Moto; Circus; Ohio; WV; 1863; Canada; 449B
Mott, Harvey; Spiritual Medium; Scotland; MO; 1845; MO; 178D
Mott, Mary; Assist. Medium; Scotland; MO; 1846; PA; 178D
Moultrie, Peter; Dead; Colleton; SC; 1830; SC; 251A
Mow, Lung; Opium Dealer; San Francisco; CA; 1833; See Yup;
    627C
Mow, On; Gambler; Yuba; CA; 1846; Canton; 428C
Moy, Lum; Gambler; Amador; CA; 1853; Canton; 47A
Muldoon, Michael; Base ballist; Hartford; CT; 1857; Ireland;
    402B
Mullen, Mary A.; Clairvoyant; Dutchess; NY; 1840; NY; 139A
Mullendore, Allen; Tramp; Saunders; NE; 1856; OH; 336B
Muller, Arthur; Tramp on public street; St. Clair; IL; 1850;
    France; 483D
Muller, Peter; Tramp on public street; St. Clair; IL; 1848; Baden;
    481D
Muller, Rich'd; Actor Circus; New York; NY; 1859; Canada;
    469C
Mullin, Tom; Circus Man; St. Louis; MO; 1859; MN; 302D

Mulllins, L. Emmitt; Dead; Washington; AR; 1879; AR; 566B
Muneger, I.H.; Tramp; Hennepin; MN; 1837; Canada; 394D
Munn, Niran; Quack Doctor; Essex; VT; 1840; Canada; 287D
Munson, George; Gambler; Ionia; MI; 1848; MI; 108C
Munson, Mandy; Dead; Owen; KY; 1857; KY; 172B
Muntsy, Hugh; Gambler; Deer Lodge; MT; 1847; Canada; 135D
Munzlinger, Mike; Dead; St. Louis; MO; 1880; MO; 443D
Muray, John; Tramp on public street; St. Clair; IL; 1855; PA; 483C
Muray, Thom; Tramp on public street; St. Clair; IL; 1829; Ireland; 484A
Muray, Thomas; Tramp on public street; St. Clair; IL; 1853; AR; 483D
Murphey, M.A.; Fortune Teller; Jefferson; AL; 1850; AL; 396D
Murphey, Mike; Tramp; Marshall; MN; 1846; NY; 143D
Murphy, Charity; Dead; Wilcox; AL; 1872; AL; 186B
Murphy, E. Lacy; Gambler; Caldwell; TX; 1862; AR; 249B
Murphy, James; Gambler; Deer Lodge; MT; 1845; IL; 110A
Murphy, Jas.; Circus; Ohio; WV; 1861; PA; 448D
Murphy, Jim; Tramp; Hennepin; MN; 1858; Canada; 395B
Murphy, John S.; Tramp; Hennepin; MN; 1847; ---; 272A
Murphy, Joseph; Tramp; Hennepin; MN; 1853; MN; 272A
Murphy, Margaret; Now dead; Stearns; MN; 1835; Ireland; 523B
Murphy, Michael; Tramp; Lackawanna; PA; 1845; Ireland; 251C
Murphy, Michael; Bummer; New York; NY; 1829; Ireland; 104A
Murphy, Mike; Tramp; Hanson; Dak. Terr.; 1854; Ireland; 56C
Murphy, Pat ; Tramp on public street; St. Clair; IL; 1856; NY; 483C
Murphy, Patrick; Tramp; New York; NY; 1842; Ireland; 581C
Murphy, Robert; Tramp; New York; NY; 1842; Ireland; 581C
Murphy, Thomas; Tramp on public street; St. Clair; IL; 1847; Ireland; 481D
Murphy, Thomas; Dead; Wayne; PA; 1866; PA; 20D
Murphy, Tom; Tramp on public street; St. Clair; IL; 1858; IL; 483C
Murray, Charles A.; Gambler; Cooke; TX; 1846; Canada; 196C
Murray, Fredrerick; Phrenologist; Pottawattamie; IA; 1848; KY; 338B

Murray, James; Gambler; Sacramento; CA; 1820; PA; 42D

Murray, John H.; Circus Manager; New York; NY; 1835; NY; 58B

Mut, Matilda; Dead; Orleans; LA; 1852; New Orleans, LA; 361D

Myers, Chas.; Tramp; Philadelphia; PA; 1822; Germany; 297D

Myers, Henry C.; Base ball player; Baltimore; MD; 1858; PA; 592B

Mysu, Wm.; Gambler; Hamilton; TN; 1842; GA; 227B

Nanaton, William; Billiard player; Suffolk; MA; 1814; MA; 225A

Napolien, Adam; Astronomer; Oneida; NY; 1835; NY; 205D

Nash, A.; Gambler; Lake; CO; 1845; PA; 352A

Nash, Anthony; Gambler; Laramie; WY; 1852; NY; 163B

Nathans, James; Traveller in Circus; New York; NY; 1821; PA; 666B

Nations, Samuel; Gambler; Butte; CA; 1830; GA; 122A

Nauhaus, John; Circus Actor; Scott; IA; 1860; IL; 579B

Nees, Elisabeth; Dead; Cook; IL; 1880; IL; 194A

Nehales, Wm.; Healer; Wapello; IA; 1830; CT; 166B

Neidafer, James; Pimp; Daviess; IN; 1852; IN; 580D

Neigle, John; Base ball player; Summit; OH; 1858; Canada; 439B

Neil, Dick; Wandering; Hawkins; TN; 1869; TN; 265C

Nelsen, John; Phrenologist; Middlesex; MA; 1835; NH; 34B

Nelson, A.; Fortune Teller; Cook; IL; 1850; Sweden; 126D

Nelson, Geo. L.; Magnetic Physician; Suffolk; MA; 1828; NH; 457A

Nelson, John; Tramp; Lancaster; NE; 1853; NE ; 173A

Nelson, John; Ball player; New York; NY; 1850; ME; 364B

Nelson, May; Clairvoyant; San Francisco; CA; 1860; NY; 143A

Nelson, William; Gambler; Warren; MS; 1857; AL; 82C

Neohr, Jacob; Gambler; Kent; MI; 1826; NY; 288C

Nepoleon; Gambler; Del Norte; CA; 1840; China; 13C

Nerson, Peter; Gambler; Deer Lodge; MT; 1860; MO; 120A

Nesbett, Charles; Dead - 1 day old; Hamilton; OH; 1880; OH; 18C

Nesbit, Phillis; Dead; Colleton; SC; 1840; SC; 251A

Nesbitt, Joseph; Gambler; Deer Lodge; MT; 1853; WI; 120B

Nesbitt, Sarah J.; Dead; Champaign; IL; 1832; OH; 191B

Netterberg, George; Dead; Cook; IL; 1874; IL; 130A

108 Name; Occupation; County; State; Birth; Birth place; Page

Neuhaus, Bernhard; Tramp on public street; St. Clair; IL; 1831;
    Switzerland; 482B
Nevels, Samuel; Gambler; Multnomah; OR; 1856; CA; 257D
Nevis, Chris; Tramp; Douglas; NE; 1857; PA; 291B
New; Gambler; Trinity; CA; 1850; China; 552B
Newall, Lizzie; Clairvoyant; Suffolk; MA; 1841; ME; 461C
Newberry, William S.; Gambler; Beaverhead; MT; 1842; MO;
    18D
Newcomb, Simon; Astronomer; Washington; D.C.; 1835; Nova
    Scotia; 80A
Newcomer, Elizabeth; Clairvoyant Physician; Cuyahoga; OH;
    1840; NY; 231A
Newcomer, Isaac; Gambler; Deer Lodge; MT; 1843; MD; 137C
Newey, Tae; Gambler; Placer; CA; 1830; China; 338C
Newil, J.; Vagrant; Buchanan; MO; 1838; MO; 41B
Newton, ---; Gambler; Lake; CO; 1845; MA; 358B
Ni, Po Wolng; Fortune Teller; San Francisco; CA; 1813; Sun
    Ning; 426C
Nicholas, Fred; B. ball player; Worcester; MA; 1852; OH; 182D
Nichols, Emma; Fest. Medium; Cook; IL; 1840; VT; 298B
Nick, Earnest; Tramp; New York; NY; 1841; Germany; 581D
Nickson, Edward; Thief; Westchester; NY; 1861; NY; 106A
Niemeyer, Fred; Tramp on public street; St. Clair; IL; 1833;
    Hanover; 483C
Nienhais, Ernest; Circus Rider; Hudson; NJ; 1854; Bern,
    Switzerland; 24C
Nieto, Logo; Pimp; Bernalillo; NM; 1860; NM Terr.; 5B
Nihart, Peter; Laborer when not too lazy; Elkhart; IN; 1828; PA;
    262B
Ning, Yong; Gambler; Storey; NV; 1840; China; 149D
Nix, Andrew A.; Dead; Rutherford; NC; 1880; NC; 581D
Nix, James; Dead; Hamilton; TX; 1879; TX; 352B
Nixon, W.M.; Gambler; Sumner; KS; 1857; OH; 282C
Nobeloft, Engan; Tramp on public street; St. Clair; IL; 1839;
    France; 482A
Noble, John; Gambler; Hennepin; MN; 1840; ME; 263C
Nolan, Ed; Baseball player; San Francisco; CA; 1857; NJ; 113B

Nolan, Edward; Professional ball player; Passaic; NJ; 1858; Canada; 471A

Nolen, James A.; Magnetic Healer; Randolph; IL; 1843; KY; 427B

Nolen, Lessie; Dead; Walton; GA; 1878; GA; 550B

Nollen, John; Thief; Franklin; OH; 1861; OH; 483D

Noon, Thomas; Gambler; Pinal; AZ; 1838; OH; 398C

Noonan, Daniel; Tramp; Santa Clara; CA; 1836; Ireland; 248B

Norcross, Reuben; Clown; Camden; NJ; 1814; NJ; 642D

Norris, Thomas J.; Vagrant; Barnstable; MA; 1851; MA; 163B

Northcott, Wm.; Circus; Ohio; WV; 1855; KY; 448D

Norton, Andrew; Wanderer; MacOupin; IL; 1812; IL; 144A

Norton, John; Tramp; St. Louis; MO; 1824; Ireland; 442A

Norwood, Sarah E.; Business Medium; Suffolk; MA; 1847; NY; 500C

Nugent, Edmond; Tramp; Rock; WI; 1838; NY; 10A

Nuttall, Richard; Prof. cricket player; Merrimack; NH; 1845; England; 231C

O Day, John; Dead Ap 9 1879; Oswego; NY; 1839; Ireland; 456A

O Donald; Tramp; Erie; PA; 1861; America; 397A

Oakes, Annie; Fortune Teller; Suffolk; MA; 1845; ME; 323D

Oakes, Iowa; Dead; Dallas; IA; 1878; IA; 246C

Oakley, Obey; Gambler; Lake; CO; 1852; IL; 354A

Oberz, Jacob; Tramp on public street; St. Clair; IL; 1840; Prussia; 481D

O'Brien, Annie; Circus Performer; Erie; NY; 1849; OH; 24D

O'Brien, Fred'k; Circus Performer; Erie; NY; 1848; NY; 24D

O'Brien, Fred'k; Circus Performer; Erie; NY; 1866; OH; 24D

O'Brien, Jno. T.; Circus Performer; Erie; NY; 1856; NY; 24D

Obrien, John; Tramp; St. Louis; MO; 1857; MO; 511C

O'Brien, William; Circus Performer; Erie; NY; 1865; OH; 24D

O'Brien, William; Baseball player; Hampden; MA; 1858; MA; 5B

Obrine, M.F.; Circus; Ohio; WV; 1857; CT; 449A

Obrion, Pat; Tramp on public street; St. Clair; IL; 1861; OH; 483D

Obryon, John; Tramp on public street; St. Clair; IL; 1856; NY; 481D

Ochee, Peter; Tramp on public street; St. Clair; IL; 1843; IN; 482A

Ock, Tip; Gambler; Elko; NV; 1848; China; 55B
Ockery, William; Tramp Blacksmith; Huron; OH; 1859; MI; 84A
Oconnel, Dan; Tramp on public street; St. Clair; IL; 1838; Ireland;
    482B
Odell, C.W.; Circus; Ohio; WV; 1858; PA; 448D
O'Dell, Wm.; Circus; Ohio; WV; 1856; PA; 449B
Odonnel, Stephan; Tramp on public street; St. Clair; IL; 1835;
    Ireland; 483D
O'Donnell, Michael; Gambler; Deer Lodge; MT; 1850; PA; 109C
Ogilliam, Pat; Tramp on public street; St. Clair; IL; 1836; Ireland;
    483C
Ogle, William; Prof. Thief; New York; NY; 1850; IL; 266C
O'Grady, Patrick; Dead; Oswego; NY; 1859; NY; 464B
O'Han, James; Gambler; Franklin; KY; 1814; KY; 112A
Ok, Kim; Gambler; Yuba; CA; 1855; Canton; 426D
Olaughlin; Gambler; White Pine; NV; 1845; LA; 334B
Oldfield, Barbary; Old age dead; Beaver; PA; 1794; England;
    430C
Oldham, G.J.; Dead head; Chariton; MO; 1819; KY; 539B
Oleston, John; Servant - Tramp; Peoria; IL; 1859; IL; 409A
Oley, Henry; Gambler; Salt Lake; UT; 1838; VA; 86B
Oliver, Robert; Tramp; St. Johns; FL; 1860; England; 145B
Olivers, Andrew; Gambler; Shasta; CA; 1828; Chile; 49A
Olmstead, Chas.; Gambler; Franklin; OH; 1829; OH; 124C
Oltmanns, Fredericke; Dead; Adams; IL; 1869; ---; 467B
Oman, Maroni; Magician; Oneida; ID; 1845; IL; 328D
Omara, James; Ran away with Barnum Circus; Suffolk; MA;
    1868; MA; 56A
On, Gong; Gambler; Washoe; NV; 1839; China; 277A
On, Owe; Gambler; Idaho; ID; 1848; Canton; 166C
On, Quong; Gambler; Idaho; ID; 1845; Canton; 166C
On, Yee; Gambler; San Francisco; CA; 1828; Kwantung; 392B
One, Chung; Propietor Opium Den; Yuba; CA; 1820; Canton;
    444D
O'Neal, Jas.; Circus; Ohio; WV; 1849; NY; 449A
O'Neil, John; Tramp; New York; NY; 1830; Ireland; 581C
O'Neil, Mollie; Hurdy dancer; Deer Lodge; MT; 1852; New
    Brunswick, Canada; 136B

Oneill, Benjamin O.; Gambler; Marion; IN; 1843; NY; 139A

O'Neill, John; Tramp; Worcester; MA; 1804; VT; 154D

Oniel, Edward; Tramp; Utah; UT; 1857; Ireland; 186A

Ordmann, Margrethe; Dead; St. Louis; MO; 1879; MO; 360A

O'Reilly, Charles; Baseball player; Providence; RI; 1856; RI; 60A

Oretga, Louis; Gambler; Webb; TX; 1857; Mexico; 322C

Orgill, Vincent; Dead; Allegheny; PA; 1874; PA; 219B

Ormsby, Joseph; Saloon keeper pimp; Manistee; MI; 1853; MI; 55A

Ormsby, Sarah; Lays out dead; Philadelphia; PA; 1836; Scotland; 445D

O'Rorke, Josephine; Listed as dead; Harris; TX; 1880; TX; 20C

O'Rorke, May; Listed as dead; Harris; TX; 1880; TX; 20C

O'Rouke, James; Base ball player; Suffolk; MA; 1850; MA; 143A

O'Rouke, John; Base ball player; Suffolk; MA; 1852; MA; 143A

Orsi, Armando; Tramp; Ascension; LA; 1853; Italy; 75A

Ortegan, Juan; Gambler; Webb; TX; 1860; TX; 326D

Osborn, Miranda B.; Dead; Breckinridge; KY; 1860; KY; 108C

Osborne, Mary; Clairvoyant; New York; NY; 1816; NY; 45B

Overdurff, Jacob; Clock Repairer & Tramp; Monroe; OH; 1815; PA; 606D

Overton, Jane; Dead; Washington; IN; 1831; IN; 478C

Ow, Wah; Gambler; Elko; NV; 1838; China; 55A

Owen, George H.; Healer; Dearborn; IN; 1850; NY; 32D

Owens, Charles; Gambler; Grayson; TX; 1850; KY; 12D

Owens, J.W.; Phrenologist; Lemhi; ID; 1852; IN; 200A

Owens, John; Dead; Madison; TN; 1880; GA; 195B

Owens, O.W.; Gambler; Will; IL; 1852; PA; 159B

Oy, Lung; Gambler; Butte; CA; 1816; China; 262D

Oyster, John H.; Gambler; Sedgwick; KS; 1850; PA; 250A

Pa, My; Gambler; Boise; ID; 1845; China; 118B

Pace, Susan; Dead; Burleson; TX; 1852; MS; 38B

Padgit, William M.; Gambler; Martin; IN; 1853; IN; 343A

Palmer, A.R.; Gambler; Gunnison; CO; 1852; MO; 98B

Palmer, H.; Circus; Ohio; WV; 1846; NY; 449B

Palmer, Isaac S.; Phrenologist; Will; IL; 1819; England; 296A

Palmer, Nathan; Magnetic Physician; New York; NY; 1820; NY; 637A

Palmer, Robert; Pimp; Delta; MI; 1852; MI; 653A
Panaja, Joseph; Lazy; Baraga; MI; 1852; MI; 624C
Pandall, H.; Gambler; Sumner; KS; 1837; MO; 293B
Pannell, Joseph; Gambler; Madison; TN; 1835; TN; 382B
Panner, Fred C.; Gambler; Arapahoe; CO; 1852; CO; 306C
Pardim, Vincent; Magnetic Healer; Mahaska; IA; 1833; NJ; 349C
Paren, Nicoline; Vagrant; New York; NY; 1820; Italy; 320C
Parker, Ada; Tramp; Cerro Gordo; IA; 1857; MI; 294C
Parker, Adam; Gambler; Spokane; WA; 1838; Scotland; 47A
Parker, Alvin; Tramp; Kalamazoo; MI; 1851; NJ; 192D
Parker, B.C.; Gambler; Pima; AZ; 1832; MS; 319D
Parker, Emma; Mother dead - put out; Gates; NC; 1880; NC; 233B
Parker, F.B.; Gambler; Grant; NM; 1855; TX; 350B
Parker, John; Tramp; Kennebec; ME; 1857; New Brunswick; 77A
Parker, Joseph; Gambler; Deer Lodge; MT; 1829; NY; 121C
Parker, O.B.; Gambler; Garland; AR; 1857; MO; 113C
Parker, R.S.; Gambler; Sumner; KS; 1856; NJ; 282D
Parker, T.J.; Gambler; Nye; NV; 1856; NY; 12B
Parker, Theodore; Magician; New York; NY; 1853; NJ; 533A
Parker, Thomas; Gambler; Cuyahoga; OH; 1854; NY; 7A
Parks, Joseph H.; Theatre dancer; Suffolk; MA; 1856; MA; 232B
Parman, James; Astronomer; New York; NY; 1835; England;
        657D
Parsons, Jno. W.; Tramp; Boone; MO; 1843; MO; 97D
Parsons, John; Tramp; Jackson; MO; 1842; IA; 368B
Pascal, Emma; Dead; Lincoln; GA; 1878; GA; 130A
Pascal, Louridine; Dead; Lincoln; GA; 1876; GA; 130A
Pasco, Laura A.; Magnetic Physician; Hartford; CT; 1837; MA;
        11A
Patterson, F.W.; Tramp; Franklin; PA; 1840; MI; 548D
Patterson, John; Clown; Baltimore; MD; 1847; Ireland; 615D
Paul, Henry; Astronomer; Washington; D.C.; 1852; MA; 98D
Paul, Mary Ella; Dead; Indiana; PA; 1878; PA; 415A
Paull, Brother; Tramp; Montgomery; PA; 1843; NY; 315B
Payne, Aaron; Prisoner for att. rape; Randolph; GA; 1862; GA;
        118C
Payne, George; Travels with Circus; New York; NY; 1846;
        Brook., NY; 368A

Payne, John; Gambler; Cooke; TX; 1851; TX; 196D
Payne, John P.; Gambler; Garland; AR; 1835; KY; 112A
Peake, Jas. J.; Gambler; Jackson; MO; 1837; VA; 554C
Pearce, Grace; Fortune Teller; Johnston; NC; 1825; NC; 500B
Pedying, Mary; With London Circus; New York; NY; 1858; NY; 374B
Peil, William; Dead; Marion; IN; 1863; IN; 503A
Pelkey, Andrew; Tramp; Rockingham; NH; 1857; New Brunswick; 257D
Pellham, Chas. H.; Gambler; Lee; IA; 1846; KY; 177B
Pendle, Sarah E.; Dead; Cook; IL; 1880; IL; 130B
Pendleton, Theodore; Gambler; Wasco; OR; 1856; CA; 181B
Penn, G.H.; Quack Doctor; Halifax; VA; 1844; IN; 189A
Penn, George; Dead; Hardin; KY; 1820; VA; 345D
Pennell, Annie; Clairvoyant; Suffolk; MA; 1842; At Sea; 192C
Penney, E.C.; Circus; Ohio; WV; 1843; NY; 449A
Peoples, Wm.; Tramp; Crawford; OH; 1810; PA; 407A
Peper, Lydia; Dead; Philadelphia; PA; 1822; PA; 83C
Percell, Mildred; Fortune Teller; Tippecanoe; IN; 1826; KY; 275A
Pereirra, Joseph; Magician; New York; NY; 1838; Portugal; 357B
Perkins, Edward; Gambler; Sacramento; CA; 1815; VT; 41A
Perkins, Isaac; Deadbeat; Jasper; MO; 1824; TN; 408B
Perkins, John; Healer; Cumberland; ME; 1825; Wales; 130B
Perkins, Wm.; Gambler; Travis; TX; 1854; TX; 184A
Perony, Peter; Gambler; Randolph; IN; 1842; Italy; 153A
Perry, A.J.; Gambler; Johnson; IN; 1858; IN; 216D
Perry, Alex; Circus Rider; Yavapi; AZ; 1831; Barbadoes; 446A
Perry, Annie P.; Claravoyant Medium; Hillsborough; NH; 1840; NH; 2C
Perry, Calvin; Gambler; Colorado; TX; 1856; TX; 311A
Perry, David S.; Quack Doctor; Mercer; NJ; 1800; NJ; 293B
Perry, James; Tramp on public street; St. Clair; IL; 1857; MO; 481D
Perry, Thos. R.; Tramp; Jackson; MO; 1848; OH; 368B
Perry, Western H.; Dead; Nash; NC; 1845; NC; 547B
Perwitt, Henry; Gambler; St. Louis; MO; 1806; GA; 65B
Peter, Laura; Vagrant; Coweta; GA; 1860; GA; 569A
Peters, George; Tramp; Douglas; NE; 1859; Germany; 318B

114 Name; Occupation; County; State; Birth; Birth place; Page

Peters, John ; Works at base ball; St. Louis; MO; 1849; LA; 322C
Peters, John J.; Ball player; Providence; RI; 1847; WI; 375C
Peters, John P.; Baseball player; St. Louis; MO; 1849; LA; 434B
Petersen, Martha S.; Dead; Montcalm; MI; 1851; Denmark; 272A
Peterson, Christ; Tramp on public street; St. Clair; IL; 1853;
        Holstein; 482A
Peterson, Frederick; Tramp; New York; NY; 1854; Sweden; 581D
Peterson, N.E.; Prisoner Tramp; Bates; MO; 1852; Denmark;
        211B
Peterson, Peter; Vagrant; Fulton; NY; 1832; Denmark; 52A
Pethon, Ambrose; Gambler; Calcasieu; LA; 1853; LA; 505B
Petri, Peter; Vagrant; Buchanan; MO; 1841; MO; 41B
Pettebone, Claude J.; Gambler; Pike; MO; 1817; NY; 487B
Pettebone, Henry; Confirmed Drunkard; Pike; MO; 1830; KY;
        491A
Pettigo, Francis; Tramp; Vanderburgh; IN; 1860; IN; 310D
Pettigrew, Geo.; Thief; Westchester; NY; 1845; NY; 107D
Pettis, John H.; Gambler; Providence; RI; 1844; RI; 120B
Pew, Chun Yee; Opium Dealer; San Francisco; CA; 1852;
        Kwantung; 389B
Pew, Lee; Opium Dealer; San Francisco; CA; 1847; Kwantung;
        392B
Pfeiffer, Matilda; Dead; Adams; IL; 1879; IL; 470C
Pfirmann, Arthur; Dead; Adams; IL; 1874; IL; 468C
Pflaum, Lizzie; Dead; McHenry; IL; 1845; Baden; 16D
Pharazyn, Adolph; Professor magic; Philadelphia; PA; 1848;
        England; 611A
Phelan, James; Ball player; Shawnee; KS; 1855; PA; 178B
Philippson, Fred; Tramp; Pima; AZ; 1865; Prussia; 373C
Philips, Leander; Drunkard; Worcester; MA; 1830; NH; 200D
Phillips, Charles; Circus Agent; Fayette; IL; 1860; IN; 163B
Phillips, Charles; Deadbeat; Eau Claire; WI; 1853; PA; 354D
Phillips, Harriet B.; Dead; Penobscot; ME; ---; ---; 379D
Phillips, Joe; Gambler; Presidio; TX; 1850; VA; 86C
Phillips, Norton J.; Magnetic Physician; Lake; IN; 1833; NY;
        608B
Phillips, P.; Circus; Ohio; WV; 1853; Canada; 449A
Phipps, John; Gambler; Storey; NV; 1853; VT; 141D

Phubury, I.T.; Circus; Ohio; WV; 1841; NY; 448D
Phy., Ann; Spirit Medium; Philadelphia; PA; 1831; PA; 153C
Pi--, Mary E.; Dead; Marshall; TN; 1832; SC; 332D
Pickens, Catharine; Dead; Monroe; OH; 1812; PA; 457D
Pickering, Edward C.; Astronomer; Middlesex; MA; 1847; MA; 329A
Pickerl, Willis; Clog dancer; New York; NY; 1862; NY; 618D
Pickett; Dead; Autauga; AL; 1880; AL; 56D
Pickett, Austin; Dead; Autauga; AL; 1878; AL; 56D
Pickett, Betsy; Dead; Autauga; AL; 1874; AL; 56C
Pickett, Frances; Dead; Autauga; AL; 1875; AL; 56C
Pickett, Maria; Dead; Autauga; AL; 1815; AL; 66C
Pickford, George W.; Gambler; Merrimack; NH; 1840; NH; 201C
Pickford,Frederick; Agent for Circus; Union; NJ; 1829; England; 532A
Pidge, John S.; Gambler; Storey; NV; 1831; RI; 137C
Pierce, B.; Vagrant; Elko; NV; 1852; CT; 49C
Pierce, Charles; Ball player; Broome; NY; 1856; NY; 218D
Pierce, James; Ball player; Broome; NY; 1858; NY; 218D
Pierson, Jane Ann; Clairvoyant; San Francisco; CA; 1830; Scotland; 585A
Pike, Levi; Magician; Shelby; AL; 1820; NY; 242A
Pike, Lipman; Ball player; Albany; NY; 1848; NY; 304A
Pike, William C.; Phrenologist; Kane; IL; 1818; NY; 334B
Pine, James; Gambler; Jackson; MO; 1850; PA; 52D
Ping, Chu; Gambler; San Francisco; CA; 1838; Kwantung; 388D
Pishoun, M.R.; Circus; Ohio; WV; 1827; ME; 449A
Pits, Catharine; Wandering; Cannon; TN; 1854; TN; 539B
Pitts, Archie; Dead; Perry; AL; 1872; AL; 441D
Pleasant, Mary; Fortune Teller; Floyd; IN; 1845; N. Albany, IN; 283A
Pleasants, Fannie; Spiritualist; Norfolk; VA; 1835; VA; 370A
Ploner, Anthony; Dead; McHenry; IL; 1823; Bohemia; 27B
Plumer, Charles; Tramp; Polk; IA; 1860; MA; 237C
Plunket, John; Pimp; Delta; MI; 1850; WI; 653A
Plutano; Circus; Ohio; WV; 1820; Isle Barneo; 448D
Poath, Giles S.; Magician; New London; CT; 1826; CT; 245A
Poff, Charles; Tramp; Schuylkill; PA; 1861; PA; 138D

Poindexter, George; Gambler; San Miguel; NM; 1843; NM Terr.;
   308D
Pointer, Mary J.; Clairvoint & Fortune Teller; Marion; IN; 1823;
   Canada; 384C
Poldsky, Rudolph; Tramp on public street; St. Clair; IL; 1846;
   Prussia; 482B
Polkhorn, Thos.; Dead; Lafayette; MO; 1872; MO; 391A
Pomeroy, Thomas; Tramp; Jackson; MO; 1838; MA; 368B
Pomroy, Annie; Layer out of the dead; Philadelphia; PA; 1833;
   PA; 576C
Pon, Chin; Opium Dealer; Sierra; CA; 1825; Canton; 187D
Pong, Wow; Opium Den Keeper; Plumas; CA; 1835; China; 390A
Pool, Rebecca; Dead; Limestone; AL; 1815; SC; 356D
Poole, Chas.; Tramp; New York; NY; 1840; NY; 424B
Poole, George; Circus Traveler; New York; NY; 1848; England;
   298C
Poole, Mary; Tramp; New York; NY; 1842; NY; 424B
Poorman, Thomas; Baseball pitcher; Clinton; PA; 1858; PA; 662D
Porgen, Geo.; Gambler; Billings; Dak. Terr.; 1870; MI; 45B
Porgen, George; Gambler; Billings; Dak. Terr.; 1870; MI; 59A
Porter, Benjamin; Tramp; Miami; KS; 1858; VA; 512D
Porter, Charles H.; Gambler; Maverick; TX; 1849; PA; 48D
Porter, Henry; With Circus; St. Louis; MO; 1864; MS; 417B
Porter, John B.; Gambler; Tippecanoe; IN; 1849; IN; 342B
Porter, John B.; Phrenologist; Tompkins; NY; 1846; NY; 263A
Porter, Mary; Clairvoyant; New York; NY; 1835; NY; 168B
Porter, Oliver; Tramp; Miami; KS; 1861; VA; 512D
Portsmouth, Mary; Clairvoyant; Cook; IL; 1846; PA; 90C
Posey, Mary; Dead; Washington; OH; 1851; OH; 230A
Poteet, John; Pimp; Buchanan; MO; 1855; NE; 153C
Potts, David; Gambler; Deer Lodge; MT; 1842; PA; 135D
Potts, Floretta; Dead; Newton; IN; 1866; IN; 222B
Powalkej, Chas. R.; Astronomer; Northampton; PA; 1818;
   Germany; 262D
Powell, Cellia; Dead; Allegheny; PA; 1872; PA; 248C
Powell, Edward; Baseball pitcher; Oswego; NY; 1863; NY; 214A
Powell, John; Gambler; Deer Lodge; MT; 1835; NY; 127D
Powell, Martin; Plays baseball; Worcester; MA; 1856; MA; 576C

Powell, William; Medium; Philadelphia; PA; 1846; MD; 167A

Powelson, Elvirah; Dead; Lapeer; MI; 1821; NY; 221C

Powers, Henry K.; Tramp; Montgomery; IA; 1853; NY; 342C

Powers, Joseph; Gambler; Fulton; GA; 1856; SC; 236A

Powers, Lucy; Medium; Santa Cruz; CA; 1854; Greece; 426B

Powers, Richard; Tramp; New York; NY; 1843; Ireland; 581D

Powers, Wm.; Circus; Ohio; WV; 1852; NY; 448D

Poydras, Eley; Tramp; W. Baton Rouge; LA; 1845; LA; 346A

Prask, E. Johanna; Dead; Bristol; MA; 1880; MA; 407C

Prater, Lorangy; Tramp; Menifee; KY; 1830; KY; 658D

Pratt, William; Gambler; Amador; CA; 1832; PA; 116A

Prentiss, Samuel H.; Clairvoyant; Worcester; MA; 1842; MA;
    329D

Pressly, Joseph; Magnetic Physician; Lucas; IA; 1843; IN; 468A

Preston, N.; Gambler; Deer Lodge; MT; 1845; England; 126C

Preston, Sarah J.; Fortune Teller; Kalamazoo; MI; 1849; NY;
    200D

Price, ---; Baseball player; Hamilton; OH; 1852; OH; 507A

Price, Billy; Clown; Juneau; WI; 1840; NY; 451C

Price, C.; Circus; Ohio; WV; 1853; NY; 448D

Price, Perry; Tramp; Warren; IN; 1864; IN; 27C

Price, Wm.; Dead; St. Louis; MO; 1878; MO; 496B

Priest, Edward; Tramp; Dakota; NE; 1858; NE ; 317A

Prior, Phil; Gambler; Muscogee; GA; 1824; GA; 667A

Pritchard, William; Vagrant; Montgomery; PA; 1815; PA; 223A

Pritchett, C.W.; Astronomer; Howard; MO; 1823; VA; 381D

Pritchett, Henry S.; Astronomer; Howard; MO; 1857; MO; 381D

Proctor, John; Vagrant; Lincoln; NC; 1852; NC; 358C

Proctor, John; Gambler; Burleigh; Dak. Terr.; 1843; IN; 214C

Pryor, John; Tramp; Davidson; TN; 1861; TN; 111C

Pryor, L.K.; Gambler; Muscogee; GA; 1853; GA; 562B

Pugh, John; Tramp on public street; St. Clair; IL; 1856; MO; 482A

Pulse, Craven; Deadbeat; Macon; MO; 1853; IL; 423D

Pulsepher, Wm.; Gambler; Billings; Dak. Terr.; 1865; MI; 45B

Pulsipher, Wm.; Gambler; Billings; Dak. Terr.; 1865; MI; 59A

Puly, Julie; Dead; Cook; IL; 1835; ---; 146A

Purcell, John; Works in Circus; Philadelphia; PA; 1864; PA; 263C

Purdy, C.B.; Gambler; Pinal; AZ; 1826; VT; 398C

Name; Occupation; County; State; Birth; Birth place; Page

Purifoy, Epr; Dead; Wilcox; AL; 1879; AL; 208A

Purtom, Francis M.; Gambler; Amador; CA; 1832; TN; 116A

Purzell, William; Tramp on public street; St. Clair; IL; 1852; WI; 481D

Qinn, Thomas; Tramp on public street; St. Clair; IL; 1838; NY; 481D

Qoneng; Propietor Opium Den; Plumas; CA; 1832; China; 395D

Quen, Wong; Fortune Teller; San Francisco; CA; 1835; Sun Ning; 429B

Quick, Frank; Dead; Orange; NY; 1880; NY; 116C

Quick, Nellie; Dead; Ulster; NY; 1878; NY; 101C

Quigley, James; Circus Showman; Franklin; OH; 1864; OH; 399C

Quigley, John; Circus Performer; Franklin; OH; 1862; OH; 399C

Quigley, Michael; Vagrant; New York; NY; 1866; NY; 622A

Quigly, Patrick; Tramp; Cheshire; NH; 1840; Ireland; 287B

Quin, Gee; Gambler; Butte; CA; 1832; China; 262D

Quintana, Martin; Gambler; Santa Fe; NM; 1833; NM Terr.; 60A

Quon, Ou; Opium Seller; Sacramento; CA; 1842; China; 4C

Quong, Ghee; Gambler; Idaho; ID; 1845; China; 184D

Quong, Loo; Gambler, Lottery, Opium Den; Plumas; CA; 1847; China; 390A

Racoff, Elizabeth; Dead; Northumberland; PA; 1810; Spain; 538C

Raescher, Henry; Tramp on public street; St. Clair; IL; 1850; Saxonia; 482A

Ragan, Patrick; Tramp; Bourbon; KS; 1818; Ireland; 244C

Ragsdale, John H.; Dead; Tarrant; TX; 1869; TN; 131B

Rahn, Elizabeth; Dead; Brown; WI; 1879; WI; 300D

Raisnor, James B.; Gambler; Owsley; KY; 1858; KY; 302B

Ralpenbach, J.B.; General Tramp; Chariton; MO; 1825; Baden; 408C

Ramon, E. Alberto; Gambler; Grant; NM; 1855; Sonora; 343C

Ramos, Guillermo; Tramp; Santa Clara; CA; 1867; CA; 356B

Ramos, Jose; Tramp; Santa Clara; CA; 1827; Chile; 356B

Ramsey, Charles; Thief; Westchester; NY; 1845; Nova Scotia; 95C

Randolph, Joseph S.; Circus Rider; New York; NY; 1840; MA; 49B

Randolph, Julia I.; Medium; Suffolk; MA; 1859; India; 454D

Rankin, Antonia; Gambling Saloon; Iberia; LA; 1840; LA; 434C

Rankin, Cary; Dead; Clark; KY; 1880; KY; 415D

Rasmussen, T.; Tramp; Douglas; NE; 1851; IN; 277B

Ratliff, Polly; Dead; Blount; AL; 1816; GA; 458B

Ratzan, L.; Circus; Ohio; WV; 1847; IL; 449B

Rawland, W.F.; Gambler; Arapahoe; CO; 1835; MO; 98D

Rawlston, Joe; Tramp on public street; St. Clair; IL; 1825; OH; 482B

Ray, Daniel; Tramp on public street; St. Clair; IL; 1855; OH; 483C

Ray, James; Tramp on public street; St. Clair; IL; 1850; NY; 483C

Ray, Jimie; Dead; Bedford; TN; 1825; TN; 166D

Ray, Joseph; Gambler; Storey; NV; 1840; MD; 141D

Ray, Mary E.; Keeps house dead; Johnson; MO; 1838; MO; 511B

Ray, Nancy; Dead; La Fayette; WI; 1832; PA; 212D

Ray, Robert; Gambler; St. Louis; MO; 1842; VA; 593A

Ray, William; Gambler; Deer Lodge; MT; 1842; MO; 127D

Rayen, Sam; Tramp on public street; St. Clair; IL; 1858; NY; 484A

Raymer, John; Tramp; Mills; IA; 1867; KS; 277C

Raymond, James K.; Wanderer; Kent; DE; 1845; DE; 50D

Raynolds, Charles de Forest; Travels with Circus; New Haven; CT; 1860; CT; 489C

Rayon, John; Tramp on public street; St. Clair; IL; 1851; CT; 484A

Reagan, Lewis; Gambler; Custer; CO; 1855; OH; 331D

Ream, Amanda; Spiritual Medium; Baltimore; MD; 1825; OH; 561C

Reams, Wm. F.; Gambler; Allegheny; PA; 1837; PA; 354B

Rean, S.B.; Tramp; Hennepin; MN; 1817; ---; 272A

Rebenack, Chas.; Tramp on public street; St. Clair; IL; 1831; Saxonia; 483C

Reddens, A.; Gambler; Davidson; TN; 1862; TN; 118D

Reddick, Charles; Gambler; Davidson; TN; 1834; TN; 145B

Reddick, James; Gambler; Grayson; TX; 1846; TN; 174C

Redding, Jane F.; Dead; Blair; PA; 1897; PA; 86D

Reddy, Norman John; Dead; Hudson; NJ; 1879; NJ; 276C

Name; Occupation; County; State; Birth; Birth place; Page

Redmeyer, Jacob; Tramp on public street; St. Clair; IL; 1826;
    Bavaria; 481D
Reed, Addie; Dead; Clark; KY; 1879; KY; 427C
Reed, Anna E.; Clairvoyant; New York; NY; 1829; CT; 465B
Reed, Buenvista; Layer out of the dead; Philadelphia; PA; 1843;
    PA; 418D
Reed, Charles; Gambler; Saratoga; NY; 1830; NY; 512D
Reed, Emma; Tramp; Daviess; KY; 1870; TN; 259D
Reed, Gabriel; Spiritualist Quack Doctor; Jefferson; KS; 1836;
    KY; 164A
Reed, Kate; Tramp; Daviess; KY; 1865; TN; 259D
Reed, Maggie; Tramp; Daviess; KY; 1867; TN; 259D
Reed, Mandy; Tramp; Daviess; KY; 1862; TN; 259D
Reed, Ophelia; Spiritualist Quack Doctor; Jefferson; KS; 1838;
    KY; 164A
Reed, Silia M.; Dead; San Francisco; CA; 1875; ---; 231B
Reed, Wilson; Gambler; Oglethorpe; GA; 1863; GA; 246D
Reese, Guido; Vagrant; Morgan; IN; 1866; IN; 143B
Reese, John; Tramp; Erie; NY; 1814; Ireland; 31D
Reeseman, Ida; Dead; Adair; MO; 1877; MO; 91A
Reetz, Augustus; Tramp; Washington; MN; 1855; Prussia; 309B
Reeves, Laomi; Clairvoyant; Essex; NJ; 1830; NJ; 257A
Reeves, Pyndapp; Dead - kept house; Ballard; KY; 1827; KY;
    400D
Reichert, Carolina; Dead; Brown; WI; 1860; WI; 301B
Reid, John; Tramp; Davidson; TN; 1860; TN; 111D
Reiley, Michael; Tramp; New York; NY; 1836; Ireland; 581C
Reiley, Thomas; Dead; Essex; NJ; 1857; NJ; 275D
Reilly, Pat; Tramp; Hudson; NJ; 1820; Ireland; 294C
Reiser, Anna; Patient Fortune Teller; Allegheny; PA; 1813;
    Switzerland; 477A
Reisley, Adolph; Circus Rider; New York; NY; 1845; NY; 354A
Renaud, May; Clairvoyant; Essex; NJ; 1844; NJ; 44B
Renner, Edward; Circus Laborer; New York; NY; 1845; NY;
    118B
Renniski, Antone; Dead (Dip); St. Joseph; IN; 1872; IN; 428A
Renniski, Helena; Dead (Dip); St. Joseph; IN; 1876; IN; 428A
Renniski, Helena; Dead; St. Joseph; IN; 1876; IN; 428A

Renniski, Joseph; Dead; St. Joseph; IN; 1874; IN; 428A

Reno, William; Tramp; Morton; Dak. Terr.; 1853; America; 46A

Rentfrow, Annie; Circus Rider; Kent; MI; 1847; England; 366D

Rentfrow, Jasper N.; Circus Clown; Kent; MI; 1850; IN; 366C

Retter, E.J.; Clairvoyant; Cook; IL; 1845; Jamaica; 309D

Reuben, Joseph; Gambler; Arapahoe; CO; 1862; Ireland; 98D

Reuschach, Lewis; Tramp; Marion; IN; 1825; Wurttemberg; 538A

Revore, Joseph; Wanderer over the earth; Clermont; OH; 1777; MI; 17A

Rhoder, James; Magnetic Physician; Guthrie; IA; 1840; IA; 79A

Rhodes, Wm.; Works in Gambling House; Jackson; MO; 1848; MO; 264B

Rhuling, John; Gambler; Storey; NV; 1825; Baden; 138B

Rice, John; Travelwilt Circus; Philadelphia; PA; 1847; PA; 351B

Rice, Tonzo; Dead; Greene; AL; 1830; Africa; 53B

Rich, Joseph C.; Gambler; Onondaga; NY; 1842; CT; 394A

Richard, Herman; Tramp; Hennepin; MN; 1850; ---; 272A

Richards, Clara E.; Dead; Sandusky; OH; 1873; OH; 157D

Richards, E. Carry; Dead; Washington; AR; 1877; IL; 564B

Richards, Franklin; Gambler; Sedgwick; KS; 1844; PA; 284C

Richards, R.; Gambler; Orleans; LA; 1838; IN; 42D

Richards, Reese; Tramp; Tama; IA; 1817; PA; 605A

Richards, Wm.; Circus; Ohio; WV; 1858; NY; 448D

Richardson, Burt; Circus Performer; Marion; IN; 1853; IN; 759A

Richardson, George; Gambler; Arapahoe; CO; 1851; MO; 98D

Richardson, Sarah; Since dead; Camden; GA; 1820; GA; 474A

Richardson, Tom; Gambler; Robertson; TX; 1860; TX; 560B

Richeson, Joshua; Lazy Laborer; Tyler; WV; 1833; OH; 99B

Richmond, ---; Baseball player; Baltimore; MD; 1854; PA; 520D

Richmond, Geo.; Tramp; Lancaster; NE; 1854; OH; 173A

Richter, Elisa; Dead; Milwaukee; WI; 1879; WI; 239B

Richter, Elizabeth; Dead; Adams; IL; 1880; IL; 483A

Riddle, Dock; Gambler; Dubuque; IA; 1820; OH; 229A

Riddle, Lizzie; Dead; Allegheny; PA; 1879; PA; 254C

Riechman, Frederick; Dead; Dubuque; IA; 1880; IA; 344B

Riely, James; Astrologer; Dutchess; NY; 1825; NY; 143A

Rienhart, Peper; Tramp; Hanson; Dak. Terr.; 1839; PA; 56C

Riggs, William; Gambler; Albany; NY; 1855; NY; 364C

Right, Dilsey; Tramp; W. Baton Rouge; LA; 1859; LA; 374A

Rigney, J.A.; Deadbeat; Monroe; KY; 1862; TN; 307A

Riley, Edward; Gypsy; Bradford; PA; 1848; Ireland; 61B

Riley, Frank; Phrenologist; Allegheny; PA; 1849; PA; 331C

Riley, Gillies; Tramp; Jackson; AR; 1848; KY; 529C

Riley, Mary; Tramp; Daviess; KY; 1831; TN; 259D

Riley, Michel; Gypsy; Bradford; PA; 1856; England; 61B

Riley, Mike; Tramp; Lapeer; MI; 1833; Ireland; 315B

Riley, Patrick; Gypsy; Bradford; PA; 1854; England; 61B

Riley, Wm.; Circus; Ohio; WV; 1859; NY; 449A

Rine, Mary; Vagrant; St. Louis; MO; 1840; Ireland; 467B

Ritter, Mck. William; Astronomer; Washington; D.C.; 1847; PA; 98D

Rivera, Masian; Gambler; Dona Ana; NM; 1830; Chihuahua; 288C

Roach, Gideon M.; Farmer and Phrenologist; Stark; OH; 1837; OH; 303D

Roache, John; Tramp; Suffolk; MA; 1849; MA; 398A

Roadman, Thomas; Travels with Circus; Washtenaw; MI; 1843; TN; 412B

Robb, Isabilla; Dead; Fairfield; SC; 1873; SC; 93D

Robberts, Rachel; Dead; Clay; KY; 1879; KY; 562C

Robbins, Burr; Owns Circus; Rock; WI; 1837; NY; 225C

Robbins, Elizabeth; With the Circus; Rock; WI; 1843; OH; 225C

Roberson, William; Tramp; Person; NC; 1805; NC; 218A

Roberts, Charles; Gambler; Presidio; TX; 1830; France; 88D

Roberts, Charles; Tramp on public street; St. Clair; IL; 1854; PA; 482B

Roberts, Ed; Tramp; Delaware; OH; 1855; PA; 374A

Roberts, Olive; Fortune Teller; Dodge; GA; 1810; GA; 508D

Roberts, Sarah; Layer out of the dead; Philadelphia; PA; 1835; PA; 30D

Roberts, Seth; Dancer; Strafford; NH; 1840; NH; 51A

Robertson, Benjamin F.; Dead; Rutherford; NC; 1874; NC; 575D

Robertson, Chas.; Tramp on public street; St. Clair; IL; 1837; IN; 483C

Robins, A.J.; Local Tramp; Henry; TN; 1843; TN; 203D

Robinson, Alexander; Circus Proprietor; Oneida; NY; 1817; NY; 18D

Robinson, Charles; Ball player; Providence; RI; 1857; RI; 512D

Robinson, Fred; Gambler; Deer Lodge; MT; 1858; Washington, D.C.; 125C

Robinson, James; Thief; Westchester; NY; 1861; NY; 94B

Robinson, Jane; Magnetic Doctor; New York; NY; 1840; Ireland; 602A

Robinson, John; Tramp on public street; St. Clair; IL; 1846; England; 483D

Robinson, Joseph; Tramp; Lorain; OH; 1856; NH; 401C

Robinson, Nathan; Vagrant; Winnebago; WI; 1831; ---; 163A

Robinson, T.; Circus; Ohio; WV; 1853; IL; 448D

Robinson, William; Vagrant; New York; NY; 1867; Ireland; 414D

Robinson, William; Base ballist; Middlesex; MA; 1860; Canada; 308A

Robledo, Manuel; Gambler; Santa Fe; NM; 1848; NM Terr.; 63D

Robmero, Ramon; Gambler; Bernalillo; NM; 1845; NM Terr.; 3A

Robson, Putnam; Gambler; Napa; CA; 1836; NY; 384C

Roche, A.; Clown; St. Louis; MO; 1856; PA; 279C

Roche, Thomas; Dead; Allegheny; PA; 1878; PA; 220D

Rockhold, Charles; Loafer & Gambler; Butler; OH; 1860; OH; 223B

Rockwell, William; Base ballist; Warren; IL; 1856; IL; 321D

Rode, Daniel; Tramp on public street; St. Clair; IL; 1855; Canada; 483D

Roderegas, Antonio; Dead keeping house; Caldwell; TX; 1851; Mexico; 195B

Rodger, West; Tramp on public street; St. Clair; IL; 1856; PA; 483C

Rodgers, James; Dead; Perry; IL; 1880; IL; 41A

Rodgers, Rebecca; Dead; Perry; IL; 1851; IL; 41A

Rodisch, Mathias; Laborer; dead; St. Louis; MO; 1830; Bohemia; 361C

Rogers, Charles J.; Retired Circus Proprietor; Philadelphia; PA; 1817; PA; 411B

Rogers, John; Dead; Schuylkill; PA; 1817; ---; 71B

Rogers, John W.; Gambler; Montgomery; IA; 1858; MI; 321A

Rogers, Thomas W.; Dead; Northumberland; PA; 1872; PA; 537A
Rogers, William A.; Astronomer; Middlesex; MA; 1833; CT;
    329A
Rohan, John; Base ball; Alameda; CA; 1860; MA; 231A
Roland, Ellen; Tramp; Barbour; AL; 1835; AL; 278D
Rolingson, Samuel; Gambler; Lawrence; Dak. Terr.; 1836; OH;
    237B
Rolla, August; Tramp on public street; St. Clair; IL; 1834; Prussia;
    481D
Rolph, Edward; Vagabond; Chautauqua; NY; 1851; NY; 343B
Rolves, Caroline; Dead; Dubuque; IA; 1879; IA; 344A
Romero, Juan; Pimp; Bernalillo; NM; 1864; NM Terr.; 7B
Rompf, Jacob; Dead; Onondaga; NY; 1835; ---; 274C
Ronnels, James; Tramp on public street; St. Clair; IL; 1823; NY;
    483D
Rooney, Patrick; Tramp; New York; NY; 1855; NY; 431C
Root, Esther A.; Medical Medium; Hartford; CT; 1823; CT; 335B
Rosalio, Garcia; Gambler; Mohave; AZ; 1844; Mexico; 128B
Rosborough, Thomas; Dead; Fairfield; SC; 1878; SC; 185A
Rose, Wm.; Circus; Ohio; WV; 1850; NY; 449A
Rosenbaum, Frederic; Phrenologist; Hardin; OH; 1845; Prussia;
    152B
Rosenbaum, Isaac; Gambler; Franklin; OH; 1845; PA; 158B
Rosenthal, Max.; Wandering Jew; Erie; NY; 1813;
    Prussia/Tomerania; 326A
Ross, Hannah B.; Clairvoyant Physician; Providence; RI; 1847;
    RI; 76B
Ross, Mary; Clairvoyant; Androscoggin; ME; 1836; ME; 78C
Ross, Matthew; Dead; Conway; AR; 1863; AR; 311B
Rotchers, John; Tramp on public street; St. Clair; IL; 1798; NC;
    483C
Roth, Anna M.; Fortune Teller; Hamilton; OH; 1832; Bavaria;
    116A
Roth, John; Circus Performer; Franklin; OH; 1862; OH; 292C
Rothbun, Oscar; Tramp; Kalamazoo; MI; 1863; MI; 192D
Rourke, Agnes; Dead; Dubuque; IA; 1880; IA; 342B
Rowe, Elvira; Tramp; Elliott; KY; 1853; KY; 648C

Name; Occupation; County; State; Birth; Birth place; Page 125

Roxburg, Laura; Magnetic Physician; New Castle; DE; 1863; DE; 135A
Royally, James H.; Gambler; Campbell; VA; 1849; VA; 375A
Royle, James; Tramp on public street; St. Clair; IL; 1858; NY; 482A
Rueben, Anna; Dead; Grundy; IL; 1844; SC; 323C
Ruff, Ellen; Dead; Fairfield; SC; 1858; SC; 92B
Rumph, John; Tramp; Hanson; Dak. Terr.; 1851; IL; 56C
Runnells, Brunnells; Circus Rider; New York; NY; 1830; GA; 24D
Runnels, William A.; Travels with Circus; Wayne; IN; 1846; IN; 315C
Ruoff, Johanna; Hskpr & Fortune Teller; Hamilton; OH; 1824; Baden; 356B
Rupert; Dead; Indiana; PA; 1880; PA; 415B
Rusch, James; Tramp on public street; St. Clair; IL; 1850; Ny; 483C
Rushton, Thomas; Drunkard & Bum; Philadelphia; PA; 1846; England; 615A
Russel, Albert; Tramp; Buchanan; MO; 1848; MO; 41A
Russel, William; Gambler; Fremont; IA; 1857; KS; 132B
Russell, Annie; Fortune Teller; Monroe; NY; 1857; NY; 68A
Russell, Asher; Dead; Essex; NJ; 1830; NY; 195C
Russell, Fred P.; Clog dancer; Cayuga; NY; 1858; MA; 398D
Russell, James W.; Gambler; Deer Lodge; MT; 1852; NY; 135D
Russell, Thomas; Off with Circus; Rock; WI; 1855; WI; 212B
Ruth, Fredrick; Dead; Sandusky; OH; 1878; OH; 170B
Rutherford, Ella; Dead; Lake; CO; ---; CO; 475C
Rutherford, Frank; Dead; St. Joseph; IN; 1856; IN; 417C
Rutlege, Ann; Tramp; Gaston; NC; 1860; NC; 107D
Ryan, Edward; Magician; Bristol; MA; 1855; England; 27B
Ryan, Ellen; Dead; New York; NY; 1832; Ireland; 283A
Ryan, James; Tramp; Charleston; SC; 1829; SC ; 151B
Ryan, James; Tramp; Hennepin; MN; 1835; ---; 272A
Ryan, John; Tramp; Polk; IA; 1854; MO; 237C
Ryan, Julia; Dead; Lapeer; MI; 1842; MI; 219C
Ryan, William; Vagrant; Davidson; TN; 1860; TN; 20D
Ryder, Arthur; Circus Tumbler; Steuben; NY; 1857; NY; 128D

Name; Occupation; County; State; Birth; Birth place; Page

Ryder, Frank; Gambler; Calcasieu; LA; 1828; PA; 505B
Ryland, George; Circus Traveller; Yavapi; AZ; 1827; MO; 439D
Ryon, John; Tramp; Stephenson; IL; 1854; IL; 63B
Safford, Charles; Gambler; Lake; CO; 1840; NY; 351C
Sages, Benjamin; Dead; Orleans; LA; 1831; Baden; 106D
Salinas, Antonio; Gambler; Bexar; TX; 1859; TX; 3A
Sallaldy, Alonso; Occultist; Davis; IA; 1818; OH; 76C
Salls, Carlos; Gambler; San Miguel; NM; 1847; TX; 412D
Sally, James; Tramp; Stephenson; IL; 1859; MA; 63A
Sally, Wm.; Tramp; Hennepin; MN; 1842; MN; 272A
Salter, John; Dead; Wilcox; AL; 1878; AL; 190B
Salter, Louisa; Dead; Orange; NY; 1852; NY; 118C
Sam, Chung; Gambler; Butte; CA; 1830; China; 262C
Sam, Ding; Gambler; Madison; MT; 1848; China; 386B
Sam, Foo Lee; Gambler; San Francisco; CA; 1842; Kwantung;
    388D
Sam, Hing; Opium Dealer; Sierra; CA; 1835; Canton; 187D
Sam, Hing; Gambler; Washoe; NV; 1854; China; 277A
Sam, Hop; Gambler; Ormsby; NV; 1844; China; 69A
Sam, Kee; Gambler; Yuba; CA; 1846; Canton; 429A
Sam, Lee; Gambler; Grant; OR; 1845; China; 36C
Sam, Qong; Gambler; Nevada; CA; 1841; China; 175A
Sambird, Mary; Medium; Philadelphia; PA; 1816; VA; 119A
Samoro, Francisco; Deadbeat; Bernalillo; NM; 1844; NM terr.; 5A
San Meguil, Gued.; Gambler; Webb; TX; 1834; Mexico; 322D
San, Tan; Opium Dealer; San Francisco; CA; 1845; China; 441B
Sanders, Eda; Vagrancy; Wilkes; NC; 1851; NC; 121D
Sanders, J.; Circus Performer; Tarrant; TX; ---; ---; 3A
Sandifer; Dead; Crawford; GA; 1880; GA; 656A
Sandoz, Stella; Dead head; St. Landry; LA; 1805; LA; 335D
Sands, Richard; Clog dancer; New York; NY; 1842; England;
    143B
Sanford, Ada E.; Clairvoyant; Bourbon; KS; 1838; ME; 193D
Sang, Toi; Gambler; Eureka; NV; 1851; China; 206D
Sang, Wing; Gambler; Eureka; NV; 1836; China; 213B
Sannick, Ellen; Magnetic Healer; Chemung; NY; 1844; NY; 321B
Santee, Charles; Drunkard; Madison; NY; 1845; NY; 63D
Santom, W.H.; Agt. for Circus; Allegheny; PA; 1835; OH; 107D

Sapeda, Pedro; Circus Actor; Atascosa; TX; 1858; Mexico; 322A

Sappington, Frank; Tramp; Washington; MS; 1855; MS; 97B

Sargent, James; Dead; Grundy; IL; 1880; IL; 317C

Sassaman, Jane; Attends to the dead; Berks; PA; 1824; PA; 314B

Saunders; Dead; Adams; IL; ---; IL; 471A

Saunders, Leonadas; Dead; Crawford; GA; 1879; GA; 666C

Savory, Henry; Tramp; Nassau; FL; 1857; Nova Scotia; 332C

Sawtell, Alexandria; Clairvoyant Physician; Worcester; MA;
    1825; Scotland; 529D

Sawyer, Carrie; Spiritualist Medium; San Francisco; CA; 1845;
    MI; 256C

Say, Louis; Base ballist; Baltimore; MD; 1854; MD; 3B

Say, Mon; Gambler; Trinity; CA; 1840; China; 570D

Say, Oo Shone; Gambler; Butte; CA; 1829; China; 148B

Scanlon, John; Teaches boxing; Middlesex; MA; 1856; MA; 256A

Schaeberle, John M.; Astronomer; Washtenaw; MI; 1853;
    Wurttemberg; 38D

Schaefer, John; Tramp on public street; St. Clair; IL; 1847;
    Wurtemburg; 482A

Schaepaly, I.; Dead; Orleans; LA; 1880; LA; 106C

Schafer, Eddie; Traveling with Circus; Kenton; KY; 1860; KY;
    279D

Schafer, J.J.; Gambler; Storey; NV; 1837; Wutenburg; 163C

Schaller, Fred; Travels with Circus; Adams; IL; 1859; IL; 544C

Schardt, Bertha; Fortune Teller; St. Louis; MO; 1853; MO; 229D

Scherrer, Juliana; Fortune Teller; St. Charles; MO; 1822; Bavaria;
    7B

Schieffal, Angus; Tramp on public street; St. Clair; IL; 1835;
    Prussia; 483D

Schlesinger, Louis; Spiritual Medium; Los Angeles; CA; 1835;
    England; 292A

Schmidt, Gustave; Dead; Redwood; MN; 1877; MN; 54A

Schmidt, Louisa; Dead; Redwood; MN; 1874; MN; 54A

Schmitt, Henry; Tramp on public street; St. Clair; IL; 1861;
    Bavaria; 482A

Schnebly, Henry; Dead; Peoria; IL; 1880; IL; 400A

Schneider, John; Tramp on public street; St. Clair; IL; 1830;
    Prussia; 482B

Schoene, Jacob; Tramp on public street; St. Clair; IL; 1845; Switzerland; 482A

Schoenfeldt, Anna; Fortune Teller; Cook; IL; 1831; Poland; 404C

Schoenknecht, Franz; Tramp on public street; St. Clair; IL; 1845; Saxonia; 482A

Scholtz, Albert; Tramp; Mercer; NJ; 1825; Germany; 10D

Schraeder, John; Tramp on public street; St. Clair; IL; 1853; Luxemburg; 482B

Schuhmann, Ths.; Tramp on public street; St. Clair; IL; 1859; Prussia; 483D

Schulz, John; Tramp on public street; St. Clair; IL; 1835; Prussia; 482A

Schulz, William; Tramp on public street; St. Clair; IL; 1825; Prussia; 482B

Schuttie, John; Dead; Milwaukee; WI; 1880; Milwaukee, WI; 286A

Schuttie, Willie; Dead; Milwaukee; WI; 1879; Milwaukee, WI; 286A

Schuzberg, Henry; Tramp on public street; St. Clair; IL; 1837; Prussia; 481D

Schwambach, John; "To lazy to work"; Suffolk; NY; 1827; Germany; 304D

Schwartz, Edward; Tramp; New York; NY; 1830; Germany; 581C

Scott, Gen. Winfield; Tramp; Hopkins; KY; 1825; KY; 379A

Scott, John; Doctor - dead; Madison; KY; 1811; KY; 350B

Scott, Moses B.; Ex Circus Man; Rice; MN; 1844; NY; 383B

Scott, O.H.P.; Agent of Circus; Washington; OH; 1839; OH; 412B

Scott, Sam; Pimp; Eau Claire; WI; 1845; NY; 481B

Scott, Susamah; Dead; Hudson; NJ; 1879; NJ; 272D

Scott, W.D.; Medium; Davidson; TN; 1815; VA; 135A

Scudder, Ralph; Gambler; Atchison; KS; 1840; OH; 309D

Scudder, Ralph; Gambler; Atchison; KS; 1850; OH; 309D

Seaborough, Mark; Gambler; Orleans; LA; 1855; KY; 51A

Seaman, Harbidge; Wizard; New York; NY; 1833; Prussia; 318C

Search, George D.; Spiritual Medium; Sedgwick; KS; 1854; MA; 348B

Searle, Arthur; Astronomer; Middlesex; MA; 1838; England; 332D

Searle, E.B.; Gambler; Pima; AZ; 1839; KY; 330D

Sebastian, Oskar; Tramp on public street; St. Clair; IL; 1865; IL; 481D

Sebastian, Romeo; Circus Rider; Hudson; NJ; 1856; NY; 121C

Sedalie, Charles; Theft; Parker; TX; 1848; KY; 321D

See, Eliza; Dead; Republic; KS; 1806; NY; 70D

See, Fung; Fortune Teller; Sacramento; CA; 1820; China; 11B

See, Joseph B.; Dead; Republic; KS; 1791; NY; 70D

See, Ton; Gambler; Boise; ID; 1845; China; 118A

Seibert, Henry W.; Dead; Sandusky; OH; 1880; OH; 158A

Sek, Sieu Lor; Gambler; San Francisco; CA; 1837; Kwantung; 392B

Sellers, Eliza; Medium; Suffolk; MA; 1793; MA; 157D

Semon, Harry; Agt. for Circus; Washington; D.C.; 1862; Washington, D.C.; 260B

Semon, Simen; Agt. for Circus; Washington; D.C.; 1845; NY; 260B

Sen, Linn; Keeps Gambling House; Calaveras; CA; 1838; China; 345B

Sensenbrenner, Barbara; Fortune Teller; St. Louis; MO; 1839; Prussia; 33A

Sepastapol, Rob't; Gambler; Sacramento; CA; 1835; KY; 52D

Seville, Edward; Tramp; Lancaster; NE; 1853; Ireland; 173A

Sew, Tan Yip; Opium Dealer; San Francisco; CA; 1844; Kwantung; 389B

Sexton, Mathew; Tramp; New York; NY; 1822; Ireland; 581D

Seymour, M.; Fortune Teller; New York; NY; 1830; Ireland; 69C

Shade, Thos. B.; Gambler; Montgomery; OH; 1843; OH; 346B

Shafer, S.C.; Tramp; Lancaster; NE; 1852; OH; 173A

Shandley, Thomas; Machinist dead; New York; NY; 1851; Ireland; 402A

Shank, Abraham; Tramp; Hampshire; WV; 1844; VA; 464D

Shanley, Frank; Gambler; Ohio; WV; 1839; OH; 232D

Shannon, Harry; Foot racer; Custer; CO; 1844; MO; 330B

Sharp, A.A.; Gambler; Estill; KY; 1848; KY; 23B

Sharp, Bessie; Gypsies; Fairfield; OH; 1878; OH; 92B

Sharp, Fred; Gambler; Oswego; NY; 1844; NY; 220C

Sharp, John; Gypsies; Fairfield; OH; 1875; OH; 92B

130 Name; Occupation; County; State; Birth; Birth place; Page

Sharp, Liza; Gypsies Fortune Teller & Trader; Fairfield; OH;
    1857; NC; 92B
Sharp, Manerva; Gypsies; Fairfield; OH; 1877; KY; 92B
Sharp, N.W.; Gambler; Arapahoe; CO; 1857; MO; 98D
Shaughnessy, Thomas; Professional baseball; Lenawee; MI; 1857;
    MI; 480C
Shaunessy, Edward; Base ballist; Middlesex; MA; 1858; MA;
    308A
Shaw, James; Gambler; Pike; MO; 1842; MO; 479A
Shaw, Mary E.; Dead; Marshall; AL; 1838; GA; 269A
Shaw, May; Trance Medium; Cook; IL; 1859; OH; 353D
Shearer, Joicy; Dead; Clark; KY; 1823; KY; 423C
Sheaver, David S.; Gambler; Dodge; WI; 1831; NY; 108A
Sheedy, John; Gambler; Lancaster; NE; 1845; MO; 117B
Sheeley; Dead; Columbia; FL; 1880; FL; 415A
Shelda, John; Gambler; Lancaster; NE; 1840; OH; 135B
Sheldon, George; Gambler; Peoria; IL; 1854; MN; 38D
Sheldon, Walt; Sport Gambler; Lancaster; NE; 1853; OH; 117B
Shellenbarger, Marshall; Dead hog dealer; Warren; IL; 1840; PA;
    236D
Sheppard, Mollie; Prize fighter; Orleans; LA; 1848; MS; 246D
Sheppard, W.H.; Circus; Ohio; WV; 1853; NY; 448D
Shepperd, A.H.; Gambler; Dallas; TX; 1840; PA; 19A
Sherdin, Peter; Tramp; Chisago; MN; 1830; Sweden; 411B

Sheridan, Ellen; Ballet dancer; Philadelphia; PA; 1863; PA; 6D
Sherman, S.; Circus; Ohio; WV; 1848; MI; 449A
Sherwood, Gilbert; Gambler; Deer Lodge; MT; 1850; WI; 129C
Shetzline, John; Baseball player; Philadelphia; PA; 1852; PA;
    451D
Shi, Yen; Keeps Opium Den; Shasta; CA; 1842; China; 2D
Shields, C.; Circus; Ohio; WV; 1854; Canada; 449A
Shields, Hugh; Tramp; Rio Grande; CO; 1849; Ireland; 329A
Shields, James; Gambler; Deer Lodge; MT; 1846; Ireland; 126B
Shields, Mary Ann; Clairvoyant; New York; NY; 1843; NY; 314D
Shields, Mathew; Tramp; Ionia; MI; 1857; Canada; 110C
Shilingburg, Jacob; Farmer dead; Grant; WV; 1808; VA; 230B
Shing, Kee; Opium Dealer; San Joaquin; CA; 1850; Canton; 12D

Shirley, Ellen; Clairvoyant; Worcester; MA; 1831; NH; 92A
Shoemaker, David; Gambler; De Kalb; IN; 1828; PA; 80B
Sholes, Erastus; Thief; St. Clair; MI; 1858; MI; 478C
Shollenberger, Jennie; Medium; Cook; IL; 1860; MN; 309A
Shook, William; Gambler; Kent; MI; 1845; NY; 288C
Shoot, Charles G.; Gambler; Jasper; MO; 1850; MO; 506C
Shoppart, William C.; With Circus; Erie; PA; 1857; PA; 306A
Shortell, Tom; Gambler; Multnomah; OR; 1853; IL; 239D
Shortlidge, Sarah; Quack Doctoress; Chester; PA; 1820; PA; 292C
Shot, Gun; Gambler; Elko; NV; 1833; China; 56C
Shuberg, Alfred; Tramp; New York; NY; 1850; Germany; 581C
Shuey, Catharine; Dead; Marion; OH; 1831; OH; 158C
Shultz, Jas.; Gambler; Gunnison; CO; 1857; OH; 98B
Shultz, Wm.; Tramp; Garland; AR; 1847; PA; 119C
Shun, Wing; Gambler; Butte; CA; 1851; China; 148B
Sick, Tom; Gambler; Deer Lodge; MT; 1845; China; 111C
Sidmore, Lewis; Gambler; Outagamie; WI; 1850; NY; 77D
Sied, William; Phrenologist; St. Louis; MO; 1830; PA; 285A
Sik, Wee; Opium Dealer; San Francisco; CA; 1838; Qwantung;
    609D
Silverstern, Louis; Thief; Westchester; NY; 1862; NY; 109C
Sim, Cong; Gambler; Deer Lodge; MT; 1849; China; 137D
Sim, John; Tramp; Santa Clara; CA; 1840; Germany; 197C
Simmons, Lucy; Dead; Calcasieu; LA; 1793; LA; 450C
Simmons, Sam'l; Tramp; Hennepin; MN; 1857; ---; 272A
Simon, Jane; Lays out the dead; Philadelphia; PA; 1831; France;
    139B
Simon, Samuel; Gambler; Kinney; TX; 1850; TX; 290C
Simpson, Rosaliee; Spirit Medium; Cook; IL; 1841; Canada; 36C
Simpson, Samuel; Gambler; Deer Lodge; MT; 1854; England;
    122A
Simson, Joseph; Gambler; Mendocino; CA; 1843; Russia; 271D
Sin, Chung; Gambler; Washoe; NV; 1835; China; 277A
Sing, Chung; Gambler; Kern; CA; 1844; China; 586C
Sing, Fong; Gambler; Boise; ID; 1855; China; 118B
Sing, Gee; Gambler; Elko; NV; 1848; China; 62C
Sing, Hi; Gambler; Lander; NV; 1855; China; 297A
Sing, Kam; General Bummer; Leander; NV; 1850; China; 297A

Sing, Loy; Fortune Teller; San Francisco; CA; 1849; Kwan Tung; 685A

Sing, Quong; Gambler; Boise; ID; 1843; China; 118B

Sing, Tie; Gambler; Eureka; NV; 1854; China; 213A

Sing, Tuck; Gambling; Yuba; CA; 1850; Canton; 427A

Sipe, Isaac; Tramp; Armstrong; PA; 1817; PA; 333A

Sirt, Thomas E.; Gambler; Ohio; WV; 1853; VA; 233B

Sise, Mary A.; Fortune Telling; Scott; KY; 1829; KY; 92A

Sisemore, David; Dead; Clay; KY; 1856; KY; 557A

Sizer, George W.; Gambler; Portage; OH; 1854; OH; 475B

Skaggs, E.M.; Gambler; Storey; NV; 1830; MO; 115C

Skellinger, Rebecca; Layout dead; Philadelphia; PA; 1841; PA; 61C

Skinner, Aaron U.; Astronomer; Washington; D.C.; 1846; MA; 184D

Skinner, Carrie; Dead; Wilcox; AL; 1880; AL; 193C

Skins, James; Tramp; Hancock; IN; 1831; Ireland; 89B

Slater, George; Billiard player; Middlesex; CT; 1841; CT; 26B

Slates, James; Dead; Sandusky; OH; 1871; OH; 166A

Slaughter, Fannie; Dead; Campbell; GA; 1852; GA; 591A

Slawson, William B.; Tramp; Wyandotte; KS; 1859; MI; 296B

Slayden, Jeff; Fortune Teller; Jackson; AR; 1805; ---; 534A

Sleckmast, H.; Circus; Ohio; WV; 1846; IL; 449A

Slen; Opium Dealer; Santa Cruz; CA; 1830; China; 521C

Slipery Dick; Gambler; Hennepin; MN; 1855; MN; 314A

Sloon, E. Pinkney; Dead; Jefferson; FL; 1876; FL; 6C

Slusler, Harry; Clog dancer in theatre; Marion; IN; 1866; IL; 495A

Small, Tursday; Dead; Colleton; SC; 1821; SC; 245A

Smalley, Fanny; Layer out of the dead; Philadelphia; PA; 1836; PA; 572B

Smiley, Sarah E.; Dead; Panola; TX; 1856; AL; 307C

Smith, Albert; Dead; St. Joseph; IN; 1874; IN; 417C

Smith, Alen; Tramp on public street; St. Clair; IL; 1860; IL; 484A

Smith, Ana; Dead; Carbon; PA; 1880; PA; 487B

Smith, Anna; Dead; Crawford; GA; 1875; GA; 655D

Smith, Anthony; Dead; Allegheny; PA; 1864; England; 222D

Smith, Archie; Advance Agent for Circus; New York; NY; 1845; England; 587D

Smith, Arther; Dead; Allegheny; PA; 1871; PA; 222D
Smith, Caroline; Gypsy; Tehama; CA; 1852; England; 475D
Smith, Charles; Tramp on public street; St. Clair; IL; 1857; NY;
 482B
Smith, Charles E.; Gambler; Richmond; GA; 1845; NY; 288A
Smith, Charles M.; Base ball player; Hamilton; OH; 1856; MA;
 165B
Smith, Columbus; Gypsy; Tehama; CA; 1867; NY; 475D
Smith, Cora; Dead; St. Joseph; IN; 1870; IN; 417C
Smith, Cornelia; Circus Performer; New York; NY; 1848; LA;
 74A
Smith, Douglass; Dead head; De Kalb; AL; 1874; AL; 582A
Smith, E.; Vagrant; Buchanan; MO; 1842; MO; 41B
Smith, Edward; Thief; Westchester; NY; 1862; NY; 94B
Smith, Edwin; Circus Man; New York; NY; 1857; NY; 390C
Smith, Elias S.; Dead; Hancock; KY; 1875; KY; 128B
Smith, Elijah; Gypsy; Tehama; CA; 1870; NY; 475D
Smith, Ellerton; Gambler; Milam; TX; 1855; TX; 269B
Smith, Frank; Vagrant; Abbeville; SC; 1856; SC ; 165A
Smith, Frank; Tramp; Lapeer; MI; 1861; MI; 315B
Smith, G.W.; Circus; Ohio; WV; 1835; DE; 449A
Smith, Geo.; Tramp on public street; St. Clair; IL; 1848; OH;
 483D
Smith, Geo. S.; Gambler; Deer Lodge; MT; 1838; England; 111C
Smith, George; Gambler; Pottawattamie; IA; 1845; MO; 291A
Smith, George; Vagrant; Licking; OH; 1877; PA; 85A
Smith, Gilbert B.; "To lazy to work"; Wabasha; MN; 1830; MN;
 507C
Smith, Gydany; Gambler; Presidio; TX; 1848; TX; 85B
Smith, Harry; Clog dancer; Floyd; IN; 1858; VA; 268A
Smith, Henry N.; Laborer - Quack Doct.; Franklin; MA; 1827;
 MA; 390B
Smith, Henry N.; Tramp on public street; St. Clair; IL; 1852; IL;
 483D
Smith, Horace; Circus Performer; New York; NY; 1814; VT; 74A
Smith, Ira; Circus; Ohio; WV; 1855; CT; 449A
Smith, Isabella; Clairvoyant; Suffolk; MA; 1848; MA; 292A
Smith, J.C.; Gambler; Buchanan; MO; 1850; LA; 211C

134 Name; Occupation; County; State; Birth; Birth place; Page

Smith, J.W.; Circus; Ohio; WV; 1834; NJ; 448D
Smith, Jack; Circus; Ohio; WV; 1855; Germany; 449A
Smith, James; Tramp on public street; St. Clair; IL; 1855; IL;
    483C
Smith, Jas. S.; Gambler; Pike; MO; 1843; MO; 498C
Smith, Jesse; Retired Gambler; San Benito; CA; 1801; GA; 414D
Smith, John; Gambler; Douglas; NE; 1853; NY; 189C
Smith, John; Circus; Ohio; WV; 1850; Ireland; 449B
Smith, John; Vagrant; Licking; OH; 1852; PA; 85A
Smith, John; Tramp; Hancock; GA; 1818; NY; 229D
Smith, John; Tramp - Prisoner; Ashtabula; OH; 1859; CT; 467C
Smith, John; Tramp on public street; St. Clair; IL; 1850; NY;
    481D
Smith, Johnnie H.; Dead; Autauga; AL; 1866; AL; 130D
Smith, Jones; Gypsy; Tehama; CA; 1876; NY; 475D
Smith, Joseph; Tramp; Hancock; ME; 1842; ME; 120C
Smith, Joseph P.; Laborer or pimp; Santa Clara; CA; 1855;
    Mexico; 393A
Smith, Julia; Thief; Bay; MI; 1838; MI; 364A
Smith, Laura; Circus Performer; New York; NY; 1852; LA; 74A
Smith, Laura; Dead; Owen; KY; 1880; KY; 169D
Smith, Leonard J.; Dead; Ingham; MI; 1843; Canada; 474A
Smith, Levi; Vagrant; Halifax; VA; 1850; NC; 522B
Smith, Malburn; Gypsy; Tehama; CA; 1870; NY; 475D
Smith, Mary; Dead; St. Louis; MO; 1818; Baden; 340D
Smith, Mont; Gambler; Garland; AR; 1845; France; 118A
Smith, Neal; Circus Man; New York; NY; 1854; NY; 390C
Smith, Noah; Gypsy; Tehama; CA; 1851; England; 475D
Smith, Peter; Tramp; Hancock; GA; 1814; NY; 229D
Smith, Queen; Gypsy; Tehama; CA; 1874; NY; 475D
Smith, Richard E.; Tramp; Jackson; MO; 1851; KS; 370B
Smith, Robert S.; Wanderer; Middlesex; MA; 1821; Nova Scotia;
    92D
Smith, Rose; Dead; St. Joseph; IN; 1864; IN; 417C
Smith, Sam; Gambler; Eureka; NV; 1850; NV; 211A
Smith, Sarah M.; Magnetic Docotor; Yankton; Dak. Terr.; 1835;
    OH; 452B
Smith, Stephen; Vagrant; Wilcox; AL; 1855; ---; 309C

Smith, Thos.; Vagrant; Leavenworth; KS; 1858; MO; 242A
Smith, William; Gambler; Storey; NV; 1846; MA; 146B
Smith, William; Cashier for Circus; Essex; NJ; 1845; NJ; 245B
Smith, William; Tramp; Hennepin; MN; 1845; NY; 272A
Smith, William; Tramp; St. Louis; MO; 1843; MD; 441C
Smith, William; Thief; Westchester; NY; 1859; NY; 94B
Sneider, William; Tramp; New York; NY; 1838; Germany; 581C
Snidow, James E.; Dead; Giles; VA; 1879; VA; 56D
Snow, Bert; Gambler; Billings; Dak. Terr.; 1849; Ireland; 46C
Snow, Bert; Gambler R.R.; Billings; Dak. Terr.; 1849; Ireland;
      59B
Snyder, Charles M.; Baseball catcher; Washington; D.C.; 1856;
      Washington, D.C.; 105C
Snyder, Elmer; Tramp; Washington; OH; 1860; PA; 285B
Snyder, Jas.; Gambler; Allegheny; PA; 1854; OH; 66A
Snyder, Sarah D.; Layer out of the dead; Philadelphia; PA; 1840;
      PA; 402C
Snyder, Solomon; Quack; Broome; NY; 1810; NY; 257D
Snyder, Thomas; Traveling with Circus; Mower; MN; 1845; OH;
      565A
Sohlke, Augusta; Ballet dancer; New York; NY; 1850; Germany;
      654B
Song, Chu; Gambling House; Calaveras; CA; 1833; China; 344C
Sor, Dat; Gambler; Mariposa; CA; 1834; China; 166D
Soroko, Andrew; Vagabond; Schuylkill; PA; 1828; Italy; 141A
Sou, Chin; Gambler; Eureka; NV; 1829; China; 206D
Sou, Lee; Opium Den; Storey; NV; 1845; China; 147C
Sough, Florence Gertrude; Dead; Bristol; MA; 1880; MA; 407D
Southwell, John; Medium; Philadelphia; PA; 1815; NY; 119A
Sowers, John; Gambler; Marion; MO; 1844; MO; 341B
Soy, Poon; Gambler; San Francisco; CA; 1851; Kwantung; 393B
Spalding, John W.; Gambler; Deer Lodge; MT; 1858; MI; 137C
Spang, John; Gambler; Duval; FL; 1845; OH; 523A
Sparks, Clem; Gambler; Arapahoe; CO; 1851; MO; 110C
Sparks, Taylor; Gambler; Estill; KY; 1851; KY; 23B
Sparks, Willie; Dead; Lee; AL; 1879; AL; 27B
Sparrow, Arthur; Gypsy; Tehama; CA; 1857; PA; 475D
Sparrow, Carrie; Gypsy; Tehama; CA; 1863; NY; 475D

Sparrow, Myrtle; Gypsy; Tehama; CA; 1876; NY; 475D

Spear, J. Monroe; Gambler; Essex; NJ; 1840; NJ; 243A

Spears, Valentine; Prisoner Deadbeat - 1yr; Brown; WI; 1834; WI; 149B

Spellman, Jack; Baseball player; Alameda; CA; 1857; NY; 61C

Spellmann, Denney; Base ball player; Alameda; CA; 1858; NY; 61C

Spence, Alex; Dead; Lawrence; MS; 1877; MS; 237D

Spencer, Wm.; Dead; Parke; IN; 1870; IN; 493C

Speria, Owen; Thief; Franklin; OH; 1859; PA; 481C

Spigler, Amanda; Dead; Washington; IN; 1844; IN; 501C

Spiller, Whitney; Clairvoyant Physician; Penobscot; ME; 1829; MA; 588D

Spore, H.S.; Gambler; Conejos; CO; 1840; Canada; 180D

Sprague, Almira; Circus Rider; Juneau; WI; 1858; NY; 451C

Sprague, Charles; Gambler; Placer; CA; 1835; RI; 242B

Springer, James M.; Professional Gambler; Spalding; GA; 1845; GA; 359B

Springfield, L.; Gambler; Waller; TX; 1860; TX; 372B

Springs, Lafayette; Witch Doctor; Cabarrus; NC; 1841; OH; 521B

Spronkle, Barbara; Fortune Teller; York; PA; 1845; PA; 291D

Sprowls, Sam'l; Dead; Hamilton; TX; 1823; KY; 355C

St. Clair, Aaron; Gambler; Mahoning; OH; 1808; OH; 76B

St. Clair, Charles F.; Magnetic Physician; Philadelphia; PA; 1843; VA; 381C

St. Germain, Eliza A.; Clairvoyant & Doctoress; Rensselaer; NY; 1821; NY; 313A

St. John, Angeline; Fortune Teller; Onondaga; NY; 1822; France; 89C

Stacks, Marshall; Gambler; St. Louis; MO; 1815; MO; 84D

Staeting, Johanna; Keeping House dead; St. Louis; MO; 1854; Prussia; 359C

Staffel, Jac.; Tramp on public street; St. Clair; IL; 1850; Wurtemburg; 482A

Staley, W.B.; Gambler; Lake; CO; 1845; OH; 358A

Stalker, John; Lazy Farmer; Lewis; NY; 1827; NY; 92D

Stamper, Susanna; Fortune Teller; Mason; WV; 1796; NC; 298C

Stamps, Peter; Quack Doctor; Halifax; VA; 1811; VA; 215A

Stanford, Charles; Dead; Schenectady; NY; 1878; NY; 142A

Stanger, Martha; Dead; Peoria; IL; 1826; England; 400A

Stanley, John F.; Register of death; Oxford; ME; 1840; ME; 271B

Stanley, Nettie; Spiritualist; Ohio; WV; 1854; WV; 205A

Stanton, John; Gambler; Douglas; NE; 1818; KY; 368C

Staphie, David; Tramp on public street; St. Clair; IL; 1861; OH;
482B

Staples, James T.; Sportsman Gambler; Choctaw; AL; 1830; VA;
117C

Starham, Mary; Tramp; Randolph; GA; 1863; GA; 103A

Stark; Medium; San Francisco; CA; 1845; Germany; 289A

Starkey, Stuart; Soldier - Deserter Prisoner; Duval; TX; 1856;
England; 240B

Starr, Jacob; Gambler; Los Angeles; CA; 1835; OH; 207C

Start, Joseph; Ball player; New York; NY; 1844; NY; 382B

Start, Joseph; Ball player; Providence; RI; 1845; NY; 375C

Stau, W.L.; Circus; Ohio; WV; 1854; NY; 449B

Stear, Carlo; Dead; Milwaukee; WI; 1869; WI; 288B

Stebbens, Charles, Mrs.; Dead; Colbert; AL; 1856; AL; 461A

Stebbins, Marion R.; Clairvoyant Physician; Plymouth; MA; 1833;
MA; 239B

Stebleton, Philip; Traveling with Circus; Miami; IN; 1858; OH;
547A

Stedge, Leonard; Gambler; Lake; CA; 1862; CA; 30B

Steel, Charles; Tramp on public street; St. Clair; IL; 1835;
Hanover; 483C

Steel, William; Gambler; Ross; OH; 1860; OH; 402C

Steele, Eliza M.; Dead; Parke; IN; 1871; IN; 488A

Steele, Geo. K.; Gen. Agt. for Circus; Marshall; WV; 1843; IA;
140B

Steele, Jack; Gambler; Sandusky; OH; 1826; NY; 55A

Stefano, Mary; Dead; New York; NY; 1879; NY; 384B

Steffis, Stephen; Dead; Monroe; MI; 1836; Prussia; 384A

Steinmetz, Byron; Phrenologist; Cameron; TX; 1855; OH; 374B

Steinmitz, John; Gambler; Lawrence; Dak. Terr.; 1848; MO; 200C

Stell, Nelly M.; Dead; Cook; IL; 1859; WI; 144A

Stent, Phillimena; Dead; Allegheny; PA; 1873; PA; 225A

Stephen, Dennis; Tramp; Hendricks; IN; 1842; Ireland; 635A

Stephen, E.; Circus; Ohio; WV; 1853; OH; 449A

Stephens, Richard H.; Gambler; Santa Fe; NM; 1834; TN; 73C

Stephenson, Lotta E.; Dead; St. Joseph; IN; 1880; IN; 417D

Sterling, James; Tramp on public street; St. Clair; IL; 1851; PA; 483D

Stevens, Lucy A.; Magnetic Healer; Fairfield; CT; 1831; CT; 35D

Stevens, Sarah R.; Spiritual Medium; San Francisco; CA; 1830; NY; 265D

Stevenson, Allen; Dead; Fairfield; SC; 1879; SC; 101B

Stevenson, George; Professional Tramp; Jackson; MO; 1854; NJ; 381D

Stewart, Chas.; Tramp; Defiance; OH; 1859; NY; 102D

Stewart, George; Tramp; Jackson; IL; 1832; NH; 186A

Stewart, Ida; Dead; Fairfield; SC; 1866; SC; 179A

Stewart, Samule; Dead; Fairfield; SC; 1805; SC; 97A

Stewart, W.H.; Circus; Ohio; WV; 1850; ME; 448D

Stile, E.H.; Circus; Ohio; WV; 1852; IL; 448D

Stile, Elizabeth; Dead; Cook; IL; 1846; IL; 148B

Stillmayer, John; Tramp on public street; St. Clair; IL; 1851; England; 483C

Stinemetz, Frank; Thief in jail; Erie; OH; 1861; OH; 12C

Stirlency, Wm. L.; Circus Actor; Vinton; OH; 1844; OH; 115D

Stober, Rosanna; Spiritualist Physic; Tippecanoe; IN; 1836; OH; 312B

Stock, Caroline; Fortune Teller & Keeping House; Hamilton; OH; 1830; Bavaria; 338A

Stocking, Belle; Dancer; Lake; CO; 1862; IN; 393B

Stockland, Jens K.; "To lazy to work"; Walworth; WI; 1854; WI; 132B

Stockwell, John M.; Astronomer; Cuyahoga; OH; 1832; MA; 60A

Stockwell, Lucy J.; Dead; Adams; IL; 1833; ME; 469B

Stoflet, G.W.; Gambler; Sumner; KS; 1840; NY; 282D

Stoflet, Geo.; Gambler; Sumner; KS; 1835; PA; 283A

Stokes, Spencer; Circus Manager; New York; NY; 1818; OH; 517B

Stone, D.P.; Circus; Ohio; WV; 1846; PA; 448D

Stone, D.W.; Clown Circus; Ohio; WV; 1824; VT; 449A

Stone, Irena; Dead; Claiborne; TN; 1880; TN; 175D

Stone, Reuben F.; Dead; Claiborne; TN; 1804; SC; 175D
Stoney, Geo.; B. ball player; Worcester; MA; 1845; IL; 182D
Stople, W.J.; Circus; Ohio; WV; 1848; KY; 448D
Storm, John; Dead; St. Joseph; IN; 1880; IN; 425D
Stormfeltz, Amelia; Attending to dead; Lancaster; PA; 1836; PA; 60D
Stoudemire, B--; Dead; Autauga; AL; 1874; AL; 67A
Stoudurmire; Son dead; Autauga; AL; 1880; AL; 57A
Stout, Catharine; Dead; Sandusky; OH; 1794; PA; 162B
Stowe, Harry D.; Baseball player; Bristol; MA; 1857; PA; 106D
Stowe, James B.; Circus Rider; Fulton; OH; 1856; OH; 180A
Straddler, John; Tramp; Oneida; NY; 1825; Switzerland; 304A
Strankamp, E.; Dead; Hamilton; OH; 1879; OH; 429C
Strassman, Max; Healer by Electricity; San Francisco; CA; 1820; Prussia; 184C
Stratton, Henry H.; Gambler; Lemhi; ID; 1833; MA; 218D
Stratton, Jarvis; Gambler; Davidson; TN; 1855; TN; 123C
Street, Simon; Tramp on public street; St. Clair; IL; 1861; MO; 483D
Streiber, Katherina; Dead; Sheboygan; WI; 1846; Hesse D.; 169A
Strickler, William; Circus Agent; Franklin; OH; 1860; OH; 140A
Striegel, Andy; Tramp on public street; St. Clair; IL; 1860; OH; 483D
Strong, Frank; Gambler; Arapahoe; CO; 1855; NY; 197A
Strong, William; Tramp; Coles; IL; 1859; IN; 212D
Strover, George; Gambler; Montgomery; IA; 1844; KY; 323A
Stuart, Henry; Stealing; Ross; OH; 1858; VA; 251C
Stuart, John; Tramp; New York; NY; 1846; NY; 581C
Stuart, Joseph R.; Gambler; Storey; NV; 1825; TN; 119C
Stuart, Sylvester; Stealing; Ross; OH; 1859; OH; 251C
Stuart, Tony; Tramp; Union; MS; 1850; AL; 315A
Stubblefield, Dan'l; Gambler; Fremont; CO; 1818; VA; 486B
Studivant, Nancy; Dead; Perry; AL; 1876; AL; 437B
Stutsman, Charles F.; Dead; Allegheny; PA; 1879; PA; 248D
Su, Chu; Gambler; Santa Clara; CA; 1844; China; 126A
Su, Up Tie; Gambler; Sweetwater; WY; 1846; China; 282C
Su, Yoke; Gambler; Amador; CA; 1845; Canton; 46D
Suay; Gambler; Trinity; CA; 1850; China; 570D

Sudith, Robert; Circus Performer; Alexander; IL; 1860; KY; 84C

Sudith, W.J.; Circus Performer; Alexander; IL; 1855; KY; 84C

Sue, Let; Gambler; Yuba; CA; 1852; Canton; 429A

Sue, Lung; Gambler; Lake; CA; 1852; Canton; 29D

Sueeney, William; Ball player; San Francisco; CA; 1857; PA;
192B

Suey; Miner and Gambler; Plumas; CA; 1832; China; 400B

Suey, Mong; Gambler; San Francisco; CA; 1858; Kwan Tung;
631C

Suliom, John; Circus; Ohio; WV; 1859; NY; 448D

Sulivan, Dennis A.; Proffic'n ball player; Onondaga; NY; 1853;
NY; 205C

Sullivan, Alex; Thief; Philadelphia; PA; 1856; PA; 293C

Sullivan, Chas.; B. ball player; Worcester; MA; 1850; MA; 182D

Sullivan, Ellen; Dead; Hudson; NJ; 1879; NJ; 272D

Sullivan, Eward; Tramp; New York; NY; 1851; NY; 581C

Sullivan, John; Tramp; Buchanan; MO; 1835; MO; 41A

Sullivan, T.J.; Baseball; St. Louis; MO; 1856; MO; 574C

Sullivan, Willie; Dead; Bristol; MA; 1878; Ireland; 44A

Summers, Rob't; Tramp; Jackson; MO; 1852; IA; 371C

Summers, Wm.; None (Tramp); Lamar; TX; 1860; IA; 247B

Sumner, Abby Maria; Clairvoyant Physician; Norfolk; MA; 1833;
MA; 92A

Sun, Law; Gambler; Eureka; NV; 1840; China; 213A

Sung, Gee; Gambler; Amador; CA; 1850; Canton; 46D

Sup, Moi; Gambler; Eureka; NV; 1856; China; 191B

Sutter, Barbara; Dead; St. Louis; MO; 1876; MO; 386C

Sutton, Ezra; Plays baseball; Suffolk; MA; 1851; NY; 434C

Sutton, Reubin; Tramp; Sanilac; MI; 1830; Canada; 267B

Sutton, William Allen; Dead; Hempstead; AR; 1875; AR; 426B

Swain, Henry E.; Phrenologist; Hillsborough; NH; 1839; NH;
232D

Swan, Prince; Dead head; St. Landry; LA; 1820; LA; 335D

Swats, Peter; Vagrant; Licking; OH; 1840; NY; 85A

Sweatman, John; Retired prize fighter; Garland; AR; 1840;
Ireland; 111D

Sweeney, Wm.; Tramp; Westmorland; PA; 1845; PA; 425C

Sweeny, John; Base ballist; Plymouth; MA; 1858; MA; 346A

Swift, Cornelia; Dead, given by mistake; Bristol; MA; ---; ---; 98C
Swift, Lewis; Astronomer; Monroe; NY; 1820; NY; 36C
Swigert, Samuel S.; Dead; Adair; MO; 1787; PA; 88B
Swinney, D.W.; Gambler; St. Louis; MO; 1848; TX; 15A
Sykes, Joseph; Astrologer Clairvoyant; Hamilton; OH; 1843;
    England; 33A
Tabors, Grace; Fortune Teller & Washer Woman; Hart; KY; 1834;
    KY; 197B
Taite, John; Gambler; San Francisco; CA; 1840; NY; 126A
Talburtt, James; Death; Jones; IA; 1849; IN; 340B
Tallenbaugh, Nathan; Tramp Saddler; Kosciusko; IN; 1837; PA;
    20B
Tam, Bak Yin; Opium Dealer; San Francisco; CA; 1839; Hop Wo;
    611D
Tam, Hok; Opium Dealer; San Francisco; CA; 1849; Hop Wo;
    611D
Tamkins, William; Gambler; Arapahoe; CO; 1843; MO; 98D
Tanner, Charles; Gambler; Amador; CA; 1844; IL; 8A
Tap, Quang; Fortune Teller; San Francisco; CA; 1840; Kwan
    Tung; 685A
Tasney, William; Baseball player; Suffolk; MA; 1861; MA; 268B
Taylor, Allice; Clairvoyant Physician; Chenango; NY; 1846; NY;
    211A
Taylor, Caroline A.; Magnetic Doctoress; Cook; IL; 1827; NY;
    561D
Taylor, Edwin A.; Healer; Suffolk; MA; 1845; MA; 371B
Taylor, Effie; Deadbeat; Henderson; KY; 1861; KY; 600A
Taylor, Frank; Gambler; Storey; NV; 1844; IL; 218D
Taylor, Henry; Gambler; Robertson; TX; 1845; TX; 363B
Taylor, Henry P.; Fortune Teller; Sullivan; TN; 1831; TN; 532A
Taylor, Horace; Gambler; Gallatin; MT; 1833; NY; 211 D
Taylor, J.; Gambler; Lake; CO; 1830; NY; 314D
Taylor, James; Dead; Washington; IL; 1864; IL; 361B
Taylor, Jane H.; Dead; Orange; IN; 1804; KY; 188B
Taylor, Jno.; Gambler; Conejos; CO; 1848; Ireland; 180D
Taylor, Lewis C.; Thief; Pottawattamie; IA; 1852; WI; 363D
Taylor, William; Tramp on public street; St. Clair; IL; 1856; OH;
    482B

Taylor, William; Base ball; Alameda; CA; 1857; NY; 228C
Taylor, William B.; Gambler; De Kalb; AL; 1816; AL; 552B
Tchein, Soon; Gambler; Union; OR; 1845; China; 177C
Tchong, How; Gambler; Union; OR; 1844; China; 177C
Tedford, Bill; Tramp; Clay; AR; 1835; TN; 31C
Tee, Yong; Gambler; Nevada; CA; 1852; China; 175A
Tell, Lee; Gambling House; Trinity; CA; 1855; China; 570D
Temple, Charles; Gambler; Hamilton; OH; 1830; NJ; 377B
Terheum, John H.; Magician; Bergen; NJ; 1866; NJ; 545B
Terner, Richard; Irish Clown; Suffolk; MA; 1856; MA; 339D
Terry, Richard; Circus Performer; Philadelphia; PA; 1838; NJ;
        401D
Terry, William; Gambler; Duval; FL; 1845; SC; 523A
Teufel, George; Tramp on public street; St. Clair; IL; 1823;
        Austria; 481D
Tew, Eudora; Dead; Wilcox; AL; 1880; AL; 189C
Tew, Toung; Gambler; Boise; ID; 1832; China; 118A
Th(?), Mary; Fortune Teller; St. Louis; MO; 1824; Baden; 343C
Thayer, Charles; Gambler; Santa Fe; NM; 1835; MA; 77C
Thayer, Frank H.; Healer; Hartford; CT; 1861; CT; 418D
Theis, Joseph; Tramp on public street; St. Clair; IL; 1855; MO;
        483D
Thibodau, Jefferson; Phrenologist; Sanilac; MI; 1854; MI; 269A
Thibodeaux, Felicia; Dead; St. Martin; LA; 1864; LA; 88D
Thistlerod, Regina; Fortune Teller; McCracken; KY; 1818;
        Bavaria; 116A
Thomas, Cliford; Tramp; Hennepin; MN; 1851; ME; 272A
Thomas, Cliford; Tramp; Douglas; NE; 1861; PA; 337D
Thomas, Esther; Dead; Marlboro; SC; 1820; SC; 526D
Thomas, Ezekel; Farmer dead; Steuben; NY; 1832; NY; 433D
Thomas, Geo.; Gambler; Jackson; MO; 1852; LA; 152A
Thomas, George; Vagrant; Buchanan; MO; 1843; MO; 41B
Thomas, Henery; Tramp; Jefferson; NE; 1845; Ireland; 629B
Thomas, Henry; Tramp; Adams; IL; 1861; OH; 467A
Thomas, J.D.; Gambler; Douglas; NE; 1820; Prussia; 301B
Thomas, Jinnie; Tramp; Morgan; GA; 1861; GA; 295D
Thomas, John; Thief; Bay; MI; 1848; NY; 364A
Thomas, Leff; Thief; Franklin; OH; 1848; OH; 482A

Name; Occupation; County; State; Birth; Birth place; Page 143

Thomas, Mary; Dead; Fountain; IN; 1850; Wales; 152B
Thomas, Tobe; Thief & Vagabond; Morgan; GA; 1852; GA; 273D
Thompson, Andrew; Gambler; Deer Lodge; MT; 1825; OH; 107D
Thompson, Edward; Thief; Westchester; NY; 1837; Canada; 108B
Thompson, Gustave; Works in Gambling House; Orleans; LA;
    1855; LA; 513B
Thompson, Henry; Dead; Milwaukee; WI; 1873; WI; 286A
Thompson, Isaac; Dead; Choctaw; MS; 1842; SC; 448A
Thompson, J.E.; Dead; Walton; GA; 1873; GA; 508A
Thompson, James; Gambler; Washoe; NV; 1854; NY; 296C
Thompson, John W.; Physician (Quack); Cumberland; NJ; 1810;
    NJ; 433D
Thompson, Leon E.; Dead; Hempstead; AR; 1864; AR; 435D
Thompson, Mary; Vagrant; Coweta; GA; 1860; GA; 569A
Thompson, S.L.; Dead; St. Joseph; IN; 1859; IN; 417D
Thompson, S.V.; Gambler; Deer Lodge; MT; 1832; PA; 108A
Thompson, Willis; Dead; Milwaukee; WI; 1877; Milwaukee, WI;
    286A
Thornton, Chas.; Thief; Philadelphia; PA; 1841; MD; 297C
Thornton, John; Laborer & Tramp; Worcester; MA; 1850; MA;
    382D
Thornton, Rich'd; Gambler; Orleans; LA; 1848; New Orleans, LA;
    19B
Thurman, Otis A.; Gambler; Montgomery; IA; 1845; OH; 323A
Tibbets, Frank; Gambler; Johnson; IA; 1847; IL; 135B
Tie, On; Gambler; Lander; NV; 1850; China; 297A
Ties, Tum; Gambler; Boise; ID; 1830; China; 118A
Tilden, Otis E.; Base ballist; Plymouth; MA; 1852; MA; 344A
Tilman, John; Vagrant; Fayette; PA; 1825; PA; 413C
Tin, Foo; Gambler; Eureka; NV; 1839; China; 192D
Tin, Yep; Gambler; Kern; CA; 1840; China; 586C
Tinnie, John; Fortune Teller; Clinton; IA; 1837; Germany; 365C
Tinsley, James; Gambler; Storey; NV; 1831; KY; 133C
Tisdale, Afred; Dead; Fairfield; OH; 1870; OH; 52B
Tittle, Alex; Gambler; Sacramento; CA; 1842; PA; 6D
Tobin, William; Ball player; Albany; NY; 1854; CT; 304A
Todd, Francis; Tramp; Allegheny; PA; 1834; PA; 30B
Todd, J.H.; Dead; Jefferson; IL; 1875; IL; 549D

Todd, Wm.; Gambler; Elko; NV; 1861; PA; 53C
Toh, Bun; Gambler; Storey; NV; 1832; China; 237D
Tolman, George C.; Gambler; Deer Lodge; MT; 1858; UT Terr.;
    136B
Tom, See; Keeping Gambling House; Storey; NV; 1848; China;
    237D
Tom, Wun; Pimp; San Francisco; CA; 1829; Kwontung; 375D
Tommey, Henry; Tramp; Dawson; GA; 1855; ---; 60C
Ton, Hung; Gambler; Trinity; CA; 1840; China; 570D
Ton, Qay; Gambler; Trinity; CA; 1850; China; 570C
Toney, D.; Gambler; Arapahoe; CO; 1852; MI; 98C
Tong, Chen; Gambler; Nevada; CA; 1849; China; 188A
Tong, Chin; Gambler; Nevada; CA; 1849; China; 188A
Tong, Gee; Gambler; El Dorado; CA; 1830; Canton; 131A
Tong, Maay; Opium Seller; San Francisco; CA; 1845; China;
    442D
Too, Wah; Gambler; Washoe; NV; 1837; China; 277A
Tookson; Circus; Ohio; WV; 1838; Canada; 449B
Toomey, John; Vagrant; Knox; TN; 1856; TN; 119A
Torrence, John; Tramp; Douglas; NE; 1839; MA; 337D
Torres, Antoino; Gambler; Santa Fe; NM; 1845; NM Terr.; 82A
Tow, Chow; Gambler; Boise; ID; 1832; China; 146B
Towel, Edward; Vagrant; Buchanan; MO; 1844; MO; 41B
Town, Frank; Tramp; Charlevoix; MI; 1845; IL; 20B
Towns, Silvia; Dead; Taylor; GA; 1780; GA; 68D
Townsend, Samuel; Dead; Athens; OH; 1806; PA; 36B
Toy, Si; Gambler; Amador; CA; 1835; Canton; 46D
Tracey, John; Irish Jig dancer; New York; NY; 1851; Canada;
    607B
Traener, N.J.; Tramp; Fayette; KY; 1835; PA; 309A
Train, Jules; Gambler; Orleans; LA; 1842; New Orleans, LA;
    414B
Trapp, Washington; Dead; Pulaski; IN; 1876; IN; 241D
Tray, James; Professional baseball; Lenawee; MI; 1859; MI; 480C
Traylor, Francis; Vagrant; Jasper; GA; 1855; GA; 46B
Trewaller, J.H.; Circus Manager; Henrico; VA; 1836; England;
    395B

Tribble, Joanne; Medium & Doctress; Plymouth; MA; 1832; ME; 316B

Trimble, Geo.; Circus; Ohio; WV; 1855; NY; 448D

Trimble, Sam; Gambler; Bexar; TX; 1850; TX; 171A

Tripp, Charles B.; With Circus Show; Richland; IL; 1856; Canada; 133A

Tripp, James; Gambler; Deer Lodge; MT; 1860; IA; 127D

Tripplet, Van. B.; Gambler; St. Louis; MO; 1840; Washington, D.C.; 484A

Tron, William; Travels with Circus; Marion; IN; 1849; OH; 513B

Tront, Ora; Dead; Benton; AR; 1879; AR; 475D

Trotman, Willis; Quack Doctor - Prisoner; Craven; NC; 1830; NC; 263A

Trott, S.W.; Ball player; Suffolk; MA; 1857; Washington terr.; 257D

Trott, Samuel W.; Base ball player; Washington; D.C.; 1859; MD; 122B

Trouble, Mary; Fortune Teller; Sangamon; IL; 1820; VA; 107B

Trouivelot, George H.E.; Astronomer; Middlesex; MA; 1856; MA; 329A

Trouivelot, Leopold; Astronomer; Middlesex; MA; 1829; France; 329A

Trout, George; Gambler; Jackson; MO; 1855; NY; 42D

Truax, Richard; Vagrant; Warren; NY; 1853; NY; 261C

Trulon, Banjamin; Too lazy to do anything; Burlington; NJ; 1838; NJ; 59A

Tuck, Yoy; Gambler; Eureka; NV; 1837; China; 212C

Tucker, Amelia; Dead head; St. Landry; LA; 1785; LA; 335D

Tun, Chan; Gambler; San Francisco; CA; 1855; Kwan Tung; 632A

Tung, Fat; Gambler; San Francisco; CA; 1857; Kwan Tung; 632A

Tung, Lee; Keeps Gambling House; Shoshone; ID; 1855; China; 361A

Tunkel, Anton; Tramp on public street; St. Clair; IL; 1827; Bavaria; 482B

Turegaus, Paul; Gambler; Orleans; LA; 1836; LA; 69C

Turner, J.R.; Fortune Teller; Accomack; VA; 1810; VA; 85A

Turner, Jno. J.; Gambler; St. Louis; MO; 1841; NY; 484A

Turner, Nancy; Keeping house & stealing; Barren; KY; 1841; KY; 40C

Turner, S.W.; Pico Gambler; Carroll; AR; 1853; MO; 152B

Tuss, Annie; Dead; Milwaukee; WI; 1880; Milwaukee, WI; 286B

Tuss, Emma; Dead; Milwaukee; WI; 1879; Milwaukee, WI; 286B

Tuss, Mary; Dead; Milwaukee; WI; 1873; MO; 286B

Tuss, Millie; Dead; Milwaukee; WI; 1878; MO; 286B

Tusselbach, Ed; Baseball player; San Francisco; CA; 1858; PA; 113B

Tutt, J.C.; Wks in Circus; Adams; IL; 1851; IL; 407B

Tuttle, Horace; Astronomer; Sweetwater; WY; 1839; ME; 317A

Tuttle, Lucina; Clairvoyant Physician; Genesee; NY; 1817; NY; 512A

Tyman, George; Gambler; Pike; MO; 1858; KY; 583B

Type, W.; Gambler; Orleans; LA; 1858; New Orleans, LA; 80C

Tyson, John; A prisoner charged of murder; Presidio; TX; 1838; AR; 90D

Un, Wang; Gambler; Deer Lodge; MT; 1834; China; 111C

Underwood, Frank; Dead; Autauga; AL; 1820; AL; 66C

Underwood, John; Dead; Wilcox; AL; 1879; AL; 199C

Unweller, William; Gambler; Modoc; CA; 1846; NV; 17B

Urann, Frederick W.; Magnetic Physician; Suffolk; MA; 1821; MA; 37A

Utzora; Circus; Ohio; WV; 1860; Canada; 449B

Utzora, Brossie; Circus; Ohio; WV; 1878; Canada; 449B

Utzora, Charley; Circus; Ohio; WV; 1874; Canada; 449B

Utzora, Harry; Circus; Ohio; WV; 1876; Canada; 449B

Vacko; Circus; Ohio; WV; 1860; Canada; 449B

Vahle, Anna; Dead; Adams; IL; 1879; IL; 482C

Vahle, William; Dead; Adams; IL; 1877; IL; 482C

Vaider, Dv. C.M.; Farmer dead; Carroll; MS; 1812; VA; 139B

Vail, Isaac S.; Thief; Westchester; NY; 1835; NY; 95C

Val, Refugio; Gambler; Dona Ana; NM; 1835; Chihuahua; 298C

Valantine, Fechter; Tramp; Lancaster; PA; 1832; Germany; 600B

Valeen, Samuel; Gambler; Deer Lodge; MT; 1844; Sweden; 125C

Valentin, Robert; Tramp on public street; St. Clair; IL; 1859; NY; 483D

Valeria, Mene; Clairvoyant & Fortune Teller; Mahaska; IA; 1840; MI; 327C
Van Houten, Willard; Pimp; Tompkins; NY; 1835; NY; 267A
Vanaukin, Martha; Magnetic Physician; Monroe; NY; 1834; NY; 13B
Vancamp, F.; Circus; Ohio; WV; 1845; MA; 449A
Vance, George; Tramp; New York; NY; 1842; NY; 581D
Vanderwaulter, James L.; On Circus; Oneida; NY; 1862; NY; 111C
Vandiwalker, E.D.; Circus; Ohio; WV; 1842; MI; 449A
Vanduzee, William; Astronomer; Erie; NY; 1812; NY; 23C
Vanghelt, Permelia; Dead; Wilcox; AL; 1835; AL; 193D
Vanoy; Gambler; Carroll; AR; 1853; (Not Given); 154B
Vanskye, George; Prof. Thief; Blue Earth; MN; 1845; IA; 463D
Vasquez, A.; In jail for murder; Eureka; NV; 1840; Mexico; 180A
Vaughn; Dead; Perry; AL; 1862; AL; 442A
Vaughn, Asberry; Vagabond; Walker; GA; 1826; SC; 335D
Vaughn, James; Gambler; Shelby; IN; 1828; KY; 297A
Vaughn, Mike; Tramp on public street; St. Clair; IL; 1848; MS; 483C
Vaughn, Virginia; Clairvoyant; Jefferson; KY; 1853; MD; 408A
Vaught, Lewis; Phrenologist; Jefferson; KS; 1860; MO; 188A
Vaugn, John; Gambler; Lake; CO; 1845; PA; 358A
Vega, Agapito; Gambler; Grant; NM; 1840; Chihuahua; 338A
Verner, August; Tramp; New York; NY; 1826; Germany; 581C
Vernett, William; Clairvoyant Doctor; Erie; NY; 1843; Mexico; 142C
Veryelva, Wm.; Vagrant; Winnebago; WI; 1826; ---; 165B
Vetter, Charles; Gambler; Lake; CO; 1842; NY; 448A
Victor, Louise; Clairvoyant; Suffolk; MA; 1853; MA; 292A
Vilas, Mary J.; Dead; Lapeer; MI; 1844; MI; 217D
Vilas, Sarah J.; Dead; Lapeer; MI; 1804; VT; 217D
Villett, Pete; Gambler; Arapahoe; CO; 1844; Canada; 98D
Villier, George; Tramp on public street; St. Clair; IL; 1856; IA; 482A
Vincentito; Oracle; Valencia; NM; 1786; NM Terr.; 442C
Vinnettin, Simon; Tramp; Montgomery; IA; 1861; Ireland; 321A

Vogel, John; Tramp on public street; St. Clair; IL; 1846; Switzerland; 482B

Volkmier, Katie; At home - dead; St. Louis; MO; 1864; MO; 506B

Von Froben, Louise; Fortune Teller; San Francisco; CA; 1850; Germany; 585A

Vonki, William; Dead; Tippecanoe; IN; 1880; IN; 205B

Wa, Choung; Gambler; Idaho; ID; 1845; Canton; 166C

Wachter, Edward; Dead; Adams; IL; 1879; IL; 479A

Waddle, Sallie; Dead head; St. Landry; LA; 1780; LA; 335D

Wade, George H.; Circus Baggage; Fairfield; CT; 1840; CT; 272B

Wade, William; Professional Thief; Montgomery; PA; 1830; PA; 40B

Wadleigh, C.D.; Gambler; Eureka; NV; 1835; ME; 184D

Waerner, Chs.; Tramp on public street; St. Clair; IL; 1853; Wurtemburg; 481D

Waggoner, Mahala J.; Dead; Clay; KY; 1870; KY; 558C

Waggoner, Martha A.; Dead; Clay; KY; 1879; KY; 558C

Wah, Hong; Tramp; Box Elder; UT; 1845; China; 115A

Wah, Kee; Sell Opium; Amador; CA; 1842; China; 52B

Wah, Lee; Keeping Opium Den; Sacramento; CA; 1846; China; 12C

Wah, Lee; Gambler; Elko; NV; 1844; China; 56C

Waight, John; Tramp on public street; St. Clair; IL; 1845; ME; 482A

Wain, Henry; Gambler; Orleans; LA; 1845; LA; 428D

Wain, Jules; Keeps Gambling House; Orleans; LA; 1843; LA; 428D

Wairick, S.; Gambler; Storey; NV; 1840; PA; 114B

Waitmann, Margret E.; Dead; Osage; MO; 1863; OH; 399A

Wakeling, Charlotte T.; Magnetic Healer; San Francisco; CA; 1840; NY; 283D

Walbarger, Mary; Fortune Teller; New York; NY; 1851; Germany; 497C

Walch, Sarah C.; Dead; Jessamine; KY; 1861; KY; 35A

Walden, Cragen; Dead; Clark; KY; 1880; KY; 420A

Walden, John L.; Dead; Washington; AR; 1874; AR; 571D

Waldhaus, Caroline; Dead; Adams; IL; 1877; IL; 474D

Name; Occupation; County; State; Birth; Birth place; Page 149

Waldhaus, Emma; Dead; Adams; IL; 1864; IL; 476D
Walk, Yu; Sell Opium; Placer; CA; 1843; China; 338D
Walker, E.D.; Tramp; Paulding; OH; 1857; MI; 502C
Walker, Jack; With Circus; Hamilton; OH; 1855; OH; 18D
Walker, Pat; Tramp on public street; St. Clair; IL; 1840; Ireland;
    482B
Walker, Thomas; Tramp; Dakota; NE; 1858; WI; 317A
Wallace, Hanna; Dead; Allegheny; PA; 1835; Ireland; 216D
Wallace, Henry; Tramp; Union; NJ; 1844; Scotland; 171C
Wallace, Leslie S.; Dead; Marshall; KY; 1872; KY; 217A
Walling, Elizabeth; Dead; Fairfield; SC; 1785; SC; 189B
Walliver, John; Gambler; Cherokee; KS; 1845; PA; 508A
Walsch, James; Tramp on public street; St. Clair; IL; 1845;
    Ireland; 483C
Walsh, John; At home - dead; St. Louis; MO; 1879; MO; 483D
Walter, John S.; Tramp; Hennepin; MN; 1857; ---; 272A
Walters, Manfred; Tramp; Wayne; IN; 1855; IN; 297A
Walton, Charles; Tramp on public street; St. Clair; IL; 1854; PA;
    483C
Walton, Edward; Tramp; Buchanan; MO; 1855; MO; 41A
Walton, Helen M.; Clairvoyant; New York; NY; 1824; MA; 344C
Wam, Wong; Gambler; San Francisco; CA; 1842; Hong San;
    449B
Wambold, Harry; Circus Performer; New York; NY; 1850;
    Canada; 74A
Wan, Chung; Gambler; Deer Lodge; MT; 1862; China; 111C
Wan, Kin; Keeps Gambling House; Beaverhead; MT; 1833;
    China; 1A
Wang, Kee; Gambler; Baker; OR; 1842; China; 8D
Wang, Qow; Gambler; Boise; ID; 1838; China; 146B
Wano; Circus; Ohio; WV; 1820; Isle Barneo; 448D
Wans, Fut; Gambler; Eureka; NV; 1836; China; 208D
Ward, James W.; Clown; Montgomery; PA; 1835; Ireland; 556B
Ward, John M.; Base ball player; Providence; RI; 1857; PA; 320C
Ward, Joseph; Tramp on public street; St. Clair; IL; 1858;
    England; 484A
Ward, Peter; Tramp; Nassau; FL; 1856; MA; 332C
Ward, Samuel; Dead; Taylor; IA; 1850; OH; 59D

Name; Occupation; County; State; Birth; Birth place; Page

Ward, W.A.; Gambler; Maverick; TX; 1842; KY; 51B
Ward, William; Dead; Cook; IL; 1853; WI; 137C
Warden, Liby; Wandering Gypsy; Clayton; IA; 1860; ---; 473D
Warden, Wm.; Wandering Gypsy; Clayton; IA; 1862; ---; 473D
Ware, Arther; Gambler; Kinney; TX; 1853; Canada; 293B
Ware, J.L.; Circus; Ohio; WV; 1850; IL; 448D
Warner, A.H.; Circus; Ohio; WV; 1828; MA; 448D
Warner, Magdelene; Dead; Pulaski; IN; 1879; IN; 242A
Warner, Mary; Circus Rider; Juneau; WI; 1861; MA; 451C
Warren, David; Phrenologist; Fremont; IA; 1851; OH; 166C
Warren, James; Tramp on public street; St. Clair; IL; 1840; OH;
    481D
Warren, Martha; Fortune Teller; New York; NY; 1840; NY; 511D
Warren, Sarah; Medium; Butte; CA; 1834; NH; 198C
Warren,Buck; Gambler; Maverick; TX; 1852; MA; 44D
Warrenburg, Cora; Dead; Washington; AR; 1880; AR; 568A
Washburn, Elsie A.; Dead; Jasper; IN; ---; IN; 298B
Washburn, W.E.; Circus; Ohio; WV; 1852; OH; 448D
Washington; Dead; Orleans; LA; 1880; LA; 109A
Washington, Alice; Tramp; Sharkey; MS; 1850; AL; 143D
Washington, George; Tramp; St. Johns; FL; 1857; GA; 145B
Washington, Henry; Tramp; Sharkey; MS; 1845; MS; 143D
Washington, Lawrence J.; Gambler; Cuyahoga; OH; 1843; OH;
    239D
Wat; Gambler; Elko; NV; 1840; China; 55B
Wateras, Modesta; Circus Performer; Maricopa; AZ; 1855;
    Mexico; 81C
Watson, Emma; Dead; Owen; KY; 1870; KY; 162B
Watson, Louis; Said to be stealing; Coffee; AL; 1861; AL; 209D
Watson, Martin A.; Traveling Agent Circus; Genesee; MI; 1841;
    MI; 145D
Watson, Richard; Gambler; Franklin; KY; 1820; KY; 157D
Watson, Wm. C.; Quack Doctor; Sagadahoc; ME; 1820; ME;
    162C
Watts; Dead; Wilcox; AL; 1880; AL; 487B
Watts, David; Clerk for Circus; Rock; WI; 1847; WI; 220A
Watts, Henry; Tramp; Lowndes; AL; 1840; AL; 246A
Weatherford, W.; Gambler; Dallas; TX; 1856; IL; 37A

Weatherly, John W.; Dead; Marlboro; SC; 1860; SC; 542D
Weaver, Earline; Wandering; Lenawee; MI; 1831; NY; 421B
Webb, John; Tramp; Delta; TX; 1852; TX; 482B
Webb, Judson; With a Circus; Dodge; NE; 1846; NY; 446D
Weber, Cint; Gambler & Thief; Clinton; MO; 1857; KY; 491B
Weber, Clint; Gambler & Thief; Clinton; MO; 1857; KY; 491B
Weber, Peter; Tramp on public street; St. Clair; IL; 1851; Nassau; 482B
Webster, Anna J.; Magnetic Physician; Suffolk; MA; 1847; NH; 274B
Weeks, Edward C.; Ticket Agent for Circus; Putnam; NY; 1845; NY; 28A
Weeks, Elbert; Tramp; Giles; VA; 1833; VA; 37A
Weeks, Mary E.; Test Medium; Cook; IL; 1830; CT; 649D
Wegmann, Jacob; Tramp on public street; St. Clair; IL; 1852; MA; 483D
Weiber, Heinddrich; Dead; Calumet; WI; 1794; Prussia; 87D
Weightman, B.L.; Magnetic Physician; Leavenworth; KS; 1848; KY; 211C
Weiler, Henry; Tramp Laborer; New York; NY; 1849; Prussia; 288B
Weiss, Frank; Tramp on public street; St. Clair; IL; 1849; Wurtemburg; 481D
Welch, Fremont; Circus Show Labor; Stark; OH; 1858; OH; 142A
Welch, Harrison; Magnetic Healer; Adams; IL; 1824; NY; 422D
Welch, O.M.; Gambler; Deer Lodge; MT; 1848; Ireland; 127D
Welch, William; Tramp; York; ME; 1856; ME; 17D
Weldon, Richard; Gambler; Storey; NV; 1824; Wales; 138B
Welfer, George; Tramp on public street; St. Clair; IL; 1841; Bavaria; 482A
Wellman, Sumner W.; Clairvoyant Physician; Suffolk; MA; 1845; MA; 164C
Wells, Anna; Medium; Green; WI; 1812; NY; 130B
Wells, Henry S.; Magnetic Physician; Chenango; NY; 1834; NY; 207B
Wells, J.; Gambler; Grant; NM; 1850; KY; 347D
Wells, Joseph; Gambler; Grant; NM; 1845; AR; 350B
Welsh, G.W.; Phrenologist; Sullivan; IN; 1837; WV; 601A

Name; Occupation; County; State; Birth; Birth place; Page

Welsh, John; Dancer; New York; NY; 1860; NY; 617B
Welsh, Michael; Baseball player; Rensselaer; NY; 1859; NY; 81A
Wender, Ambrose S.; Tramp; Mercer; NJ; 1846; NJ; 299B
Wendleton, David; Dead; Cooper; MO; 1807; Germany; 241C
Wensean, George; Tramp; Kankakee; IL; 1850; NY; 179D
Werner, Frederick; Baseball player; Washington; D.C.; 1855; PA;
    378B
Wernike. Henry; Dead; Adams; IL; 1878; IL; 479B
Wesley, Lewis; Dead; St. Joseph; IN; 1878; IN; 408B
Wesly, John; Tramp; Johnson; IL; 1855; IL; 592B
West, Abby; Dead; St. Louis; MO; 1879; MO; 500B
West, Carrie; Vagrant; Alexandria; VA; 1858; VA; 448C
West, J.D.; Circus; Ohio; WV; 1843; AL; 449B
West, Thomas; Tramp; Cecil; MD; 1850; MD; 211D
Wetzler, Lewis A.; Dead; Juniata; PA; 1877; PA; 395A
Weurch, Mary; Fortune Teller; Cuyahoga; OH; 1834; Switzerland;
    242A
Wheeler, Charles; Dead; Hamilton; OH; 1841; OH; 7B
Wheeler, Geo.; Tramp; Ramsey; MN; 1847; USA; 147C
Whilstadt, Ed; Gambler; Tippecanoe; IN; 1850; IN; 271B
Whitaker, Francis; Ringmaster Circus; New York; NY; 1819; NY;
    68A
Whitall, Henry; Astronomer; Camden; NJ; 1818; NJ; 157B
White, Chan; Tramp; Marshall; MN; 1857; NY; 143D
White, Chas. F.; Gambler; Deer Lodge; MT; 1851; OH; 135D
White, Edward; Tramp; New York; NY; 1829; England; 581C
White, Frank; Magnetic Physician; Washington; D.C.; 1840; CT;
    102C
White, George; Barnum Circus; Middlesex; NJ; 1851; NY; 329C
White, James; Tramp; New York; NY; 1817; Ireland; 581C
White, Mary M.; Keeping House Fortune Teller; Nodaway; MO;
    1838; IN; 205C
White, Napolian; Gambler; Orleans; LA; 1824; Washington, D.C.;
    369C
White, Patrick; Vagabond; Penobscot; ME; 1850; Ireland; 197C
White, Rob't; Circus; Ohio; WV; 1852; MI; 449A
White, W.H.; Base ball player; Hamilton; OH; 1854; NY; 165A
Whitfield, Andrew; Gambler; Robertson; TX; 1845; AL; 373A

Whitie, Jane; Dead; Hempstead; AR; 1849; SC; 437D

Whiting, George; Tramp; New York; NY; 1829; Germany; 581C

Whitington, Gracie; Dead; Crawford; GA; 1879; GA; 666D

Whitkin, Simon; Gambler; Columbia; WA; 1856; Prussia; 117A

Whitlemeyer, Cathrine; Pick Human Hair; Philadelphia; PA; 1836; Baden; 194B

Whitly, Louis; Tramp; Marengo; AL; 1830; AL; 704B

Whitman, Catharine; Dead; McLean; KY; 1815; KY; 271C

Whitmarsh, Abbie O.; Clairvoyant Physician; Plymouth; MA; 1829; MA; 611A

Whitney, Arthur; Baseball player; Worcester; MA; 1858; MA; 22B

Whitney, Charles; Base ball player; San Francisco; CA; 1856; IA; 136D

Whitney, Frank; Gambler; Eureka; NV; 1835; LA; 210C

Whitney, James; Base ball player; San Francisco; CA; 1858; NY; 136D

Whitney, John W.; Boxing master; New London; CT; 1832; NY; 42C

Whitney, Stephen; Vagrant; Winnebago; WI; 1835; IL; 162C

Whitney, Wm.; Gambler; Eureka; NV; 1845; LA; 210C

Wick, Chas.; Thief; Licking; OH; 1855; OH; 390C

Wicks, James; Tramp; Knox; IN; 1815; Co. Limerich, Ireland; 269B

Wicks, Lotetia; At home dead; Davidson; TN; 1840; TN; 88C

Wieger, Katy; Dead; St. Louis; MO; 1879; MO; 499B

Wiehr, Joseph; Tramp on public street; St. Clair; IL; 1848; Hanover; 483C

Wiggat, Charles; Tramp on public street; St. Clair; IL; 1835; Sweden; 483D

Wiggin, Frank E.; Astronomer; Suffolk; MA; 1856; MA; 489B

Wiggins, Abram; Avoiding the law (for murder); Swain; NC; 1850; NC; 167C

Wiggins, Andrew; Dead; Crawford; GA; 1878; GA; 657C

Wiggins, Jimmie; Dead; Walton; GA; 1880; GA; 507C

Wiggins, William; Thief; Franklin; OH; 1843; New Brunswick, Canada; 483C

Wigginton, Charlotte; Dead head; Lowndes; AL; 1800; VA; 214D

154 Name; Occupation; County; State; Birth; Birth place; Page

Wigginton, Nancy; Dead head; Lowndes; AL; 1781; VA; 214D
Wilbich, George; Tramp on public street; St. Clair; IL; 1846; Ny;
    483D
Wilbur, Joseph; Magnetic Physician; Cook; IL; 1811; NY; 6D
Wilburn, Mary; Fortune Telling; Cherokee; KS; 1839; TN; 455B
Wilburn, Walter P.; Gambler; Shasta; CA; 1853; MO; 13B
Wilcox, Effie E.; Dead; Miller; MO; 1879; MO; 160B
Wilde, Robert T.; Magnetic Physician; Cumberland; ME; 1832;
    MA; 209D
Wildheck, Henry; Dead; New York; NY; 1833; Prussia; 167B
Wiley, Minnie; Dead; Owen; KY; 1879; KY; 165D
Wiley, Thos.; Circus; Ohio; WV; 1855; NY; 448D
Wilison, Abraham; Tramp; Belmont; OH; 1862; OH; 478A
Wilkins, Lynford; Engineer out with Circus; Philadelphia; PA;
    1856; PA; 144D
Wilkins, Renitta; Dead head; St. Landry; LA; 1824; VA; 335D
Wilkins, Scepio; Dead head; St. Landry; LA; 1805; VA; 335D
Will, George; Gambler; Howard; IN; 1845; OH; 446C
Will, Granny; Fortune Teller; Sauk; WI; 1808; Prussia; 239B
Willam, John; Dead; Montgomery; PA; 1793; PA; 203A
Willard, James; Magician; Tuolumne; CA; 1860; NY; 134B
Willard, Jno.; Circus Man; St. Louis; MO; 1845; MO; 107C
Willday, Richard; Bummer; Amador; CA; 1861; CA; 9B
Willey, Pulaski M.; Magnetic Physician; Cook; IL; 1842; NH;
    64A
William, Chas.; Tramp; Jackson; MO; 1844; NH; 368B
William, Edwin A.; Circus Agent; Livingston; NY; 1839; NY;
    158B
Williams; Tramp - Prisoner; Ashtabula; OH; 1858; ---; 467C
Williams, A.B.; Magnetic Physician; Brown; WI; 1819; OH; 55B
Williams, A.C.; Dead; Walton; GA; 1814; GA; 550A
Williams, A.M.; Magnetic Doctor; St. Louis; MO; 1819; VA;
    111B
Williams, Bob; Gambler; Robertson; TX; 1850; TX; 421C
Williams, Dilla; Fortune Teller; Edgefield; SC; 1861; SC ; 331B
Williams, Edward; Tramp; Hardin; OH; 1875; OH; 209A
Williams, Ellen; Tramp; Coweta; GA; 1860; GA; 453D
Williams, F.M.; Tramp; Phelps; MO; 1850; MO; 307C

Name; Occupation; County; State; Birth; Birth place; Page 155

Williams, Felix; Tramp; Buchanan; IA; 1846; KY; 506B
Williams, Frank; Tramp; Butler; IA; 1850; NY; 101D
Williams, Frank; Tramp; Douglas; NE; 1858; England; 337D
Williams, Geo.; Thief; Philadelphia; PA; 1854; NY; 289C
Williams, Geo.; Thief; Westchester; NY; 1856; NY; 97D
Williams, George E.; Dead; Giles; VA; 1878; VA; 59D
Williams, J.S.; Tramp; Douglas; NE; 1848; PA; 277B
Williams, James; Tramp on public street; St. Clair; IL; 1834; NY;
    482B
Williams, James; Tramp on public street; St. Clair; IL; 1860; PA;
    483D
Williams, Jeremiah; Gambler; Cook; IL; 1859; MO; 244D
Williams, Jno. O.; Vagrant; Kennebec; ME; 1829; ME; 78C
Williams, John; Gambler; Deer Lodge; MT; 1850; KY; 125C
Williams, John; Tramp - Prisoner; Tippecanoe; IN; 1852; ---;
    237C
Williams, John; Tramp on public street; St. Clair; IL; 1848; OH;
    482B
Williams, John; Tramp; Hennepin; MN; 1859; Canada; 272A
Williams, John; Tramp; Hennepin; MN; 1857; MI; 272A
Williams, John; Tramp; Lancaster; NE; 1856; NE; 173A
Williams, M.F.; Phrenologist/Fortune Telling; Jackson; AR; 1820;
    WV; 533C
Williams, Martha; Dead; Orleans; LA; 1833; VA; 102C
Williams, Mary A.; Dead; Limestone; AL; 1828; NC; 355B
Williams, Mary L.; Dead; Baltimore; MD; 1826; Germany; 290C
Williams, Milly; Tramp; W. Baton Rouge; LA; 1862; LA; 341D
Williams, Minnie; Vagabond; Rutherford; TN; 1859; TN; 101A
Williams, Needham; Tramp; King George; VA; 1861; VA; 551B
Williams, R.P.; Tramp; Monroe; AR; 1857; TN; 323D
Williams, Silas; Tramp; Scott; KY; 1855; Prussia; 10C
Williams, Thomas; Tramp; Sullivan; IN; 1838; England; 512B
Williams, Thomas; Tramp; Montgomery; IA; 1849; MO; 321A
Williamson, Thomas; Base ball player; San Francisco; CA; 1848;
    NY; 583B
Willie, Edward; Dead; Allegheny; PA; 1879; PA; 247B
Willis, James T.; Dead; Autauga; AL; 1866; AL; 132D
Willison, James; Tramp; Belmont; OH; 1856; OH; 469D

Name; Occupation; County; State; Birth; Birth place; Page

Willson, L.; Dead; Madison; KY; 1879; KY; 346B
Willson, William; Tramp; Orleans; LA; 1863; LA; 25C
Wilmer, Henry; Tramp on public street; St. Clair; IL; 1846; LA; 482B
Wilson, Anna; Clairvoyant; Suffolk; MA; 1832; MA; 314A
Wilson, Arthur G.; Gambler; Montgomery; IA; 1852; OH; 328C
Wilson, Biddie A.; Tramp; Belmont; OH; 1848; OH; 475C
Wilson, Charles H.; Gambler; Franklin; OH; 1848; OH; 399C
Wilson, Daniel; Drunk; Beaufort; NC; 1850; NC; 171A
Wilson, Edward; Tramp on public street; St. Clair; IL; 1857; NJ; 483D
Wilson, Eliza; Layer out of the dead; Berks; PA; 1821; PA; 152C
Wilson, Florence; Fortune Teller; Suffolk; MA; 1852; France; 110B
Wilson, George; Tramp; Stephenson; IL; 1858; NY; 63B
Wilson, Howard; Gambler; Montgomery; IN; 1853; IN; 337A
Wilson, James; Tramp; New York; NY; 1831; England; 284B
Wilson, John; Tramp on public street; St. Clair; IL; 1854; NY; 483D
Wilson, Mary; Fortune Teller; Scott; IA; 1825; NY; 595A
Wilson, Samuel; Dead; Norfolk; VA; 1877; VA; 408B
Wilson, W.; Circus; Ohio; WV; 1850; OH; 449A
Wilson, W.H.; Gambler; Arapahoe; CO; 1862; OH; 98D
Wilson, William; Master Medium; McLean; IL; 1840; IL; 190A
Wilson, Wm.; Tramp on public street; St. Clair; IL; 1842; NY; 483C
Wiltermood, Lucinda G.; Fortune Teller; Jasper; MO; 1845; OH; 506D
Win, Soon; Gambler; Washoe; NV; 1840; China; 277A
Winegar, Clarence; Dead; Bristol; MA; 1879; MA; 411D
Winkler, Henry; Phrenologist; Knox; IN; 1840; OH; 427B
Winkler, John; Dead; St. Louis; MO; 1875; MO; 338D
Winson, Jacob; Tramp on public street; St. Clair; IL; 1845; Hungary; 483D
Winston, Henry; Gambler; Warren; MS; 1856; MS; 333C
Winters, Drury; Tramp; Talladega; AL; 1864; AL; 164C
Winters, Fanney; Dead; Allegheny; PA; 1845; PA; 249A
Winters, George; Tramp; Talladega; AL; 1869; AL; 164C

Name; Occupation; County; State; Birth; Birth place; Page 157

Winters, J.M.; Tramp; Talladega; AL; 1825; AL; 164C
Winters, Sallie; Fortune Teller; Clark; OH; 1830; VA; 341A
Wintress, David H.; Magnetic Healer; New York; NY; 1844; NY; 353A
Wisby, Charles; Tramp; Hennepin; MN; 1856; NY; 272A
Wiseman, Frederick; Dead; St. Louis; MO; 1879; MO; 485C
Wiseman, Rebecca; Dead - crossed out; Ritchie; WV; 1859; VA; 331D
Wisenen, Girty M.; Dead; Grundy; IL; 1880; IL; 323D
Wite, Lorne; Tramp on public street; St. Clair; IL; 1845; MO; 483D
Witney, Lewis; Circus; Ohio; WV; 1839; RI; 448D
Wmery, Peter; Tramp; Hennepin; MN; 1859; MN; 272A
Wolf, James; Tramp; Ionia; MI; 1847; PA; 108D
Wolf, Michael; Dead; Sandusky; OH; 1811; PA; 157D
Wolfe, James; Tramp - Prisoner; Ashtabula; OH; 1859; NY; 467C
Wolsey, James; Dead; Benton; AR; 1859; AR; 463C
Wong, Chung; Opium Dealer; San Joaquin; CA; 1845; Canton; 12D
Wong, Keon; Gambler; Storey; NV; 1855; China; 147D
Wong, Kun; Gambler; San Francisco; CA; 1827; Qwantung; 609C
Wong, Lin; Opium Dealer; San Francisco; CA; 1820; Qwantung; 609D
Wong, Sing You; Opium Merchant; Sacramento; CA; 1840; China; 4C
Wong, Tak; Opium Dealer; San Francisco; CA; 1855; See Yup; 629C
Woo; Opium Den; Yuba; CA; 1850; Canton; 445B
Woo, Fou; Gambler; Ormsby; NV; 1851; China; 74C
Wood, George A.; Professional baseball player; Suffolk; MA; 1859; Prince Edward Island; 179B
Wood, J.B.; Tramp on public street; St. Clair; IL; 1858; TN; 483C
Wood, James; Gambler; Shackelford; TX; 1854; NM Terr.; 466C
Wood, John; B. ball player; Worcester; MA; 1850; MA; 182D
Wood, Joseph G.; Gambler; Butte; CA; 1848; AL; 135C
Woodhead, James; Baseball player; Suffolk; MA; 1852; MA; 79D
Woodhead, James; Base ballist; Middlesex; MA; 1852; MA; 308A
Woodland, John; Gambler; Sierra; CA; 1829; IL; 149B

Name; Occupation; County; State; Birth; Birth place; Page

Woodridge, John; Gambler; Harrison; TX; 1851; TX; 363D
Woods, James; Gambler; Lake; CO; 1843; PA; 352A
Woods, Lafayette; Magician; Solano; CA; 1860; CA; 310A
Woods, Lou; Vagrant; Lafayette; MS; 1854; VA; 336D
Woods, Mary; Magician; Solano; CA; 1864; CA; 310A
Woods, Phil; Gambler; Travis; TX; 1850; NY; 267C
Woodworth, Homer; Magician; Steuben; IN; 1843; IN; 376B
Woolsayer, Margaret; Dead; Allegheny; PA; 1807; Switzerland;
    230C
Wooster, Norman; Tramp; Berkshire; MA; 1866; MA; 150C
Wooten, Samuel; Tramp; Marion; SC; 1860; NC; 118B
Wooton, Mariah; Dead; Fairfield; SC; 1879; SC; 197C
Workmans, Meredith; Professional Thief; Franklin; OH; 1830;
    VA; 480B
Worthmour, Henry; Gambler; Ionia; MI; 1854; MI; 108C
Worton, Louisa; Gypsy; Tehama; CA; 1841; England; 475D
Worton, Nathan; Gypsy; Tehama; CA; 1879; CA; 475D
Worton, Pheobe; Gypsy; Tehama; CA; 1867; NY; 475D
Worton, Sunnyside; Gypsy; Tehama; CA; 1872; NY; 475D
Woteras, Curola; Circus Performer; Maricopa; AZ; 1855;
    Chihuahua; 81C
Wren, Josie; Crossed out listed as dead; Adair; MO; 1878; MO;
    84C
Wright, Chas. W.; Gambler; Rio Grande; CO; 1846; NY; 323A
Wright, Della; Dead; Halifax; NC; 1879; NC; 663A
Wright, George; Baseball player; Suffolk; MA; 1848; NY; 34C
Wright, Harry; Tramp; Adams; IL; 1858; NY; 467A
Wright, Henry; Dead; Claiborne; TN; 1823; TN; 173A
Wright, Jane E.; Dead; St. Louis; MO; 1878; MS; 500B
Wright, John R.; Gambler; Salt Lake; UT; 1835; IL; 94B
Wright, Joseph W.; Dead; Autauga; AL; 1876; AL; 132D
Wright, Josiah; Dead; Crawford; GA; 1879; GA; 657C
Wright, Mary; Clairvoyant Physician; New Haven; CT; 1843;
    Ireland; 318C
Wright, Mary; Quack Doctoress; Butler; OH; 1820; OH; 382D
Wright, Mary; Dead; Taney; MO; 1849; TN; 272C
Wright, Samuel; Baseball player; Suffolk; MA; 1855; NY; 36C
Wurtz, Henry; Tramp; New York; NY; 1842; Germany; 581C

Wy, Kee Wong; Gambler; San Francisco; CA; 1845; Kwantung; 388D

Wyatt, Aggie; Dead; Autauga; AL; 1848; AL; 62D

Wyatt, Jno. R.; Gambler; Conejos; CO; 1849; Canada; 178C

Wynne, John; Gambler; Davidson; TN; 1840; KY; 66A

Wyrnesk, Stanslaugh; Dead; St. Joseph; IN; 1879; Prussia; 431A

Xase, Duvas; Tramp; Cuyahoga; OH; 1840; Hungary; 86A

Yah, Siah; Gambler; Deer Lodge; MT; 1850; China; 110A

Yan, Chin; Fortune Teller; San Francisco; CA; 1855; Kwantung; 385A

Yang, Chong; Gambler; Boise; ID; 1847; China; 118B

Yang, M.; Circus; Ohio; WV; 1862; MS; 449A

Yee, Cum; Gambling House Keeper; Boise; ID; 1843; China; 118B

Yee, Hoy; Opium Dealer; San Francisco; CA; 1840; Kwantung; 379B

Yee, Jan; Opium Dealer; San Francisco; CA; 1840; Kwantung; 379B

Yee, Loy Hing; Opium Dealer; San Francisco; CA; 1826; Canton Sun Ning; 378C

Yee, Sing; Opium Seller; Sacramento; CA; 1842; China; 4C

Yee, Soon; Gambler; San Francisco; CA; 1844; Kwantung; 393B

Yek, Pat; Opium Shop; Santa Clara; CA; 1852; China; 125C

Yeldell, Mahaley; Dead 2 yrs; Wilcox; AL; 1876; AL; 185C

Yen; Gambler; Tehama; CA; 1842; China; 489A

Yen, Sik; Gambler; San Francisco; CA; 1835; Kwan Tung; 677A

Yeney, Que; Gambler; Boise; ID; 1850; China; 118B

Yep, Gun; Opium Dealer; San Joaquin; CA; 1831; Mikoo; 12A

Yet, Gee; Gambler; Eureka; NV; 1846; China; 191A

Yeu, Yip; Gambler; Washoe; NV; 1833; China; 276C

Yeung, Wo; Gambler; Lander; NV; 1850; China; 298B

Yew King, Fong; Gambler; San Francisco; CA; 1839; Kwantung; 392B

Yew, Gang; Gambling House Keeper; Boise; ID; 1840; China; 118B

Yik, Foo; Gambler; Eureka; NV; 1841; China; 213A

Yik, Yun Ben; Opium Seller; Sacramento; CA; 1829; China; 4C

Yik, Yung; Gambler; Eureka; NV; 1850; China; 191A

Yin, Hoy; Gambler; Amador; CA; 1839; Canton; 46D
Ying, Chu; Opium Dealer; San Francisco; CA; 1840; Kwantung; 392B
Yoder, James; Magnetic Physician; Guthrie; IA; 1838; PA; 81B
Yong, Lee; Gambler; Nevada; CA; 1858; China; 175B
Yorba, Jose; Gambler; Los Angeles; CA; 1840; CA; 422D
Yost, James; Gambler; Grayson; TX; 1850; LA; 12C
You, Sing; Gambling House; Yuba; CA; 1830; Canton; 444D
Young, Charles; Gambler; Lake; CO; 1853; England; 355D
Young, Charles; Wandering; Coffey; KS; 1866; IA; 316C
Young, Fin; Keeping Gambling House; Storey; NV; 1829; China; 237D
Young, J.L.; Gambler; Decatur; IA; 1857; IA; 340B
Young, James; Tramp; Monroe; KY; 1848; TN; 308D
Young, John; Vagrant; Fulton; NY; 1833; NY; 47D
Young, Milton; Gambler; Henderson; KY; 1852; KY; 399C
Young, Moses; Shoemaker - dead; Adams; IL; 1791; NY; 476D
Young, Wan; Gambler; Boise; ID; 1850; China; 136A
Young, William H.; Dead; St. Mary's; MD; 1842; MD; 94C
Youngblood, Judia; Dead; Wilcox; AL; 1860; AL; 213C
Youngman, Bill; Tramp; Williamson; TN; 1835; TN; 134B
Youngman, Bill; Tramp; Menifee; KY; 1852; KY; 658D
Youngs, Anna; Wandering Gypsy; Clayton; IA; 1865; ---; 473D
Youngs, Buttler; Wandering Gypsy; Clayton; IA; 1874; ---; 473D
Youngs, Carol; Wandering Gypsy; Clayton; IA; 1876; ---; 473D
Youngs, Dan; Wandering Gypsy; Clayton; IA; 1864; ---; 473D
Youngs, Dina; Queen of Wandering Gypsys; Clayton; IA; 1856; ---; 473D
Youngs, Elia; Wandering Gypsy; Clayton; IA; 1857; ---; 473D
Youngs, Ema; Wandering Gypsy; Clayton; IA; 1850; ---; 473D
Youngs, Esau; Wandering Gypsy; Clayton; IA; 1873; ---; 473D
Youngs, Jimy; Wandering Gypsy; Clayton; IA; 1830; ---; 473D
Youngs, Jo; Wandering Gypsy; Clayton; IA; 1858; ---; 473D
Youngs, John; Wandering Gypsy; Clayton; IA; 1840; Gt. Britain; 473D
Youngs, Lidia; Wandering Gypsy; Clayton; IA; 1878; ---; 473D
Youngs, Linra; Wandering Gypsy; Clayton; IA; 1870; ---; 473D
Youngs, Lorina; Wandering Gypsy; Clayton; IA; 1872; ---; 473D

Youngs, Louisa; Wandering Gypsy; Clayton; IA; 1866; ---; 473D
Youngs, Oliver; Wandering Gypsy; Clayton; IA; 1863; ---; 473D
Youngs, Pinkey; Wandering Gypsy; Clayton; IA; 1876; ---; 473D
Youngs, Setha; Wandering Gypsy; Clayton; IA; 1879; ---; 473D
Youngs, Sweety; Wandering Gypsy; Clayton; IA; 1872; ---; 473D
Yu, Gie; Opium Shop; Santa Clara; CA; 1840; China; 125C
Yu, Wo; Gambler; Eureka; NV; 1847; China; 213B
Yum, One; Gambler; Eureka; NV; 1855; China; 208D
Yun, Chun; Gambler; San Francisco; CA; 1858; Kwantung; 392B
Yun, Lo; Gambler; Kern; CA; 1846; China; 586C
Yun, Tong; Opium Seller; San Francisco; CA; 1861; China; 442D
Yuncker, Sarah; Dead; Sandusky; OH; 1861; OH; 164B
Yung, Fat; Gambler; San Francisco; CA; 1840; Kwan Tung; 630B
Yung, Sang; Oracle; Amador; CA; 1835; Canton; 46D
Yung, Wing; Gambling House; Yuba; CA; 1845; Canton; 445A
Yut, Ming Yat; Fortune Teller; San Francisco; CA; 1840; Quong
        Tong Nan Hoi; 444C
Zaiser, Christian; Dead; Adams; IL; 1794; Wurtenburg; 472D
Zcotack, Woycech; Dead; Milwaukee; WI; 1880; WI; 237B
Zele, John; Vagrant; Hudson; NJ; 1857; Canada; 398D
Zerby, George; Tramp; Schuylkill; PA; 1856; PA; 138D
Zigler, Peter; Gambler; Franklin; OH; 1845; Germany; 134C
Zimmermam, John; Bum; Licking; OH; 1830; PA; 390C
Zimmerman; Dead July; Washington; IL; 1880; IL; 363B
Zirbel, Willie; Dead; Milwaukee; WI; 1879; WI; 233A

ABOUT THE AUTHOR

JANA SLOAN BROGLIN is a Certified Genealogist and an Ohio native. She is the Vice-President of Membership for the Federation of Genealogical Societies and a Trustee of the Ohio Genealogical Society. Memberships include the Ohio Genealogical Society, the National Genealogical Society, the Association of Professional Genealogists, Genealogical Speakers Guild, and the International Society of Family History Writers and Editors. She has published over sixty books on Ohio and Kentucky and was named a Kentucky Colonel for her work on Kentucky. As a lecturer, she has spoken at local, state, and national conferences. She currently works as a freelance indexer for Gateway Press in Baltimore, Maryland.

www.ingramcontent.com/pod-product-compliance
Lightning Source LLC
Chambersburg PA
CBHW070840300326
41935CB00038B/1156

* 9 7 8 0 7 8 8 4 4 5 5 0 7 *